PERSONAL PATRONAGE UNDER THE EARLY EMPIRE

PERSONAL PATRONAGE
UNDER THE
EARLY EMPIRE

RICHARD P. SALLER

Assistant Professor of Classics
Swarthmore College, Pennsylvania

CAMBRIDGE UNIVERSITY PRESS

CAMBRIDGE
LONDON NEW YORK ROCHELLE
MELBOURNE SYDNEY

PUBLISHED BY THE PRESS SYNDICATE OF THE UNIVERSITY OF CAMBRIDGE
The Pitt Building, Trumpington Street, Cambridge, United Kingdom

CAMBRIDGE UNIVERSITY PRESS
The Edinburgh Building, Cambridge CB2 2RU, UK
40 West 20th Street, New York NY 10011–4211, USA
477 Williamstown Road, Port Melbourne, VIC 3207, Australia
Ruiz de Alarcón 13, 28014 Madrid, Spain
Dock House, The Waterfront, Cape Town 8001, South Africa

http://www.cambridge.org

First published 1982
First paperback edition 2002

A catalogue record for this book is available from the British Library

Library of Congress Cataloguing in Publication data
Saller, Richard P.
Personal patronage under the early empire
1. Patron and client
I. Title
937′.04   DG83.3   80-42226

ISBN 0 521 23300 3 hardback
ISBN 0 521 89392 5 paperback

Contents

Tables

Preface

Patronage is a social practice of considerable importance in most Mediterranean societies today. Few historians of ancient Rome would deny its existence during the early Empire: patronage of communities has been studied in a full-scale work, and in its personal form it is mentioned frequently in political and social histories. But patron-client relations between individuals have not yet received the systematic treatment that this study aims to provide for the period from Augustus to the Severan emperors. As the title indicates, municipal patronage falls outside the scope of this work, and patronage of freedmen is also excluded on the ground that, in being subject to legal regulation, it differed fundamentally from voluntary associations between freeborn men. Further, owing to the nature of the evidence, the aristocracies of Rome and the provinces will claim the greatest part of our attention; patrons and clients lower on the social ladder certainly existed, but they left little record of their activities (except perhaps in the special case of Egypt). No attempt has been made to examine all provinces comprehensively, since it seemed that much could be learned from an intensive study of a single area of special significance, the North African provinces.

This volume originated as a doctoral dissertation written at the University of Cambridge, where I received help and encouragement in an environment made stimulating by Professor Sir Moses Finley and by teachers and fellow students too numerous to list. I wish to thank those who read and commented on various chapters: Mr D. Cohen, Dr R. Duncan-Jones, Professor Sir Moses Finley, Professor F. Millar, Professor M. Ostwald, Mr S. Price, Miss J. M. Reynolds, Dr B. D. Shaw, Mr W. Turpin, and Mr C. R. Whittaker. A special acknowledgement of gratitude is due Professor John Crook, who was kind and patient enough to read three drafts of my work — when submitted as a fellowship thesis, as a doctoral dissertation, and finally as a manuscript for publication. I have followed much of his advice, and where it has seemed better to accept alternative suggestions, I have done so only after serious consideration. My deepest appreciation is reserved for my dissertation supervisor, Dr Peter Garnsey, without whose guidance and criticism at all stages of research and composition this book would not have been written. Needless to say, these generous readers are not to be blamed for errors which remain in the text. Most of the research and writing was done while I was a member of Jesus College, Cambridge, whose years of financial assistance, including a research fellowship, made it possible for an American to profit from the special Cambridge environment. Finally, Swarthmore College is to be thanked for a grant to prepare the typescript.

Swarthmore, Pennsylvania   R.P.S.
July 1980

TO CAROL

Abbreviations

The abbreviations used here for journals are the standard ones found in *L'Année Philologique*. The following abbreviations are used for standard reference works.

AE   *Année Epigraphique*

CIL   *Corpus Inscriptionum Latinarum*

ILAfr. *Inscriptions latines d'Afrique*, ed. R. Cagnat, A. Merlin, L. Chatelain (1923)

ILAlg. *Inscriptions latines de l'Algérie*, ed. S. Gsell, H.-G. Pflaum (1922 and 1957-)

ILLRP   *Inscriptiones Latinae Liberae Reipublicae*, ed. A. Degrassi (1957-65)

ILS   *Inscriptiones Latinae Selectae*, ed. H. Dessau (1892-1916)

ILTun. *Inscriptions latines de la Tunisie*, ed. A. Merlin (1944)

PIR   *Prosopographia Imperii Romani*

RE   Pauly-Wissowa-Kroll, *Real-Encyclopädie der classischen Altertumswissenschaft* (1894-)

TLL   *Thesaurus Linguae Latinae*

Introduction

Our study begins with a problem. Patronage is as difficult to define precisely as are other types of complex behavior, because it shares characteristics with other categories of relations into which it merges. The Roman use of the word *patronus* does not offer much help, for reasons discussed in the following chapter. Anthropologists who have studied the institution intensively in the context of the modern Mediterranean world have argued about a suitably exact definition which is not so broad as to be useless.[1] One specialist on the subject has offered the following definition: 'Patronage is founded on the reciprocal relations between patrons and clients. By patron I mean a person who uses his influence to assist and protect some other person, who becomes his "client", and in return provides certain services to his patron. The relationship is asymmetrical, though the nature of the services exchanged may differ considerably.'[2] Three vital elements which distinguish a patronage relationship appear in this passage. First, it involves the *reciprocal* exchange of goods and services. Secondly, to distinguish it from a commercial transaction in the marketplace, the relationship must be a personal one of some duration. Thirdly, it must be asymmetrical, in the sense that the two parties are of unequal status and offer different kinds of goods and services in the exchange — a quality which sets patronage off from friendship between equals.

Something recognizable as patronage, thus defined, appears in histories and monographs concerning the Principate, but it has not received a systematic treatment. Nor has it received more than scattered attention in the recent social histories of the early Empire. For instance, Ramsay MacMullen in his *Roman Social Relations* decided to exclude the subject from consideration, commenting that 'we need not repeat the investigations of other scholars at this level'.[3] In his footnote two studies of the Empire reaching diametrically

1 E. Gellner, 'Patrons and clients', in *Patrons and Clients*, ed. E. Gellner and J. Waterbury, Ch. 1; Robert R. Kaufman, 'The patron-client concept and macro-politics: prospects and problems', *CSSH* 16 (1974), 287ff.

2 J. Boissevain, 'Patronage in Sicily', *Man* n.s. 1 (1966), 18. Kaufman, 'Patron-client concept', 285, offers a similar definition.

3 *Roman Social Relations, 50 B.C. to A.D. 284*, 8.

opposed conclusions are cited without comment: de Ste Croix's examination of *suffragium* emphasizing the central importance of patronage during the Principate, and Harmand's monograph on *Le patronat* in which it is concluded that 'cette clientèle "privée", à forme individuelle, n'est pas plus qu'une relique sous l'Empire'.[4] Harmand, on the basis of this conclusion, focuses exclusively on municipal patronage for the period of the Principate. His idea that personal patronage became insignificant during the early Empire to re-emerge in the form of rural patronage during the late Empire represents a commonly held view: in a recent textbook, reference can be found to 'un relâchement des liens personnels', and in the most extensive recent treatment of Roman imperial society, municipal patronage is said to have taken the place of the Republican type of personal patronage which underwent a 'réduction à l'insignifiance'.[5]

There is another group of studies which diverges from Harmand's and recognizes the continuing function of patron-client relations in imperial politics. Perhaps the best-known exponent of this position is R. Syme, who argues persuasively in his *Roman Revolution* that the emperor's position was based on patronal ties to his supporters: under Augustus 'political competition was sterilized and regulated through a pervasive system of patronage and nepotism'.[6] Unlike some historians who see the role of patronage declining as other institutions of the Principate developed, Syme thinks it of continuing importance: in his *Tacitus* political history is written in terms of 'webs of intrigue for office and influence', 'secret influence', and 'managers of patronage'.[7] A similar view is expressed in G. Alföldy's social history of Rome, in which the emperor's position as a great patron is recognized, as is the need of the *novus homo* for the support of well-placed aristocrats such as the younger Pliny.[8] Alföldy's treatment of patronage seems to me a step in the right direction, but is too limited in the understanding of its function in Roman imperial society in several respects. As in most other works mentioning patronage, it is treated as an almost exclusively political phenomenon with a focus on the emperor. The social, economic, legal and ideological aspects receive little or no attention, and even the political side is not examined systematically (for instance, patronal support does not appear in the discussion of equestrian appointments).

A broader approach to patronage is taken by J. Michel in his *Gratuité en droit romain*. This book examines at length the ideology and the economic and

---

4 *Un aspect social et politique du monde romain: le patronat sur les collectivités des origines au Bas-Empire*, 467f. For discussion of de Ste Croix's views, see below p.3.
5 P. Petit, *La paix romaine*, 232; J. Gagé, *Les classes sociales dans l'Empire romain*, 77.
6 *The Roman Revolution*, 386.
7 *Tacitus*, 8, 55, 24.
8 *Römische Sozialgeschichte*, 105f.

social significance of reciprocal exchange during the Roman Republic.[9] But for many of the same reasons expressed by other historians, Michel believes that the role of this exchange declined during the Empire, a decline which is reflected in the legal texts of the time.[10]

In my judgement the best analysis of personal patronage in the early Empire is to be found in G. E. M. de Ste Croix's article about *suffragium*. It is 'the growth of patronage', in his view, 'which provides the key to the working of the Roman constitution in the imperial period', for the reason that 'with the collapse of the Republic and the virtual elimination of the democratic features of the constitution in the last half-century B.C., patronage and clientship became as it were the mainspring of Roman public life'.[11] De Ste Croix considers the influence of *suffragium* on the allotment of offices and on legal hearings, and gives attention to the growth of its sale and its distribution at all levels of government. The brevity of de Ste Croix's remarks, however, invites a more complete description and analysis of the political and judicial aspects of the subject, as well as consideration of its many other facets.

This book is intended to contribute to the understanding of Roman imperial society in several ways. The systematic collection and presentation of the available evidence should make possible a sounder evaluation of the divergent claims about the place of patronage in imperial politics. Furthermore, the evidence suggests that the importance of patronage extends beyond the realm of politics, just as in many Mediterranean societies today where the institution influences the ways in which people view their world, earn their living, associate with their fellow townsmen, and relate to the state administration.[12]

Demonstrating the mere existence of patron-client relationships in imperial Rome is of limited value, since they can be found in one form or another in most societies. It is much more valuable to know how patronage functioned in relation to other political, economic and social institutions. Function is more difficult to prove than existence, and so at times suggestions under this head will necessarily be tentative. For instance, lack of evidence makes it impossible to prove for imperial Rome a connection between strong patron-client ties and attitudes towards capital investment, such as has been observed in some better-documented societies.[13] More can be said about the relationship between Roman government and patronage. Patrons supply protection and special access to certain goods and services for their clients; as state administrations expand, providing protection and services to all citizens on the basis of universal, impersonal criteria, the clients' need for patrons declines. A.

---

9 *Gratuité en droit romain*, espec. 503ff.
10 *Ibid.*, 553ff. See p.119 with n.2 below.
11 'Suffragium: from vote to patronage', *British Journal of Sociology* 5 (1954), 33, 40.
12 For the many facets of patronage, see the contributions in *Patrons and Clients*, ed. Gellner and Waterbury, and J. K. Campbell, *Honour, Family, and Patronage*.
13 See below, p.126.

Blok conceptualizes this interrelationship between government and patronage in a typology in which different kinds of states are related to the various functions which patronage performs. Blok singles out four types of states, characterized by vassalage, brokerage, friendship, and disguised patronage. These 'may be conceived of in terms of a continuum on which patronage and bureaucratization (i.e., centralized authority) "move" in opposite directions. One pole of this continuum is feudal society in which patronage is full-fledged: patron-client ties are the dominant social relations which have a clear public face, while bureaucratic authority is near to zero. On the other pole, authority is fully centralized; patronage is dysfunctional and is likely to be absent'.[14] The two intermediate types, characterized by brokerage and friendship, are most relevant to the study of the Roman Empire. The former is often found in segmented societies where sections of the population are not yet fully integrated into the state by direct contact with government. Thus broker-patrons are left to mediate between the central administration and the people in gaps where no formal administration exists to perform the tasks. In the state characterized by friendship, on the other hand, an extensive central organization exists and the patron's main task becomes that of expediting contact with the bureaucracy. These two types are distinguished according to whether patronage operates in place of state machinery or 'lubricates' machinery that exists by offering preferential treatment to those who have effective patrons. Blok also suggests that the language and ideology of patronage vary along the same continuum. At the feudal end, patronage has 'a clear public face' and the language of patronage does not carry immoral or unethical implications; at the opposite end of the continuum, 'patronage is a bad word' so that 'in public neither the patron nor the client is allowed to refer to his mutual contacts, let alone take pride in maintaining these relationships...'.[15]

There would be little point in devoting a great deal of space in this book to categorizing the Roman state of the Principate: pure ideal types rarely occur in history and attempts at categorizing are often futile. But it seems to me that Blok's typology throws much light on the issue of the function of patronage vis-à-vis the state and allows us to pose a central question more clearly. In much work on the growing bureaucracy of the Principate it is assumed or argued that the Roman state moved some considerable distance along the continuum toward fully centralized authority which eliminated or minimized

14 'Variations in patronage', *Sociologische Gids* 16 (1969), 365-78. The historical example closest to the ideal type of fully centralized authority is probably modern Scandinavia. It has been pointed out to me that the word 'patronage' cannot be translated into the Swedish or Norwegian languages. Kaufman, 'Patron-client concept', 290, prefers not to allow feudal relations under the heading of patron-client relations, but this does not seem to me to detract from the value of Blok's continuum.
15 Blok, 'Variations in patronage', 373.

the importance of patronage. Further, it is argued that concurrently the ideology changed so that patronage became an evil to be suppressed, losing its 'clear public face' of the Republic.[16] This position is examined in the first chapter on language and ideology. During the Republic patron-client relations, far from being thought an evil, were reinforced by law and religious mores. Did this ideology change during the rule of the emperors? In order to answer the question, the social roles (e.g., emperor, administrative official) which the patronal ideal continued to shape will be considered. The remaining chapters will examine the web of patron-client relationships, beginning with the emperor and his court and moving out through the imperial aristocracy to the provinces. At each level the recurring issue of the impact of the growing bureaucracy on patronage will arise in the form of the question: to what extent did the state change from a brokerage to a friendship type, with patronage functioning only as a 'lubricant' for the newly created administrative machinery?

Finally, an explicit statement about method may serve as a useful preliminary to what follows. The theme of patronage looms large in recent studies of contemporary Mediterranean societies.[17] Of course, the historian of antiquity who wishes to examine similar phenomena faces the problem that he does not enjoy the same opportunities for observation: the examples of patron-client bonds to be found in the literature from the Principate are scattered and not enough is known about any of them. Therefore, it is necessary to resort to indirect approaches in addition to the accumulation of specific examples. The first of these is a word study. Explicit statements about how patrons and clients should behave are not common in our texts and are to be treated with care when they are encountered. The fact that they are self-conscious and often philosophical means that they may be as unrepresentative of the ideas and expectations of men in everyday life as a sermon preached from a pulpit today. A study of the contexts and connotations of key words may be more revealing, and so a word study of patronage-related words is offered in Chapter 1.

The ancient historian rarely has enough data to prove by simple induction that a particular kind of social behavior was typical rather than the exception. For instance, several or even a dozen cases of patronal influence on the appointment of officials do not prove that such influence normally played a part. This obstacle to generalization can be overcome in several ways. One is a sensitivity to the expectations of the writer and people involved: do they write or act as if influence was an essential factor in securing offices? Even expectations can sometimes be misleading. Another indirect approach is to ask what alternatives to patronage were available for securing appointments. It

16 See below, p.79.
17 An extensive bibliography can be found in *Patrons and Clients*, ed. Gellner and Waterbury.

has been widely suggested that senatorial and equestrian careers became highly structured during the second century, with the result that the emperor's discretion was normally very limited and patronal influence of little value. Much of Chapter 3 is devoted to a critique of this position, on the grounds that if careers were not highly regulated personal influence was more likely to have been decisive in the vast majority of appointments for which no positive evidence is available.

A third indirect approach utilized here is comparative analysis.[18] The body of anthropological material on patronage has grown enormously over the past few decades.[19] I cannot claim to have read all of it, but I have looked at a great deal concerned with modern Mediterranean cultures and have found it useful in several respects. The ongoing discussion and debate among anthropologists have produced new and more sophisticated analyses of patronage, some of which suggest new questions and ways of analyzing the evidence of the Roman world. Studies of the Turkish Empire, to take one example, indicate a link between the quality of provincial administration and the integration of officials and their subject populations in the same patronage networks — a link which is worth considering for the Roman Empire. In addition, knowledge of patronage and bureaucracy in other states should give us a better perspective on the government of the Principate. For those who are uncomfortable with Blok's ideal types, comparison with other pre-industrial states, such as China or early modern European countries, can provide some standard by which to measure the significance of patronage and the extent of bureaucratization at Rome. A monograph on a particular social institution inevitably runs the risk of presenting an unbalanced view by overemphasizing the subject under study. This is especially true when our evidence is so inadequate: for instance, how could a Roman historian possibly measure with any precision the relative influence of patronage vis-à-vis wealth on social mobility with the information available? Knowledge of better-known societies cannot tell us what we do not know about Rome, but it can at least indicate realistic possibilities for the place of patron-client relationships in Roman society.

18 A critique of the uses of comparative analysis can be found in William H. Sewell, Jr, 'Marc Bloch and the logic of comparative history', *History and Theory* 6 (1967), 206ff.
19 A recent lengthy bibliography can be found in the notes of S. N. Eisenstadt and L. Roniger, 'Patron-client relations as a model of structuring social exchange', *CSSH* 22 (1980), 42-77.

1

The language and ideology of patronage

Several reasons may be offered for beginning this study of patronage with an examination of the related vocabulary. Most simply, in order to understand the testimony of the ancient sources, it is necessary to know the meaning of the words used to describe the phenomena under study. But this, of course, hardly constitutes a sufficient reason, since the lexical definitions of the important words, such as *patronus, cliens* and *beneficium*, are satisfactory. What is of real concern here is to discover in what social contexts and with what connotations the words were used. As these questions are answered, we shall begin to understand the way in which Roman aristocrats categorized their social relationships and the attitudes and ethics appropriate to each category.[1]

While a language study can be useful as an avenue of entry into the Roman *Weltanschauung*, it has potential pitfalls. Just as problems are encountered if no distinction is drawn between ideals and behavior, so will mistakes be made if we fail to distinguish between conscious statements about the usage of patronage-related words given by Roman authors and actual usage in the extant literature. Moreover, there may be a temptation to assume a simple one-to-one relationship between words and categories. For example, in a recent study it was thought significant that both Roman poets and their aristocratic supporters were called *amici*, adhering to the 'familiar code of *amicitia*'.[2] But, as will become clear in this chapter, the fact that men of varying social statuses could be called *amici* does not indicate that all *amicitiae* fit into a single category of social relationships with a single code of conduct. Conversely, we should not jump to the conclusion that patronage existed only where the words *patronus* and *cliens* were used. Both of these pitfalls can be avoided by close attention, not only to the definitions of words, but also to the way in which they relate to behavior in all their usages.

---

1 Bryan Wilson ('A sociologist's introduction', *Rationality*, ed. B. Wilson, xvii) makes this point, but emphasizes that it is only a preliminary step and not sufficient in and of itself. The observer must attempt to supersede the actors' understanding and pose his own questions.
2 P. White, 'Amicitia and the profession of poetry in early imperial Rome', *JRS* 68 (1978), 74. See notes 11, 15, 91 and 94 below for criticism.

KEY WORDS AND DEFINITIONS

Initially, the vocabulary of patronage must be identified and the most important words for this study selected. No attempt will be made to provide a comprehensive examination of all patronage-related words, an endeavor which would require a separate work the length of Hellegouarc'h's *Le vocabulaire latin des relations et des partis politiques sous la république* (1963). Given a definition of patronage as 'an exchange relationship between men of unequal social status', two groups of basic terms would seem to be particularly important: those applied to the people involved in the relationship and those describing the goods and services which passed between them. The first group includes *patronus, cliens* and *amicus,* and the second *officium, beneficium, meritum* and *gratia.*[3] Much has been written about this language for the period of the Republic and has been summarized in recent studies by Hellegouarc'h, Moussy and Brunt.[4] Their work provides a convenient starting point for our purposes here, since the basic meanings of the words changed very little in the period under consideration. Furthermore, a brief review of the Republican meanings will allow us to emphasize the continuity of the social contexts in which they were used.

Patronus and cliens

Before undertaking a language study, one might assume that the words *patronus* and *cliens* would be the terms most frequently used to describe patronage relationships. In fact, this does not seem to be the case. (Perhaps the relative rarity of these words explains the claim of some scholars that patronage of individuals was unimportant or even absent in the Principate.)[5]

---

3 I have chosen not to discuss *fides* here for two reasons: (1) the most frequent meanings of the word in the literature from the Principate are 'honesty' or 'credibility', which do not imply the existence of a social exchange relationship; (2) the importance of the moral aspect of the patronage relationship is very difficult to evaluate. From his study of the Bedouin in modern Cyrenaica, E. L. Peters concluded: 'the significance of the moral bond varies as widely as the vast number of local communities there are with patrons and clients living together. Therefore the *fides* part of the relationship, always present in one of its multiple forms, cannot be given the analytical priority ascribed to it by Badian—a catalysis of all sets of relationships which are caught up in it—but must be relegated to the place of an attribute, which commonly occurs in combination with it.' ('Patronage in Cyrenaica', in *Patrons and Clients,* ed. Gellner and Waterbury, 280). For Badian's position, *Foreign Clientelae,* Introduction. P.A. Brunt in his review of Strasburger, *Zum antiken Gesellschaftideal, Gnomon* 51 (1979), 443, stresses material interests.

4 J. Hellegouarc'h, *Le vocabulaire latin des relations et des partis politiques sous la république;* Claude Moussy, *Gratia et sa famille;* P. Brunt, '"Amicitia" in the late Roman Republic', *PCPhS* n.s. 11 (1965), 1-20; also consulted were Erik Wistrand, 'Gratus, grates, gratia, gratiosus', in his *Opera Selecta,* 11-20; Victor Pöschl, *Grundwerte römischer Staatsgesinnung in den Geschichtswerken des Sallust,* 82ff.; Hans Volkmann, 'Griechische Rhetorik oder römische Politik?', *Hermes* 82 (1954), 475f.; E. Badian, *Foreign Clientelae,* 1-14; Emile Benveniste, *Indo-European Language and Society,* 159ff.

5 E.g., Petit, *La paix romaine,* 232 and Harmand, *Le patronat,* 476f.

The use of *patronus* in the literature of the early Empire was restricted to legal advocates, patrons of communities and ex-masters of freedmen; in none of the major prose writers of the post-Augustan Principate (Seneca, Tacitus, Pliny the Younger and Suetonius) is *patronus* used in the general sense of an 'influential protector'. This represents a continuation of the literary usage of the late Republic: of the 23 appearances of the word in the corpus of Cicero's letters, for example, 21 fall into one of these three categories of technical usage, while only two have the more general meaning of 'protector' or 'influential supporter'.[6] In the same way (though not to the same extent) the word *cliens* was not used freely by authors with reference to any member of an exchange relationship of inferior status. It was usually reserved for humble members of the lower classes. Pliny, for instance, never referred to any of his protégés as *cliens* in his letters.

The reason for the infrequent appearance of *patronus* and *cliens* in literature lies in the social inferiority and degradation implied by the words. Thus, Seneca, referring to the *cliens'* duties, scorned those for whom not even their love and hate were under their own control.[7] Fronto never referred to himself as a *patronus* of his protégés and used the word *cliens* only once. In a *commendatio* he explained to the emperor Verus how intimate he and Gavius Clarus, a senatorial protégé, were.

From an early age Gavius Clarus has attended me in a friendly fashion not only with those *officia* by which a senator lesser in age and station properly cultivates a senator senior in rank and years, earning his goodwill; but gradually our *amicitia* developed to the point that he is not distressed or ashamed to pay me the sort of deference which *clientes* and faithful, hard-working freedmen yield—and not through arrogance on my part or flattery on his. But our mutual regard and true love have taken away from both of us all concern in restraining our *officia*.[8]

This single occurrence in Fronto of the association of a protégé with the word

---

6 The two uses in the general sense are *Ad Fam.* 7.29.2 and *Ad Att.* 1.16.10. Both passages illustrate the point to be made below concerning the use of *patronus*. In neither of these passages does Cicero use the word to describe himself: in the first M'. Curius, Cicero's banker friend from Patrae, uses the word to describe Cicero—a sign of Curius' deference; in the second, Cicero applies the label to C. Scribonius Curio in a sneer at Clodius' relationship with him. In both cases, then, the connotations of social subordination and/or degradation are clear. See Walter Neuhauser, *Patronus und Orator,* for a complete description of uses of *patronus* in Republican and Augustan literature (64-118) and White, 'Amicitia', 79.

7 *De Brev. Vitae* 19.3; a comparison between this statement and Seneca's plea for help in securing return from exile in *De Cons. ad Polyb.* leaves little doubt about Seneca's hypocrisy in this respect. Cf. Brunt, 'Amicitia', 8.

8 *Ad Verum* 2.7: 'sed paulatim amicitia nostra [Fronto and Gavius Clarus] eo processit ut neque illum pigeret nec me puderet ea illum oboedire mihi, quae *clientes,* quae liberti fideles ac laboriosi obsequuntur: nulla hoc aut mea insolentia aut illius adulatione; sed mutua caritas nostra et amor verus ademit utrique nostrum in officiis moderandis omnem detrectationem.' All translations are mine unless otherwise indicated.

cliens is the exception which proves the rule: Fronto employs the word to emphasize the mutual affection which makes the normally offensive *officia clientium* acceptable. Tacitus used the word *cliens* more often than any other extant author of the Principate. As might be expected, the connotation of degradation is skillfully exploited to reinforce Tacitean themes. More than once the chaotic effects of civil war are emphasized by scenes of rich and dignified senators compelled to seek refuge in the houses of their *humillimi clientes*.[9] *Clientes* was a potent label for those undergoing the degradation of pandering to Sejanus.[10]

The epigraphic usage of *patronus* and *cliens* differs markedly from the literary, in a way which is to a large extent explicable.[11] In the corpus of inscriptions from North Africa *patronus* occurs relatively frequently in the general sense of 'protector' or 'benefactor'. For instance, a municipal aristocrat from Lambaesis, M. Sedius Rufus, dedicated an inscription to his *patronus*, the governor of Numidia, Q. Anicius Faustus.[12] Numerous similar dedications could be adduced, but it is enough to say at this point that a notable uniformity among them shows clearly that *patronus* was a term of deference and social superordination:[13] though stones were dedicated by friends and relatives to men of all *ordines*, only senators and *equites* of imperially granted rank or office were called *patroni* in the general sense. (Others were so called by their freedmen.)

How should we account for this difference between literary and epigraphic usages? Certainty is impossible, but the best explanation seems to lie in distinguishing which member of the patronage relationship was using the words. The language of social subordination may have seemed arrogant when used by the patron, a tactless advertisement of his superiority and the relative weakness of his client. The collections of letters which have come down to us were, of course, written by leading men of the Roman aristocracy, i.e., men in the position of patron. On the other hand, the inscriptions were set up by clients. One of the duties of a recipient of a favor was to publicize the favor and his gratitude for it;[14] dedications were an important vehicle for such publicity, as the use of *patronus* and *cliens* on the stone served to exalt the benefactor by emphasizing his superiority. This explanation for the absence of

---

9 *Hist.* 1.81; 3.73, 74 and 86.

10 *Ann.* 4.2; 4.34.

11 The epigraphic usage vitiates White's conclusion that during the Empire *patronus* 'is not even used in a general way to describe the role in society of the lordly man who receives the respectful attentions of lesser men and who dispenses favours and rewards to them'. ('Amicitia', 79).

12 *AE* (1911), 99.

13 *Patronus* appears in the following inscriptions in the table of patronage inscriptions in Appendix 5: nos. 2-4, 9-12, 20, 21, 23, 24, 25, 27, 28, 30, 32, 33, 36, 37, 38, 40, 41, 43, 45, 46, 48, 49, 51, 52.

14 Seneca, *De Ben.* 2.23; see P. Veyne, *Le pain et le cirque*, 698 for a similar point.

patronus in the general sense pertains most directly to usage in the various collections of *epistulae,* especially those addressed to protégés; but the absence of *patronus* in this sense in other prose genres may be similarly explained as a reflection of the restricted use of the word in polite society (though it must be admitted that in these other genres *cliens* is on occasion used to describe protégés). Whatever the precise reasons, the divergence of literary and epigraphic usages cannot be doubted. The clear corollary is that the appearance or absence of the words *patronus* and *cliens* is not indicative of the presence or absence of the phenomenon of patronage, but is a reflection of the circumstances in which it was described.

Amicus

In contrast to the words *patronus* and *cliens,* the language of *amicitiae* did not carry any inherent notions of differential social status, since the word *amicus* was sufficiently ambiguous to encompass both social equals and unequals. This ambiguity was exploited and there was a tendency to call men *amici* rather than the demeaning *clientes* as a mark of consideration. The tendency did not produce any levelling effect or egalitarian ideology in the hierarchical Roman society.[15] Quite the contrary — a new grade in the hierarchy was added as relationships with lesser *amici* were labelled *amicitiae inferiores* or *amicitiae minores.* With some aristocratic houses this group seems to have been formally defined. Seneca claimed that the practice could be traced back to C. Gracchus and Livius Drusus who divided their friends/followers into three groups: the first comprised peers who were received in private; the second included those lesser *amici* permitted into the *atrium* in groups for the morning salutation; the lowliest group was made up of humble *clientes* who were admitted *en masse* and might be humiliated by being kept out of the house by slave *nomenculatores.*[16] Though Seneca disapproved of this practice, several

---

15 White's argument on this point ('Amicitia') confuses the language with the reality: while acknowledging Roman attention to distinctions of status (81), he nevertheless concludes that 'it would be incorrect even to divide the great man's *amici* into peers and dependants, and to suppose that the benefits I have enumerated are the special perquisites which fall to dependants' (92). Yet, as the following passages demonstrate, the Romans certainly made distinctions in classes of friends and carried on the exchange of *officia* and *beneficia* in accordance with the distinctions: *amici* of lower status attended the morning salutation of friends of higher status, receiving food or money for their effort, not *vice versa; wealthy amici* gave their less well-to-do friends *viatica* or estates, not *vice versa* (see Chapter 4 for a full discussion). For a recent discussion of friendship, see R. Seager, 'Amicitia in Tacitus and Juvenal', *AJAH* 2 (1977), 40-50: Seager takes the comments of Tacitus and Juvenal about the decline of *amicitia* far more seriously than I would—the letters of Pliny and Fronto do not give the impression that the mores of friendship were 'hollow shams', and it may be argued that they are more reliable guides than pessimistic moralists such as Juvenal and Tacitus. For the element of caricature in Juvenal's treatment of *amicitia,* see Richard A. LaFleur, 'Amicitia and the unity of Juvenal's First Book', *ICS* 4 (1979), 158ff.

16 *De Ben.* 6.33.3ff.

of his dialogues indicate that it continued in his day.[17] Pliny implicitly accepted the hierarchical classification of friends, speaking of the need to attend to 'amicitiae tam superiores quam minores'. At the same time, he disapproved of some of the manifestations of arrogance encouraged by such a classification —for example, the custom of serving at the same dinner table different grades of food and wine to *amici* according to their status.[18] In a less moralizing mood, Seneca also seems implicitly to have taken the classification for granted: in a letter to Lucilius he suggested that different sets of precepts were appropriate depending on whether a man was seeking *amicitiae regum, pares amicitiae* or *amicitiae inferiores*.[19]

Despite variations in precepts and the treatment of friends of different statuses, there was a core of ideals which were thought to be applicable to all friendships. Since most of the participants in the patronage relationships under consideration were called *amici* rather than *patroni* or *clientes*, some attention needs to be devoted to clarifying these precepts. In the analysis we shall need to distinguish the ideals of the philosophers from the common values and expectations which affected everyday life. This distinction will enable us to explore the following paradox, which is found in other societies:[20] although friendship was ideally to be based on mutual affection with no thought for profit, a necessary part of friendship was a mutually beneficial exchange of goods and services.

The ideals concerning *amicitia* changed very little in the transition from the Republic to the Principate: Seneca's views differ little from Cicero's. Moreover, Seneca is a good source for the ideals of friendship in our period because most of his ideas are not uniquely Stoic; rather they represent the common philosophical currency of the aristocracy of his day, as shown by their repetition in the works of orators such as Pliny and Fronto.

True friendship, in Seneca's view, was thought to be one of the highest goods, reflecting a natural human need.[21] *Amicitia* was supposed to be based

17 E.g., *De Tranq. Animi* 12.6-7; *De Brev. Vitae* 14.3.
18 *Ep.* 7.3.2; 2.6.2.
19 *Ep. ad Luc.* 94.14.
20 J. Pitt-Rivers, in *The People of the Sierra*, describes this paradox in the context of contemporary Spain: 'For friendship to be real it must be disinterested. The language echoes the point continually. People assure one another that the favor they do is done with no afterthought, a pure favor which entails no obligation, an action which is done for the pleasure of doing it, prompted only by a desire to express esteem. On the other hand, the suggestion that someone's friendship is "interested" is a grave one. Honorable people fight shy of accepting a favor which they will not be able or will not wish to return. The other may wish for one's friendship in order to exploit it. Yet having once accepted friendships one cannot refuse to fulfil the obligations of friendship without appearing oneself the exploiter, for one has entered falsely into a contract... The paradox, then, is this: that while a friend is entitled to expect a return of his feelings and favor he is not entitled to bestow them in that expectation' (138 f.).
21 *Ep. ad Luc.* 109. Indeed many of these precepts are not particularly Roman: Aristotle

on virtue (especially *fides*) and not *utilitas*: an *amicus* tied only by *utilitas*, according to Seneca, will abandon his friend as soon as he falls on hard times.[22] One assurance of fidelity is that friends should hold everything in common and should share similar interests and character.[23] (This ideal of similarity of character will have interesting implications for *commendationes* based substantially on character.)[24] One can also find a number of frequently repeated specific ideals: a friend should be forgiving but frank in advice and criticism;[25] a man has an obligation to spread his friend's fame and reputation (an obligation which also carries interesting implications for the objectivity or otherwise of *commendationes*);[26] a man should attend to a friend when ill and look after his family, interests and reputation after his death;[27] on the one hand, friends should attend to petty formalities and expressions of affection, such as *vota* on birthdays, congratulations on reaching office, and letter writing; on the other hand, close friends may be allowed the liberty of dispensing with the formalities.[28] Clearly, there is little in these ideals that the political changes from Republic to Principate would have altered.

The ideals of common interests and selfless service represent a philosophical view of *amicitia*. In the correspondences and histories, on the other hand, it can be seen that in the common view *amicitia* was expected basically to entail reciprocal exchange of *officia* and *beneficia*. Even Seneca admits this exchange to be a necessary part, though not the purpose, of *amicitia*.[29] Fronto, however, drawing on the more common meaning of *amicitia*, distinguishes *amicitia* from *amor* which is based on affection rather than mutual services. In a letter to Marcus Aurelius, Fronto rejoices that their relationship is one of *amor* instead of *amicitia*, because the former, unlike the flame of burning logs, continues and grows without tending. *Amicitiae* by contrast require the constant nourishment of new *officia*.[30]

The range of goods and services exchanged will be outlined in later chapters. It is enough to say at this point that the fundamentally instrumental nature of Roman friendship was a corollary of the underdevelopment of rational,

conveys many similar ideas in *Nicomachean Ethics* 8 and 9. For a more detailed discussion, see Brunt, 'Amicitia'.

22 *Ep. ad Luc.* 9.8f.; 48.2-4; Pliny, *Ep.* 9.30.1.
23 Pliny, *Ep.* 4.15; 5.14; Seneca, *De Prov.* 1.5; *Ep. ad Luc.* 6.3. Cf. Brunt, 'Amicitia', 1f.
24 See below, p.109.
25 Seneca, *De Ben.* 6.33.1f., *De Ira* 3.13.3-4; *Ep. ad Luc.* 25.1; 112.1f.
26 Pliny, *Ep.* 3.11.1 and 9; 7.28.
27 Pliny, *Ep.* 1.12.7f.; 1.17.2; 2.10.5; 3.5.3; Tacitus, *Ann.* 2.71; 15.62 and 71; Seneca, *Ep. ad Luc.* 78.4; 85.29.
28 Pliny, *Ep.* 9.37.1; *Paneg.* 61.8; Fronto, *Ad M. Caes.* 3.9; 5.31; *Ad amic.* 1.17. See Michel, *Gratuité en droit romain*, 534ff.
29 *De Ben.* 1.5.5. Michel, *Gratuité*, 502-29, emphasizes the two threads in the thought of the Latin moralists: (1) pragmatic reciprocal exchange, pervasive in the society, and (2) selfless, spiritual friendship.
30 *Ad. M. Caes.* 1.3.4f.

impersonal institutions for the provision of services.[31] Writing about the whole
of antiquity, A. R. Hands summarized the point well: 'for this [aristocratic]
class of men the need to maintain "friendships" turned in part on the fact...
that even in a money economy there were still a considerable number of
services essential to comfort and security which could not be bought for
money... "friends" supplied services analogous to those provided by bankers,
lawyers, hotel owners, insurers and others today'.[32]

In all of the relevant literature, the reciprocal nature of the exchange is
emphasized. An *amicus* in receipt of a favor was expected to return it at an
appropriate time and to show gratitude. Nothing was baser than an *ingratus
amicus*, and ingratitude was seen as just cause for the breaking off of *amicitia*.[33]
Even Seneca accepted this reciprocity ethic, which together with the ideal of
eschewing *amicitia* based on *utilitas* produced the paradox mentioned above:
a man was not supposed to form a friendship or distribute a favor with a view to
the return, and yet he knew that his *amicus*/recipient was in fact obliged to
make a return. This paradox does not seem to have troubled men less
self-conscious than Seneca: the exchange of *beneficia* and the cementing of
amicitiae were ordinary parts of everyday life — the subtleties of purity of
motive were easily ignored. For Seneca, on the other hand, the paradox
created problems. The Stoic wise man should not form *amicitiae* for the
purpose of *utilitas*, yet *utilitas* inevitably results from *amicitia* — how can that
utilitas not enter into the wise man's thoughts? The answer: what virtue does
not have *utilitas* as a by-product? 'But that is said to be desired for its own sake
which, even though it possesses some outside advantages, would still be
pleasing even if those advantages were stripped off and removed.'[34] Seneca's
argument here would seem to underline the instrumental nature of Roman
amicitia: even the self-sufficient wise man would be expected to exchange
beneficia, and so it requires a logical argument to show that this would not be

---

31 Eric Wolf argues for the usefulness of the distinction between instrumental and emotional in
'Kinship, friendship, and patron-client relations' in *The Social Anthropology of Complex
Societies*, ed. M. Banton. In a legitimate argument against the equation of *amicitia* with
political alliance, Brunt, 'Amicitia', 1, stresses that in Cicero's view friendship arises 'from
natural affection and benevolence from which in turn reciprocal services result'. Brunt's
emphasis is somewhat different from that in the Fronto passage above. The relative
importance of emotional attachment vis-à-vis exchange of *officia* is impossible precisely to
evaluate, nor would the two have always been clearly separable. For my purposes it is
enough to say that neither Cicero nor Brunt denies that reciprocal exchange was a
fundamental part of *amicitia*.
32 *Charities and Social Aid in Greece and Rome*, 32ff.; also Veyne, *Le pain*, 17 and Michel,
Gratuité, 562.
33 Seneca, *De Ben.* 7.31.1. See Michel, *Gratuité*, 589ff., for the sanctions enforcing
reciprocity, and Hands, *Charities and Social Aid*, for a good treatment of reciprocity in
general.
34 *De Ben.* 4.20: 'Sed id propter se expeti dicitur, quod, quamvis habeat aliqua extra
commoda, sepositis quoque illis ac remotis placet.'

the aim of his friendships. In short, the Romans could hardly conceive of friendship without reciprocal exchange.

The above description of the role of the *amicus* in terms of reciprocal exchange has begun to introduce aspects of interest for the study of patronage. But neither the word *amicus* nor the words *patronus* and *cliens* are fully satisfactory pointers to patronage relationships. The latter two were avoided for reasons of politeness except in inscriptions. The category of *amicitia*, on the other hand, encompasses a larger group of social relations than we are concerned with in this study, since it includes exchange relationships between men of equal, as well as unequal, social status. Where the term *amicus* occurs with respect to a friendship between men known to be of unequal status, we can assume a patronage relationship. But where the respective statuses are unknown, the relationship cannot be assumed to meet our definition of patronage and so cannot be used as evidence.

Since patron-client relationships were essentially instrumental — that is, based on the exchange of goods and services — the words which describe the exchange are perhaps the best pointers to patronage. The basic words set out for discussion here are *officium, beneficium, meritum* and *gratia*. The list could be expanded, but limitations of space require some selection, and a discussion of these four basic words will provide a clear idea of the reciprocity ethic which is the *sine qua non* of patronal societies.

Officium

The meaning and social significance of *officium* in the Republic, according to Hellegouarc'h, can be summarized in the following way.[35] The Romans themselves recognized *officium* as a basic element in their social relations. Originally *officium* was the activity proper to a particular category of people (e.g., craftsmen). This developed into an idea of the 'rules' or 'obligations' proper to certain categories, especially categories of social relationships such as between *necessarii* or *amici*. *Officium* in the sense of 'a favor' came to be the concrete expression of the *fides* implicit in such relationships. Like *fides*, *officium* entailed an element of reciprocity — thus an *officium* from a patron to a client was possible, just as from a client to a patron. This reciprocal aspect is reflected in the language of debt associated with *officium*: a man receiving an *officium* is often said 'to owe' (*debere*) one in return, and the phrase *officium reddere* expresses the idea of acquitting oneself of a debt.

During the Empire reciprocity continued to be an important element in the meaning of *officium*, but it should not be understood in an overly simplified manner as a direct one-for-one exchange.[36] Cicero exhorted the readers of his

35 Pp. 152-63.
36 As the anthropologist Marshall Sahlins has pointed out: 'the casual received view of reciprocity supposes some fairly direct one-for-one exchange, balanced reciprocity, or a

De Officiis 'to become good calculators of duty (*boni ratiocinatores officiorum*), able by adding and subtracting to strike a balance correctly and find out just how much is due to each individual'.[37] This passage, together with another from the *De Officiis* (1.47), has been used to show that *officia* had a material value capable of measurement and that this 'money of exchange' was allotted to friends, patrons, and clients only in the measure that they could be expected to repay.[38]

Cicero's statement should not, however, be interpreted too literally. In the same paragraph (1.59) Cicero suggests that the recipient's need should also be considered when distributing *officia* — a factor likely to be in conflict with the criterion of expected return.[39] Furthermore, whatever Cicero's exhortations in a moral tract, strict accounting, precise evaluation and exact repayment of debt were rarely possible in the realm of day-to-day social favors. Cicero's letters provide a clear illustration of why this was true. Before civil war broke out in 49 Cicero twice successfully defended a certain Acilius in capital cases.[40] After Caesar's victory at Pharsalus, Acilius was appointed proconsul of Sicily, during which time Cicero requested from him a number of favors for clients and friends. What was one of these — for instance, Acilius' recognition of Demetrius Megas' citizenship[41] — worth in comparison with Cicero's services as advocate? It was surely impossible for either of them to say with precision. In Book 13 of the *Epistulae ad Familiares* ten *commendationes* addressed to Acilius are preserved:[42] how many favors was Acilius required to perform before he absolved his debt to Cicero? By the very nature of *officia* the exchange of services operated outside of an impersonal market context in which their value could be quantified in terms of a common standard, and so ambiguity must inevitably have surrounded their exchange in the Republic and the Principate as well. (The only exceptions to this rule were the few instances in which monetary values could be assigned.)[43]

near approximation of balance... [However, in primitive societies] balanced reciprocity is not the prevalent form of exchange. A question might even be raised about the stability of balanced reciprocity. Balanced exchange may tend toward self-liquidation' ('On the Sociology of Primitive Exchange', in *The Relevance of Models for Social Anthropology*, ed. M. Banton, 178).

37 *De Off.* 1.59: 'Haec igitur et talia circumspicienda sunt in omni officio, ut boni ratiocinatores officiorum esse possimus et addendo deducendoque videre, quae reliqui summa fiat, ex quo, quantum cuique debeatur, intellegas'.

38 Hellegouarc'h, *Le vocabulaire*, 154f.

39 *De Off.* 1.47. Other considerations suggested by Cicero include bonds of affection and relationship to the benefactor.

40 Cicero, *Ad Fam.* 7.30; for the identification of Acilius, D.R. Shackleton Bailey, *Cicero: Epistulae ad Familiares*, 435f.

41 *Ad Fam.* 13.36.

42 *Ad Fam.* 13.30-39.

43 The unquantifiable quality of *officia* in my view makes much modern exchange theory, as described by Anthony Heath, *Rational Choice and Social Exchange: A Critique of Exchange Theory*, useless for the study here. How can one demonstrate that Romans were

The effect of this ambiguity on the durability of patronage and friendship bonds has been explored in anthropological work about the social ramifications of exchange. It has been suggested that 'balanced exchange may tend toward self-liquidation', for the reason that a precise one-for-one exchange — that is, a complete and conscious absolution of debt — leaves both parties free to break off the relationship without moral recriminations.[44] Ambiguity of the kind illustrated in Cicero's letters to Acilius generally precluded a clear, exact balance. It was difficult for an exchange partner to opt out of a relationship on the grounds that his debts were paid up, when he could not be sure whether the repayment was commensurate with the initial favor. It is Cicero once again who offers the clearest illustration of this point in a letter to Curio.

Curio, if only my *officia* to you were as great as you yourself are accustomed to proclaim rather than as I evaluate them, I would be more reserved in my effort in requesting some great favor. For it is a serious matter for a man of modesty to request something great from another from whom he believes he deserves well; he does not wish to appear to demand what he requests rather than to ask it, and to count the request as payment instead of a *beneficium*. But since your *beneficia* for me are known to everyone... and it is the mark of a noble spirit to wish to owe more to the same man to whom you are already in great debt, I have not hesitated to make my request...[45]

Here the ambiguity of balance and the perceived (or pretended) imbalance proclaimed by each in favor of the other permits each to ask favors of the other without the arrogance of demanding repayment. It also rather commits the other to fulfill the requests, since each pretends to be under obligation to the other. Though we have no passage of similar clarity in Pliny's or Fronto's letters, the obligation of reciprocity continued, and so the ambiguity inherent in the exchange must have continued to make people reluctant to break off *amicitiae*.

Beneficium and meritum

Beneficium, which basically means 'kindness' or 'favor', carries much the same force as *officium* when the latter is used with regard to exchange. In studies of Republican usage, an attempt is frequently made to distinguish the two words

naturally manipulating the *officia* exchanges to maximize their gain when there was and is no means of precisely measuring the gain?

44 See note 36 above.

45 Cicero, *Ad Fam*. 2.6.1-2: 'Ego, si mea in te essent officia solum, Curio, tanta, quanta magis a te ipso praedicari quam a me ponderari solent, verecundius a te, si quae magna res mihi petenda esset, contenderem. Grave est enim homini pudenti petere aliquid magnum ab eo, de quo se bene meritum putet, ne id, quod petat, exigere magis, quam rogare et in mercedis potius, quam beneficii loco numerare videatur. Sed quia tua in me vel nota omnibus vel ipsa novitate meorum temporum clarissima et maxima beneficia exstiterunt, [I will ask the favor].'

with reference to their varying connotations or the different social contexts in which each is appropriate. For instance, it has been suggested that the initial favor was labelled *beneficium*, which created an obligation for the recipient to return an *officium*. Hellegouarc'h has rightly dismissed this notion, pointing out that both can give birth to *amicitia*.[46]

With more justification the two words have been distinguished on the basis of whether the favor was bestowed within an already existing *fides*-relationship. This distinction finds support in Seneca's comment that 'beneficium esse quod alienus det (alienus est qui potuit sine reprehensione cessare), officium esse filii, uxoris, earum personarum quas necessitudo suscitat et ferre opem iubet'. ('A *beneficium* is that which a stranger gives (a stranger is one who is in a position not to give without incurring blame); an *officium* is given by a son or a wife or other persons whom a prior relationship moves and requires to provide help.')[47] From this passage, Hellegouarc'h remarks, 'il en résulte que les *officia*, qui sont imposés par une sorte de contrainte sociale, sont moins prisés que les *beneficia*, marque d'un cœur généreux'.[48] It should be noticed, however, that these lines from Seneca represent a view of 'some men' (including the Stoic Hecaton), which Seneca regards as mistaken. Whatever the outcome of this philosophical disagreement, there can be no doubt that Hecaton's distinction did not govern common usage. It is not uncommon to find *beneficium* used of exchanges in established relationships. At the most extreme, a slave could perform a *beneficium* for his master (in the words of the elder Cato, no less),[49] a son for his father,[50] an allied or subordinate city or state for Rome,[51] and a citizen for his country.[52] It might be suggested that we should not expect rigid distinctions in usage and that these are some of the few confusing cases which ought to be set aside.[53] It should be pointed out, however, that the largest concentration of Republican uses of *beneficium* falls into the category of 'favors between aristocratic friends'. A survey of the usages listed in the *Thesaurus Linguae Latinae* shows that for every one use of *beneficium* which might qualify as a 'spontaneous favor' three refer to exchanges in established *amicitia* relationships. With these two words, then, it is not a question of occasional confusion and overlap; rather, a basic

---

46 *Le vocabulaire*, 165.
47 *De Ben.* 3.18.1.
48 *Le vocabulaire*, 165.
49 Cato, *Agr.* 5.2; Val. Max. 6.8.3.
50 Livy 40.10.9.
51 Sallust, *Iug.* 14.3.f.; Livy 37.49.3.
52 Cicero, *De Invent.* 2.104, 106, 115; *De Leg.* 3.25; *Ad Fam.* 12.1.2; 10.14.2; 7.28.3; *Mil.* 83; *Cael.* 74; *Sulla* 26; *Domo* 74f.; *Phil.* 3.11; 5.37; *Verr.* 2.2.112; *Sest.* 49; Ps-Cicero, *Ad Heren.* 1.24; Sallust, *Iug.* 31.28; Livy 2.2.7; 6.20.10; Val. Max. 6.2.3. The passages from Cicero are particularly interesting because of his position that a man's foremost obligation is to serve his state (*De Off.* 1.57)—the fulfillment of the obligation can be a *beneficium*.
53 Hellegouarc'h, *Le vocabulaire*, 165.

distinction drawn by some modern scholars does not conform to the majority of uses of *beneficium*. Further, if *beneficium* is often found where we might expect *officium*, the reverse occurs as well. In *De Officiis* (1.48) Cicero suggests that a man might initiate a relationship by performing an *officium* in the hope of receiving a *beneficium* in return (a sequence in which the traditional model is reversed).

Another of Seneca's statements is sometimes used to draw a third distinction between *beneficium* and *officium*. He wrote: 'beneficium enim id est quod quis dedit, cum illi liceret et non dare'. ('For a *beneficium* is that which someone gives when it is also permitted for him not to give.')[54] Thus a *beneficium* is said to have been a purely gratuitous act which, in contrast to an *officium*, did not give the benefactor a right to repayment. For, as Seneca noted, 'nemo beneficia in calendario scribit nec avarus exactor ad horam et diem appellat'. ('No one writes down *beneficia* in his debt-book, nor does an avaricious collector demand them at a given hour and day.')[55] But the explanation for these statements does not lie in the fact that reciprocity was less a fundamental element in the meaning of *beneficium* than of *officium*.[56] Rather, it lies in the ethical rule that a benefactor was not supposed to bestow a favor (*beneficium* or *officium*) with its return in mind. A return was nevertheless expected from the recipient, and his failure to reciprocate brought moral condemnation, the *ingratus homo* being among the lowest forms of social life, according to Cicero and Seneca.[57] For the good of the recipient's character, a benefactor might even regard it as proper to prod him to fulfill this obligation.[58] Though this ethic of reciprocity may not have commanded universal adherence, it is beyond doubt that it was taken seriously, as an example from the time of the civil wars shows. Asinius Pollio refused to join Octavian's fight against Antony on the grounds that 'illius [Antonii] in me beneficia notiora [sc. sunt].' ('Antony's *beneficia* to me are very well known.')[59] Apparently Octavian accepted this moral reason as sufficient justification for neutrality. Here, as with most other uses of *beneficium* in Republican and imperial literature, the ethic of reciprocity is expressed or implied.[60]

One final distinction found in Republican studies is expressed by Hellegouarc'h: 'ce qui caractérise *beneficium* par rapport à *officium*, c'est qu'il implique une superiorité de celui qui l'accorde sur celui qui le reçoit'.[61] Though

---

54 *De Ben.* 3.19.1.
55 *De Ben.* 1.2.3.
56 As suggested by Hellegouarc'h, *Le vocabulaire*, 163ff.
57 Cicero, *De Off.* 1.47f.; Seneca, *De Ben.*, *passim*, esp. 1.10.4.
58 Seneca, *De Ben.* 7.23.3.
59 Vell. Pater. 2.86.3.
60 The only significant exception is legal usage in the *Digest*.
61 *Le vocabulaire*, 167

not entirely accurate, this comment provides a useful insight into the significance of *beneficium*-exchange in the dynamics of social ranking, and helps us to understand certain kinds of behavior, especially the reluctance to accept or publicize the receipt of *beneficia*, commented upon by Seneca.[62] That one man could deliver a needed favor to another served as public proof that the former was more powerful than the latter and hence more worthy of cultivation as a patron. But this principle had an effect only when the benefactor and recipient were of sufficiently similar social status to make competition between them for social prestige conceivable. Another class of exchange relationships between unequal partners existed, and *beneficium* was used to describe the favors from both sides, while in no way implying that the inferior's *beneficium* to his social superior proved the former's ascendancy. Provincials could deliver *beneficia* to their governors and soldiers to their commanders,[63] but there was no question in such cases of a superiority of the former.

In sum, the distinction between *officium* and *beneficium* is far from clear. In his *De Officiis* Cicero uses the word *officium* in the general sense of 'duties appropriate to men'. One of the duties described is generosity, that is, the distribution of favors.[64] These specific favors are also called *officia*. Clearly, *officium* in its general sense of duty carries a different meaning from *beneficium*. But in its specific sense of an act of generosity (the sense of interest in this study) the meaning of *officium* overlaps with that of *beneficium* almost completely. Indeed, Cicero himself uses the two words interchangeably in this passage from the *De Officiis*. For our purposes here we may conclude that both words are used to describe patronage relationships and so are of concern to us when they appear on inscriptions or in the literature.

A third word, *meritum*, is equally difficult to distinguish from *beneficium* or *officium*.[65] As with *officium*, passages can be cited in which *meritum* is used interchangeably or in parallel with *beneficium* with no clear distinction.[66] In a single passage in his *De Beneficiis* Seneca uses all three words synonymously.

A favor (*beneficium*) is owed in the same spirit in which it is given, and therefore it should not be given carelessly. For a man owes only himself for what he receives from an unwitting giver. A favor should not be given late, because in view of the fact that in every favor (*officium*) the goodwill of the giver is considered of great importance, the tardy giver has not wished to give for a long time. In particular, the favor should not be bestowed in an abusive fashion; for since nature has ordained it that insults sink in deeper than quickly forgotten favors (*merita*), the memory stubbornly retaining the

62 *De Ben.* 2.21.5 and 2.23.1.
63 Cicero, *Verr.* 2.3.44; Caesar, *B.C.* 2.32.1f. To support the same point one could add the references in notes 49 through 52 above.
64 *De Off.* 1.42ff.
65 Hellegouarc'h, *Le vocabulaire*, 170.
66 E.g., Cicero, *Domo* 74f.; *Post red. in Sen.* 1; *Mil.* 100.

former, what should a benefactor expect if he offends at the same time as he puts the recipient under obligation?[67]

What is to be made of this overlap of meaning among the three words? The above arguments are not meant to show that *officium, beneficium* and *meritum* in their senses of 'favor' never had different shades of meaning. Individual writers in specific contexts may well have intended certain differences at times. But nothing approaching a universal distinction can be pinpointed.

Gratia

Gratia differs from the above synonyms in that it represents an attitude rather than an action, and basically means 'goodwill'. It was used of animate and inanimate objects simply to mean 'pleasing', while in connection with social exchange it took on a more specific sense analogous to *favor* or *voluntas*. *Gratia* was often provoked by a *beneficium* or *officium* for which it constituted a kind of repayment. Hence, it frequently appears with verbs such as *debere, referre, pendere, persolvere* and *reddere*, an indication that the relationship was thought of as something like that of debtor and creditor. In Republican politics, according to Hellegouarc'h, the *gratia* of friends and clients was manifested essentially by their votes; with the decline of the voting assemblies in the Principate, the manifestations, though not the concept of *gratia*, underwent some change (though the change should not be overestimated, as will be shown in later chapters).[68] Like other words in the *grates* family, *gratia* could have an active and a passive sense: as well as expressing the active return of a favor, *gratia* could also have the passive sense of the 'influence' of the man who is dispensing favors and to whom return is owed. In its active sense, it has been suggested, *gratia* was especially appropriate to clients in relationships of dependence (as opposed to *amicitia* between equals).[69] This may be doubted, since in Book 13 of Cicero's *Epistulae ad Familiares*, for example, *gratia* in its active sense is used more frequently in connection with *amici* of equal status than with regard to relationships of dependence.

In sum, the Latin words describing favors and their return are no more susceptible of precise definitions or delimitations of appropriate social contexts than is *amicus*. The attempt to draw distinctions with the aid of

---

67 *De Ben.* 1.1.8: 'eodem animo beneficium debetur, quo datur, et ideo non est neglegenter dandum; sibi enim quisque debet, quod a nesciente accepit; ne tarde quidem, quia, cum omni in officio magni aestimetur dantis voluntas, qui tarde fecit, diu noluit; utique non contumeliose; nam cum ita natura comparatum sit, ut altius iniuriae quam merita descendant et illa cito defluant, has tenax memoria custodiat, quid expectat, qui offendit, dum obligat?'

68 Hellegouarc'h, *Le vocabulaire*, 202-8.

69 *Ibid.*, 206.

comments and definitions offered by Roman writers, who were frequently interested in ideals or caught up in philosophical debate, has led to confusion and error. In ordinary usage *beneficium, officium, meritum* and *gratia* were not closely related to specific, mutually exclusive categories of social relationships, just as *amicitia* did not represent a single category.

Having explored the general meanings and connotations of the basic language, we may proceed in two directions. First, it has become clear that a common element in all this language is the notion of reciprocity, and in the process of discussing it we have in effect described the Roman ideology of exchange, one similar to that which Marcel Mauss explored in relation to other societies.[70] The remainder of this chapter will be devoted to identifying the main social roles (parent, advocate, administrator, etc.) which were significantly affected by this ideology. In the later chapters the key words will be used as indicators of concrete patronage relationships. For in addition to *patronus* and *cliens*, it is clear that *amicus, beneficium, officium, meritum* and *gratia* can be used as signs of reciprocal exchange relationships which, if the additional qualification of inequality of status is met, can be used as evidence of patronage.

LANGUAGE AND SOCIAL ROLES

The political changes brought by Augustus and his successors do not seem to have altered the basic lexical meanings of the key words. Hellegouarc'h implicitly attests to this when he uses Seneca as well as Cicero as evidence for the Republican meanings of the same words. Hellegouarc'h and others working on this language do seem to think, on the other hand, that the words no longer possessed any real force in the ideology of the Empire. Moussy in his study of *gratia* came to the conclusion that

en effet, sous l'Empire, la disparition progressive des institutions républicaines transforme profondément les conditions de la politique, et les relations du clientèle ou amitié ne jouent plus qu'un rôle secondaire dans l'acquisition de l'autorité, de l'influence d'un homme d'État. Cette évolution fait sentir ses effets dans le domaine du vocabulaire politique, jusqu'alors peu fixé: 'Avec la disparition de toute vie politique digne de ce nom, ce vocabulaire se stabilisera, il se sclérosera aussi'.[71]

It should be noted that in coming to this conclusion Moussy does not offer a detailed study of usages of *gratia* in the political context of the Principate. Instead he cites Hellegouarc'h who puts the point more strongly in the conclusion of his book: 'd'un vocabulaire tout rempli de la passion et de l'ambition de ceux qui l'emploient, l'on aboutit peu à peu à un jargon de

---

70 *The Gift*, transl. I. Cunnison.
71 Moussy, *Gratia*, 390f.; quotation is from Hellegouarc'h, *Le vocabulaire*, 570.

bureaucrates, de fonctionnaires et de mandarins'.[72]

Hellegouarc'h and Moussy rightly perceive that the force of the patronal language and ideology is closely related to the administrative structures of a society. With the introduction in modern times of rational-legal bureaucracies, patronage may continue to exist covertly, but the ideal social roles of administrators and others cease to be defined in patronal terms. Hellegouarc'h and Moussy seem to be suggesting that the same sort of development occurred in the Principate, that the impact on society of the ethic implicit in words such as *officium* came to be overshadowed by impersonal administrative structures. In the remaining pages of this chapter their hypothesis will be tested by pinpointing the social roles which continued to incorporate the expectation of reciprocal exchange. In view of the evidence which can be adduced to illustrate the continuing effect of the ethic in virtually all walks of life, the hypothesis must seem dubious.

Before proceeding to discuss the various social relationships which fall within our definition of patronage, it should be noted that reciprocity continued in the Principate to be a basic element in other types of social relations. Just as in the Republic, the language of exchange was used to conceptualize man-god, family and friendship relations.

The contractual nature of Roman religion, often remarked upon, is reflected in the use of words such as *officium, beneficium* and *gratia*, and these words continued to be used in the Principate. For instance, references to prosperity and good luck as *beneficia* of the gods, Fortuna or Nature are scattered evenly through the literature of the Republic and Principate.[73] As far as can be seen, the feeling that the gods deserved *gratia* in return also continued with little change.[74] At Claudius' prompting the Senate passed a *senatus consultum* in order that 'benignitati deum gratiam referendam'.[75]

Although there is no statistical evidence available on which to base conclusions about the continuity of customs related to Roman family life, it can

---

72 Hellegouarc'h, *Le vocabulaire*, 570.
73 Pliny, *N.H.* 12.1; Quint., *Decl.* 268; Seneca, *Ep. ad Luc.* 8.3.In a recent essay('When the saints go marching out: Reflections on the decline of patronage in Malta', in *Patrons and Clients*, ed. Gellner and Waterbury, 81) Boissevain used recent changes in Malta to emphasize the connection between the conceptualization of man-god and patron-client relationships. In past ages the saints played a crucial part in the Catholicism of Malta as mediators. But with the recent modernization in Maltese society and the gradual disappearance of the powerful patrons mediating between villages and central institutions, the role of the saints has also gradually diminished and the religion has become more Christocentric. It thus seems that 'religious and political patronage reinforce each other'. That such a change did not occur in Roman religion argues against any major changes in social relations away from patronage.
74 Seneca, *Ep. ad Luc.* 119.16.
75 Tacitus, *Ann.* 11.15. Unlike 'gratiam agere', 'gratiam referre' is not a banal idiom meaning 'to thank'. It is appropriate specifically as a response to a *beneficium*.(*TLL* VI.2, 2219, 29.)

at least be suggested that the *beneficium-gratia* concept remained a part of the mores of kinship. A new husband, having been given his wife's virginity, was said to be *beneficio obstrictus*.[76] Pliny used the language of exchange to explain how the less-than-praiseworthy Domitius Tullus partially redeemed himself after his death. Although he had courted legacy-hunters, in the end '*pietas, fides* and *pudor* wrote his will in which gratitude (*gratia*) was returned to all of his relatives in proportion to the *officium* of each, especially his wife'.[77] Inscriptions dedicated to kin *ob merita* or *ob beneficia* also suggest that these words were commonly linked with kinship relations.[78]

With respect to the wider group of the *familia* it was briefly suggested in the section concerning *beneficium* that master-slave and patron-freedman relationships were to some extent governed by notions of reciprocal exchange. Though passages from Republican literature were cited, it can be shown that this aspect of *familia* relationships continued into the Empire. Manumission, for instance, is frequently referred to as the most important *beneficium* a master might bestow, one which put the freedman under a heavy moral as well as legal obligation.[79] Exchange in the reverse direction also was possible, and not only in the view of the moralizing Seneca. In several cases in the *Digest* the jurists wrote on the assumption that a slave or freedman could perform some service (*beneficium* or *meritum*) deserving reward.[80] An inscription from Lower Germany (*CIL* XIII. 8658) records the dedication of a *patrona* to her freedman *ob merita*.

The Roman ideal of friendship between equals has already been explored in the process of defining the word *amicus*. We may add here that the language of reciprocity continued to be used casually in day-to-day communication in a way which suggests that the reciprocity ethic remained basic in shaping the social role of the *amicus*. Pliny, for instance, was asked by his friend Statius Sabinus to take on a legal case on behalf of Firmum (of which Sabinus was patron). Noting that Sabinus sought his friendship for the sake of 'praesidium ornamentumque', Pliny accepted the case: 'for I desire to bind to myself (*obstringere*) both a distinguished town by *officium advocationis* and you by this *munus* which is *gratissimum* to you'.[81] In addition to illustrating the use of the *officium-gratia* language between friends, this passage suggests an element of the ideology which contributed to the extension of networks of mutual

---

76 Apuleius, *Apol.* 92.
77 *Ep.* 8.18.7: 'pietas fides pudor scripsit [sc. testamentum], in quo denique omnibus adfinitatibus pro cuiusque officio gratia relata est, relata et uxori'.
78 E.g., *CIL* III.6833 (= *ILS* 7199), III.7644, VII.189.
79 Often in the *Digest*, e.g., 38.2.1.
80 *Dig.* 24.3.64.5; 38.2.47.2.
81 *Ep.* 6.18.1: 'Cupio enim et ornatissimam coloniam advocationis officio, et te gratissimo tibi munere obstringere'. See Sherwin-White, *Letters of Pliny,* 375, for the identification of this Sabinus as 'a military man and man of letters'.

obligation: friends not only exchanged personal favors between themselves, but they also exchanged and were bound by favors for their clients and other friends. Indeed, to judge by the letters of Pliny and Fronto, one of the largest categories of *beneficia* binding aristocratic friends together were favors for clients and protégés. Further, the client, obligated by the *beneficium* to both his original patron and his new benefactor, was thought to be in an ideal position to draw the two patron-friends closer together. Pliny again provides an illustration. He apparently recommended an equestrian protégé Pompeius Saturninus to a friend Priscus (which Priscus is uncertain). We have three letters concerning the relationship written some time after the initial introduction. In the first two (7. 7-8) Pliny relays expressions of gratitude and affection from Priscus to Saturninus and then back again. In the third letter (7.15) to Saturninus Pliny indicates that Saturninus has been staying with Priscus and enjoying his companionship. 'I had known of his (Priscus') frankness and his charming companionship, but I am experiencing now what I was less aware of, that he is *gratissimus*, since you write that he has such happy memories of my services (*nostra officia*)'.[82] Saturninus seems here to have strengthened the bond of friendship between his patrons by providing a personal channel of communication for expressions of mutual respect and gratitude.

One final indication of the strength of the reciprocity ethic in the social role of the *amicus* in the Principate is the use of buried treasure and investment metaphors with respect to *beneficia* bestowed on friends. Because friends were so strongly obliged to return favors, all *beneficia* distributed to them were felt to be insurance against misfortune since in time of need they could be called in. As Seneca says, a *beneficium* should be stored away like a buried treasure (*thensaurus*), 'which you would not dig up, except from necessity'.[83] The recipient, on the other hand, should be content to guard the *beneficium* until a time of need. He should not contrive a situation to make the return, but should wait: 'if [the benefactor] prefers that [the favor] should remain in our custody, why do we dig up the treasure (*thensaurus*)?'[84] In addition to other investments (houses, ships, cattle, slaves) about which people are careless, Columella cites *beneficia* bestowed on friends: 'for many destroy by fickleness the *beneficia* which they had conferred on friends'.[85]

---

82 *Ep.* 7.15.3: 'Noveram simplicitatem eius, noveram comitatem; eundem esse (quod minus noram) gratissimum experior, cum tam iucunde officiorum nostrorum meminisse eum scribas.' For the identification of Priscus compare Sherwin-White, *Letters of Pliny*, 412, with C. P. Jones, 'A new commentary of the Letters of Pliny', *Phoenix* 22 (1968), 128, relying on Syme, 'The jurist Neratius Priscus', *Hermes* 85 (1957), 480.

83 *De Vita Beata* 24.2: 'beneficium conlocetur, quemadmodum thensaurus alte obrutus, quem non eruas, nisi fuerit necesse'.

84 *De Ben.* 6.43.3: 'si illud apud nos custodiri mavult, quid thensaurum eius eruimus?'

85 *De Re Rustica* 4.3.2. 'multi etiam beneficia quae in amicos contulerunt, levitate destruunt'.

The above evidence demonstrates that the language of reciprocity did not become exclusively 'un jargon de bureaucrates, de fonctionnaires et de mandarins' in the Principate. Romans continued to use words such as *beneficium* and *gratia* in their private lives to conceptualize social roles involved in man-god, familial and friendship relations. Can the same be said for the social roles associated with public and professional life? Hellegouarc'h and Moussy clearly think not. But to uphold their position it would have to be demonstrated that a dichotomy developed in the language and thinking about *familia* and friends on the one hand and public roles on the other. Before examining the Roman evidence, we may note that comparative material from the modern Mediterranean suggests that such a dichotomy is unlikely; that a strong reciprocity ethic between family and friends is usually reflected in the expectations of men involved in public life.[86] During the Principate there were great obstacles to the development of such a dichotomy, most importantly, the lack of specialized and professional roles for aristocratic administrators.[87] The consequences of this will be explored in later chapters. For our purposes here it is important to note that in the Principate, as in the Republic, aristocratic social roles straddled the public and private sectors, making it highly unlikely that the reciprocity ethic of private life would not also affect the role of the official.

The patron-protégé and advocate-client relationships illustrate the point: each has a public and a private aspect which are inextricably linked and which the Romans never tried to separate. The best source for what the Romans thought a patron-protégé relationship should be is Pliny's idealistic description of his friendship with his late patron, Q. Corellius Rufus. Clusinius Gallus had written to Pliny reminding him of his duty to defend the daughter of Corellius in court. In his reply Pliny described his relationship with Corellius as so intimate that Pliny could never doubt that the legal defense of the daughter was his duty.

I came to love him through admiration, and, contrary to the general rule, when I knew

---

86 The observations of anthropologists in Mediterranean countries today suggest that such a dichotomy is not to be expected. Jeremy Boissevain suggests that in Sicily the strong family morality is reflected in official administration ('Patronage in Sicily', *Man* n.s. 1 (1966), 18); see p.162 below. In *The People of the Sierra* (126ff.) Julian Pitt-Rivers describes a system of friendship strikingly similar to the Romans' (see note 20 above). No dichotomy existed between the morality expected from officials and the morality of reciprocity expected from family and friends. Officials could not be integrated into the community and expect to remain impartial when they performed their duties. The local officials assumed patronal roles with no pretense of impartially enforcing the laws. Outside officials who interfered to enforce laws strictly had to remain aloof, refusing offers of hospitality which might require reciprocation (unlike Roman officials). Altogether, a heavy burden of proof rests with those who wish to argue that a rational-legal bureaucracy can coexist with the kind of values outlined.

87 Two important recent articles which will be heavily relied upon in later chapters for this assertion are Brian Campbell, 'Who were the "viri militares"?', *JRS* 65 (1975), 11, and in the same volume P. A. Brunt, 'The administrators of Roman Egypt', 124.

him intimately I admired him even more. For I did know him intimately; he kept nothing hidden from me, whether grave or gay, joy or sorrow. I was only a young man at the time, and yet he showed me the regard and, I venture to say, the respect he would have shown an equal. When I sought office he gave me his support as sponsor (*suffragator*); I was introduced and attended by him when I entered upon my duties, and had him for guide and counsellor while I discharged them... Moreover, when he was dying he told his daughter (it is she who tells the story) that he had made many friends for her in the course of a long life, but none like Pliny and Cornutus Tertullus.[88]

Most of the essential aspects of the patron-protégé exchange relationship are represented in this passage. The patron was intended to serve as a general mentor. He helped his protégé's career financially, if necessary, and politically in his capacity as *suffragator* (i.e., 'one who recommends for office').[89] Once the protégé reached office, the patron accompanied and advised him in his duties. For his part the younger man was expected to praise his patron and so enhance his reputation; he also provided companionship for the older man in later life. The protégé was supposed to follow the political advice of his elder while in the senate and in office, thus allowing the patron to exercise political influence after his own *cursus* was completed. Finally, it was the protégé's duty to protect his friend's family and reputation after his death, and it was this responsibility which Pliny said that he was about to fulfill by his defense of Corellia.

In Pliny's letters (though not in this one), all of these duties, public and private, are described in terms of *beneficia, officia* and *gratia*.[90] Clearly, the

88 *Ep.* 4.17.4f.: 'Obversatur oculis ille vir quo neminem aetas nostra graviorem sanctiorem subtiliorem tulit, quem ego cum ex admiratione diligere coepissem, quod evenire contra solet, magis admiratus sum postquam penitus inspexi. Inspexi enim penitus: nihil a me ille secretum, non ioculare non serium, non triste non laetum. Adulescentulus eram, et iam mihi ab illo honor atque etiam (audebo dicere) reverentia ut aequali habebatur. Ille meus in petendis honoribus suffragator et testis, ille in incohandis deductor et comes, ille in gerendis consiliator et rector, ille denique in omnibus officiis nostris, quamquam et imbecillus et senior, quasi iuvenis et validus conspiciebatur... Quin etiam moriens filiae suae (ipsa solet praedicare): "Multos quidem amicos tibi ut longiore vita paravi, praecipuos tamen Secundum et Cornutum."' (Loeb translation.)

89 G. E. M. de Ste Croix has constructed an excellent essay about patronage around the changes of meaning in the word *suffragium* ('Suffragium', 33). He notes that the change of meaning from 'vote' in the Republic to 'patronal support' in the Principate reflects the elimination of the democratic elements in the Roman political system. His study obviously adds a qualification to the general assertion of continuity of language argued in this chapter. But it should be noted that in fact the qualification is not a major one: the patronal character of Republican politics and society cannot be doubted and it is only words tied to specific political institutions such as voting assemblies which undergo a substantial change of meaning. Even other words with the same root as *suffragium* but without ties to particular institutions (such as *suffragator*) do not change in meaning in the Principate, as de Ste Croix points out.

90 Financial and political aid: Pliny, *Ep.* 1.19; 2.13.2; 10.51; 7.22; 4.15; 3.8; 4.4; *Paneg.* 45, 91, 93. Advice while in office: Pliny, *Ep.* 2.1.8. Expressions of gratitude: Pliny, *Ep.* 2.13.9; also see 3.8.4.

whole of the relationship was being conceptualized in terms of exchange with a reciprocity ethic. This is especially noticeable in a particular sub-type of this relationship, that between literary patron and protégé.[91] Attendance at recitations of each other's compositions was a (wearisome) *beneficium* which had to be returned. The generous Pliny, after listening to the works of others, declined to have a formal reading of his own 'lest it seem that I was not a listener but a creditor of those whose recitations I attended. For, as in other things, so in the duty of listening (*audendi officium*) the gratitude (*gratia*) is lost if return is demanded.'[92] Side by side with this private aspect of their exchange is the public aspect: literary patrons attended to the welfare of their less wealthy protégés by appointing them to salaried posts on their own staffs while governing provinces or by using their influence to secure other posts in the imperial administration. Pliny showed this kind of concern for Suetonius and praised Titinius Capito for promoting the careers of young authors.[93] As Pliny noted, the traditional rewards for poets were *pecunia* and *honores*; the former derived from the patron's private resources and the latter from his public position.[94] Pliny's lament that the distribution of these *beneficia* had gone out of fashion need not be taken too seriously in view of the evidence

91 White's recent discussion of literary patronage ('Amicitia') seems misleading and contradictory in several respects. His conclusion is that 'poets attached themselves to wealthy households for reasons which had little to do with poetic interests, and much to do with the composition of Roman society... And once established in the *amicitia* of a rich man, poets received material benefits which were the perquisites of friends rather than the due of poetry' (92). While we may agree that literary patronage was one type of patronage which resembled other types, the exchange which it involved was distinct in important respects: (1) as White himself argues, the poet hoped for support and publicity for his work from his patron (85); (2) most importantly, the poet offered his verses and *libelli* as his part of the exchange (for example, Pliny, *Ep.* 3.21, explicitly says that he made Martial a gift of his travelling expenses back to Spain 'in recognition of our friendship and *the verses he wrote about me'* and that 'it was the custom in the past to reward poets who had sung praises of cities or individuals with gifts of office or money'). See note 94 below.

92 *Ep.* 1.13.6: 'ne videar, quorum recitationibus adfui, non auditor fuisse sed creditor. Nam ut in ceteris rebus ita in audiendi officio perit gratia si reposcatur'.

93 *Ep.* 1.24, 3.8, 8.12. White, 'Amicitia', 83, doubts whether 'provehere' in 8.12 means 'promote' with regard to public office. In view of Pliny's comment that *honores* were the traditional reward for poets, Radice's translation in the Loeb edition seems reasonable.

94 Pliny, *Ep.* 3.21. White ('Amicitia') attempts to play down the material aspect of the exchange between the poet and his friend or patron. He cites the Seventh Satire of Juvenal as evidence of the reluctance of the rich litterateurs to support poor poets, but Juvenal's satire would lack any point if such wealthy men were not *expected* to support poor poets (as poets and not just as friends). Moreover, Martial explicitly acknowledges the support of his Spanish patrons, one of whom gave him a house and an estate (*Epig.* 12.31), while the other relieved him of the need to work (the gift of the 'ingenuae ius pigritiae', 12.4). The fact that Martial was an *eques* does not mean that his own income was sufficient to support a household of the kind Martial desired, nor does any of White's evidence (89) show that it was. Moreover, the dearth of references to gifts of money in Martial's poems is of no significance whatever (*pace* White, 90)—Martial's epigram for Pliny (10.19) makes no mention of Pliny's gift; further, non-monetary gifts of the kind mentioned by Martial in other poems could be of great value.

provided by Pliny and others to the contrary.[95]

The second major example of a social role which straddled the public and private sectors is that of the advocate. In the Principate as in the Republic the advocate was called *patronus* and his services continued to be described by the words *beneficium*, *officium* and *meritum*. Indeed, since, as Quintilian points out, it was not honorable for an aristocratic advocate to set a fee for his services, he depended on the custom of reciprocity from his client-friends.

> The orator (i.e., advocate) will not wish to acquire more than is sufficient for him. And not even a poor orator will accept compensation as if it were pay; but he will enjoy a mutual generosity (*mutua benivolentia*) in the knowledge that his generosity has exceeded his compensation. Nor ought his service (*beneficium*) come to nothing because it ought not be sold. Finally, the man in debt (i.e., the client) has the primary responsibility to display his gratitude (*gratus*).[96]

Pliny uses the language of *gratia* with respect to the return for his legal services and indicates that such services were part of the duty of an *amicus*.[97] The entire argument for taking up oratory in Tacitus' *Dialogus* is based on a view of the advocate as patron-friend: in contrast to poetry, effective oratory in court attracts to the advocate *amici* and *clientes* whom he puts in his debt with *beneficium*.[98] The debt could be repaid in a variety of ways: it might take a financial form (e.g., legacies from wealthy and especially childless clients), or it could be in the shape of political support (so Eprius Marcellus and Vibius Crispus possessed formidable followings in the senate). The repayment from more humble clients might simply consist of public deference demonstrated by joining the patron's following in public places (*togatorum comitatus*).[99] Concrete instances of the advocate as patron will be examined in Chapter 4, but enough evidence has been presented here to illustrate how minimal was the degree of differentiation of aristocratic social roles in the Principate. Pliny thought of his legal services as one element in the stock of *beneficia* available for exchange with his friends, a stock in which *beneficia* of a public and private nature were not distinguished.[100]

95 Martial, *Epig.* 12.4 and 31. Pliny is known to have helped Martial and Suetonius (in *Ep.* 1.24 Pliny speaks of Suetonius' need for an estate *as a scholar*).
96 *Inst.* 12.7.12: 'Nihil ergo acquirere volet orator ultra quam satis erit; ac ne pauper quidem tamquam mercedem accipiet, sed mutua benivolentia utetur, cum sciat se tanto plus praestitisse. Non enim, quia venire hoc beneficium non oportet, oportet perire.Denique ut gratus sit ad eum magis pertinet qui debet.'
97 *Ep.* 3.4.7, 6.18.1
98 *Dial.* 9.4.
99 *Dial.* 5ff.; the advocate's receipt of legacies seems to be the point of mentioning the childless at the head of the list of important clients (6.2).
100 In *Patronus und Orator* Neuhauser shows how *patronus* and *orator* came to be used interchangeably for the barrister of the late Republic. This conclusion is interesting and his summary of work on various aspects of Republican patronage is useful, but his concluding remarks about the word *patronus* in the Empire seem dubious (205f.).

To summarize the argument so far, there is no evidence that the importance of the reciprocity ethic as described by the language of *beneficium* and *gratia* diminished in private relationships in the Principate. Furthermore, we have seen that in the Roman *Weltanschauung* there was no strong differentiation between Roman aristocrats' public and private social roles, with the idea that the exchange of favors was appropriate only in the latter. As a result, it is unlikely that a dichotomy developed between private and public morality (comparable to the dichotomy between the affection expected of parents and the impartiality expected of public officials today).[101] So as we come finally to the roles and expectations of officials in the Roman world, we should be skeptical of any view which suggests that when officials used the language of *beneficium* and *gratia* they meant something different from private individuals, something banal and without any implication of reciprocity.

In nearly all societies officials may sometimes deliver favors to family and friends. What sets Rome and other pre-modern societies apart from modern bureaucracies is that according to the ideology in Roman society public figures, from municipal administrators to the emperors, were not only expected, but were supposed to use their positions to bestow *beneficia* on friends. This is evident in the longest essay of practical advice to a public official which has come down to us, Plutarch's *Praecepta Gerendae Reipublicae*. The essay, written for an aspiring young municipal statesman Menemachus, contains a section about the proper use and treatment of friends while in office. When the statesman enters office he should not try to detach himself from his friends, but should call on them to help with public business,

The claim that the word *advocatus* completely replaced *patronus* after Tacitus' age is demonstrably false. A younger contemporary, Suetonius, used *patronus* as often as *advocatus* in his *Lives of the Caesars* to designate barristers (*Claud.* 16.2, *Iul.* 55.1, *Nero* 7.2). Nearly a half century after Tacitus Apuleius actually preferred *patronus* to *advocatus* when referring to legal representation in his *Apologia*. The paucity of Latin prose literature extant from the next century makes speculation about trends in usage useless.

The claim that technical legal argument replaced oratorical persuasion in the courts is more difficult to assess. Certainly, professional jurists came to be prominent in the emperor's *consilium*, but the examples of Fronto and Apuleius prove that the orator still had a place in legal hearings in the mid-second century. Indeed, we possess a request from Marcus Aurelius to Fronto that the latter restrain his oratory and suppress his invective in his case against Herodes Atticus (*Ad M. Caes.* 3.2-6).

Finally, the assertion about the danger involved in patronage as a result of political changes would, if true, have broad consequences for my argument. Two points should be made: (1) while there were some legal cases with dangerous political consequences (as there were in the Republic), the majority of them must have been of an ordinary nature unaffected by the institution of the Princeps or imperial politics; (2) politically inspired trials, far from discouraging patronage altogether, encouraged leading aristocrats to build up a clientèle in the senate (see below, p.141f.).

101 Roger Brown, *Social Psychology*, 157, discusses the sort of difference of roles (and possible conflicts) of interest here. For a discussion of the distinction between personal obligations and impersonal, bureaucratic morality, see P. Stirling, 'Impartiality and personal morality' in *Contributions to Mediterranean Sociology*, ed. J.-G. Peristiany, 49ff.

utilizing the particular talent of each. In return, the statesman should help his friends acquire honor and wealth. Their honor could be increased by giving the friends a share of the credit for popular acts or by sending them on embassies.[102] 'In public life means of assistance for needy friends in the acquisition of money exist which are not dishonorable... To one entrust the paid advocacy of a case at law, to another introduce a wealthy man in need of care and protection. And for another help in negotiating some profitable contract or lease.'[103] So what would look like graft to the modern eye is openly recommended to the young Menemachus as part of the ideal role of the statesman. One other passage may be cited to reaffirm the point made above concerning lack of differentiation of public and private roles: in addition to his public duties, Plutarch advises the good statesman to show himself 'a well-disposed adviser and an advocate charging no fee and a kind mediator between husbands and wives and between friends'.[104]

Though Plutarch was writing with a municipal statesman in mind, the same ideals can be documented for officials of the imperial aristocracy. As will be suggested in more detail in Chapter 5, the governor's role was conceived of partially in paternalistic terms. Like a father, a proconsul was praised for his indulgence toward his subjects, tempering their desires and restraining them with gentle remedies.[105] Most people thought of and appreciated the governor in his capacity as benefactor. Apuleius sets himself apart from the masses in this respect in a speech before the governor of Africa Proconsularis, Séverianus:

Philosophy has taught me not only to love *beneficium* but also to repudiate *maleficium* and to attach greater importance to justice than to private interests and to prefer what benefits the community rather than myself. Therefore, while most esteem the profit which they can derive from your *bonitas*, I esteem your *studium*. I have come to this position as I watch your moderation in the affairs of provincials, by which you have acted so that those in contact with you should love you on account of *beneficium* and those not coming into contact ought also to love you on account of your example. For you have favored many with *beneficium* and have benefited all by your example.[106]

---

102 *Moralia* 808Bf.
103 *Moralia* 808Ff.: εἰσὶ δὲ καὶ πρὸς χρηματισμὸν οὐκ ἀγεννεῖς ἐν πολιτείᾳ τοῖς δεομένοις τῶν φίλων αἱ συλλήψεις... τῷ μὲν ἐγχείρισον συνηγορίαν ἔμμισθον ὑπὲρ τοῦ δικαίου, τῷ δὲ σύστησον πλούσιον ἐπιμελείας καὶ προστασίας δεόμενον· ἄλλῳ δ' εἰς ἐργολαβίαν τινὰ σύμπραξον ἢ μίσθωσιν ὠφελείας ἔχουσαν .
104 *Moralia* 823B: ἔπειτα σύμβουλον εὔνουν καὶ συνήγορον ἄμισθον καὶ διαλλακτὴν εὐμενῆ πρὸς γυναῖκας ἀνδρῶν καὶ φίλων πρὸς ἀλλήλους παρέχων ἑαυτόν.
105 Apuleius, *Flor.* 17.
106 *Flor.* 9: 'Sed philosophia me docuit non tantum beneficium amare, sed etiam maleficium ⟨negare⟩ magisque iudicio impertire quam commodo inservire et quod in commune expediat malle quam quod mihi. igitur bonitatis tuae diligunt plerique fructum, ego studium, idque facere adortus sum, dum moderationem tuam in provincialium negotiis contemplor, qua effec⟨is⟩ti ut te amare debeant experti propter beneficium, expertes propter exemplum, nam et beneficio multis commodasti et exemplo omnibus profuisti.'

Apuleius disclaims any motivation of self-interest behind his esteem for the governor, but it is not because personal profiteering by the governor's friends is improper (so long as it is kept within certain boundaries). On the contrary, Apuleius praises Severianus for his generosity, adding that the generosity is not the only reason for his esteem. This view of the governor's role was held not only by the provincials who stood to benefit, but even by the emperor. Marcus Aurelius addressed a *commendatio* to Fronto just before his intended departure for Asia. The letter was written on behalf of a friend of Marcus' philosophy teacher and requested Fronto to extend to him more than the justice due to all the subjects of Asia, to extend *consilium, comitatem* and all the things due to friends 'which *fides* and *religio* permit a proconsul to bestow without injury to anyone else'.[107] For their part, provincials were legally entitled to show their gratitude in moderation by gifts (*xenia*) to the governor (the degree of moderation to be determined in the first instance by the governor).[108] A description of the variety of concrete *beneficia* available to provincial officials and provincials is left to the last chapter. The conclusion to be drawn here is that it would be wrong always to interpret the *beneficia* as evidence of bribery, graft or injustice. The inscriptions set up in public, advertising the governor's patronage, make it clear that within certain limitations, provincial officials were expected to play a patronal role.[109]

At the center of the imperial administrative apparatus stood the emperor. The patronal aspect of his role has long been recognized. In the late 1930 s Premerstein and Syme published their classic works stressing the importance of clientèle relationships in the maintenance of the emperor's position.[110] The consequences of the emperor playing a patronal role, rather than one of an impartial administrator, have been worked out over the past decades, and recently Fergus Millar published his *Emperor in the Roman World* in which he documents with massive detail the emperor's personal distribution of *beneficia*. In his introduction Millar summarizes his view of the emperor's role.

[When the emperor had leisure from his military expeditions, society] demanded not a programme of change but a willingness to listen; a willingness to respond to demands, to grant gifts and privileges, to give justice, to issue legal rulings... This whole conception of course ran directly counter to that of the emperor as... office-holder dependent on the senate and people of Rome... The emergence of the monarchy to some extent transformed those very republican institutions themselves into instruments of patronage: so the 'public horse', membership of the jury-panels, entry

107 *Ad M. Caes.* 5.36: 'quae amicis sine ullo cuiusquam incommodo propria impertire fides ac religio proconsulis permittit...'
108 *Dig.* 1.16.6.3; see below, p.165.
109 See the table of patronage inscriptions (pp.195ff.) which contains dedications to governors.
110 Premerstein, *Vom Werden*; R. Syme, *Roman Revolution*.

to the senate or appointment to a wide range of senatorial offices became things to be petitioned for, and to be granted as a favor by the emperor; while, besides these ranks and posts, there evolved the whole pattern of equestrian office-holding which was from the beginning entirely dependent on imperial patronage.[111]

Now it seems to me that the crucial quality which gave the emperor his patronal character was the expectation that he would distribute *beneficia* in accordance with particularistic rather than universalistic criteria.[112] That is, the distribution depended upon individual approaches to and relationships with the emperor, who was supposed to be generous to family, friends and those who could approach him in person. In his *Third Discourse on Kingship* Dio of Prusa speaks of the great pleasure which a king should derive from rewarding his kin and friends out of his great resources of *beneficia*. Further, the emperor should use these *beneficia* to bind as friends those men in the state who are talented and have ambitions to be administrators and generals. For 'who is better able to appoint governors? Who is in need of more administrators? Who has it in his power to give a share in greater deeds? For whom else is it possible to entrust to a companion the activities of war? From whom are honors more brilliant? Whose table is more honored? If friendship could be purchased, who is better endowed with resources so that he may have no one acting against him?'[113]

Very recently a challenge to the view of Premerstein has been raised which is of particular interest to us at this point because part of the argument revolves around the understanding of the word *beneficium*. The essential premise is that 'to imagine that an immense State, where the relations between sovereign and subject are anonymous and of obedience, was similar to a band of faithfuls is, to speak frankly, to lose sight of historical realities...'[114] With regard to *beneficium*, this analysis distinguishes several different meanings: (1) the mechanical application of a rule to an individual case, as when a veteran is given certain rights on his discharge from the army; (2) the individualization of the letter of the law in the name of justice and equity; and (3) 'an unjustifiable favor, a royal caprice which one embellishes with the label "grace"'... Practically, the word is used most especially of the most banal administrative decisions, because they are the most frequent: concession of the right of

111 *Emperor*, 11.
112 Jean Béranger notes the personal nature of the *tutela* in the ideology (*Recherches sur l'aspect idéologique du Principat*, 259;) see also Hans Kloft, *Liberalitas Principis*, 127.
113 *Third Discourse on Kingship* 132, 110, 120: τίς οὖν δύναται μᾶλλον ἄρχοντας αποδεικνύειν; τίς δὲ πλειόνων δεῖται τῶν ἐπιμελουμένων; τίς δὲ κύριος μειζόνων μεταδοῦναι πραγμάτων; τίνι δὲ μᾶλλον ἔξεστιν ἑτέρῳ πιστεύειν τὰ πρὸς πόλεμον; αἱ παρὰ τίνος δὲ τιμαὶ φανερώτεραι; ἢ παρὰ τίνι δὲ εὐδοξοτέρα τράπεζα; εἰ δὲ ὠνητὸν ὑπῆρχε φιλία, τίς εὐπορώτερος χρημάτων, ὥστε μηδένα ἔχειν τὸν ἀντιποιησόμενον; The benefactor ideology is found elsewhere, e.g., in Dio's report (71.34.3) of Marcus Aurelius' dedication of a temple to Εὐεργεσία and in Philo, *Leg. ad Gaium, passim.*
114 Veyne, *Le pain*, 620.

citizenship, admission to the equestrian order, authorization given to a private individual to draw water from an aqueduct.'[115] In these kinds of cases the phrase *beneficio imperatoris* means simply 'in virtue of a decision of the emperor'. The word *beneficium* with its positive connotations is used, not because the decision or act constitutes a personal favor, but because the emperor, being essentially good, can do nothing but good deeds (*beneficia*), even in his impersonal administrative activities.[116]

The introduction of these distinctions is useful: *beneficium* cannot be assumed to have the same meaning in every context and there are certainly instances where *beneficium* is a banal word of administration.[117] But certain problems with this analysis seem to me to cast doubt on the weight of the objections to Premerstein (and implicitly to Millar). It should be noted at the outset that the three categories of meanings for *beneficium* are not exhaustive. Part of the argument hinges on the claim that very few uses of *beneficium* fall into the third category of royal caprice and that the first two categories are consistent with the emperor's role as rational administrator. But clearly there is a fourth possibility which falls between the second and third categories — i.e., decisions or favors which are entirely at the emperor's discretion, not being an extension of existing laws on the basis of equity and not being in violation of the law. For instance, appointment to a procuratorship was a gift given at the discretion of the emperor — given not on the basis of firm administrative guidelines, but given to friends or friends of friends.[118] Most of the instances of *beneficium principis* listed in the *Thesaurus Linguae Latinae* fall into this category characterized by the emperor's discretion.

Indeed, it is precisely the lack of administrative guidelines and the wide scope for personal discretion which Max Weber cites as one characteristic of patrimonial bureaucracies. In a modern rational-legal bureaucracy management is guided by general rules, relatively stable and exhaustive, which produce abstract regulation; 'this stands in extreme contrast to the regulation of all relationships through individual privileges and bestowals of favor, which is absolutely dominant in patrimonialism...'[119] While it cannot be claimed that there were no regular administrative mechanisms in the Principate, it is the great merit of Millar's book to have shown in detail the great range of goods, statuses and honors at the disposal of the emperor for *ad hominem* or *ad civitatem* grants.

115 *Ibid.*, 622f.
116 *Ibid.*, 624.
117 Examples of passages where *beneficium* is used with regard to the universal application of a favorable rule or imperial decision include *Dig.* 35.2.18 and 22. pr; 35.1.63; 23.2.48.1. Outside of the *Digest*, the great majority of uses of *beneficium* in the Principate listed in the *Thesaurus Linguae Latinae* carry implications of personal reciprocity.
118 Fronto, *Ad Pium* 9; see below, pp.47 ff.
119 M. Weber, *Economy and Society*, ed. G. Roth and C. Wittich, 958.

In favor of the view of the emperor as an impersonal administrator, citizenship grants, admission to the equestrian order and permission to tap aqueducts are singled out as illustrations of banal administrative decisions labelled *beneficia*. But when these grants are examined in detail, there seems to be no evidence to show that the emperor was firmly guided by any administrative rules of universal application. The evidence which we have concerning extension of citizenship and water supplies suggests that the grants were not mechanical decisions. Full discussion of these two kinds of *beneficia* can be left to later chapters. It is enough to show here that the word *beneficium* continued to contain an element of reciprocity in imperial grants, even the most common sort of grants such as citizenship and water rights. Pliny sent three letters to Trajan requesting citizenship for one Arpocras. In the opening lines of the first, he described his motivation: 'when I was seriously ill last year, and in some danger of my life, I called in a medical therapist whose care and attentiveness I can only reward *tuae indulgentiae beneficio*. I pray you therefore to grant him Roman citizenship' (*Ep.* 10.5). Trajan granted citizenship to Arpocras, but since he was an Egyptian and since (as Pliny was unaware) Egyptians had to have Alexandrian citizenship to be eligible for Roman citizenship, a second *beneficium* had to be requested in another letter. Pliny explicitly indicates his gratitude (*gratia*) in this letter and notes that the extra *beneficium* would further obligate (*obligare*) him to Trajan (10.6). The emperor in his response says that he does not intend to grant Alexandrian citizenship indiscriminately, but that in this case he cannot refuse (10.7). *Beneficium* here is clearly used in the sense of a favor in a reciprocal exchange relationship. Arpocras received citizenship not because he met any universal qualification, but because he had provided a service for a Roman aristocrat who happened to be a personal friend of the emperor. For his part, Pliny uses the language of *gratia* and there is no reason to doubt that his loyalty to Trajan was strengthened by the emperor's generosity on various occasions.

In connection with the privilege of tapping the aqueducts, Frontinus uses the word *beneficium*, but does not comment on how it could be obtained. In the only example available as to the form of the requests, the form is not an impersonal application in which an applicant tries to demonstrate that he meets certain prerequisites; rather it is a poem from Martial of the kind which he addressed to Domitian requesting other gifts such as money.[120] The poet Statius also sought this *munus* from Domitian and after receiving it acknowledged his gratitude.[121]

---

120 *Epig.* 9.18. Friedlaender denies that Martial received the water supply because there is no poem of gratitude for it (*Roman Life and Manners under the Early Empire*, vol. 3,59); Millar, *Emperor*, 496, comes to the opposite conclusion on the grounds that Martial published the request. Neither argument seems particularly compelling. For the request of money, *Epig.* 6.10.
121 Statius, *Silv.* 3.1.61f.

Altogether, the evidence adduced above and in the following chapter suggests that the assumption that the emperors could not possibly have distributed such mundane rights to such large numbers of people as personal favors is anachronistic.[122] What is important to note here is that, like Pliny, the ordinary beneficiaries of imperial grants seem to have treated them as matters of the emperor's personal discretion, deserving demonstrations of gratitude in return. On any other assumption it is difficult to explain why people in the provinces erected the numerous and expensive inscriptions which thanked the emperor for various *beneficia*.[123] For, as the anthropologist J. Boissevain has pointed out with respect to Malta, as the role of the official changes from patron to impersonal administrator guided by regulations, the attitude of the citizens towards administrative decisions changes from obsequious gratitude for the official's exercise of his discretionary powers to demands for what is felt to belong to the citizens by right.[124] The inscriptions leave little doubt that no such change had taken place in the Roman citizens' and subjects' view of their emperor.

It seems to me, then, that the anecdote about Titus' generosity recorded by Suetonius ought to be taken seriously. Titus initiated the policy of ratifying all *beneficia* granted by preceding emperors *en bloc*.

Moreover, in the case of other requests made of him, it was his fixed rule not to let anyone go away without hope. Even when his household officials warned him that he was promising more than he could perform, he said it was not right for anyone to go away sorrowful from an interview with his emperor. On another occasion, remembering at dinner that he had done nothing for anybody all that day, he gave utterance to that memorable and praiseworthy remark: 'Friends, I have lost a day'.[125]

It is doubtful whether Titus in fact uttered these precise words,[126] but the passage is to be taken seriously as evidence of the patronal element in the social role of the emperor.

122 Space is not available to deal with all of Veyne's other peripheral arguments concerning this issue in detail here. For example, he devotes several pages to a discussion of Seneca's *De Clementia* (625ff.). His argument that Seneca was concerned with true Platonic justice rather than mercy in the ordinary sense does not carry conviction. Veyne is forced to explain away Seneca's plea for mercy *instead of deserved punishment* as a tactic designed to persuade the unphilosophical. M. Griffin in her *Seneca: A Philosopher in Politics*, 159f. offers a much more plausible resolution of the difficulties which does not require believing that Seneca did not mean what he said.
123 For example, *ILS* 9399, 9400.
124 'When the saints go marching out', in *Patrons and Clients*, ed. Gellner and Waterbury, 87f.
125 Suet., *Titus* 8: 'In ceteris vero desideriis hominum obstinatissime tenuit, ne quem sine spe dimitteret; quin et admonentibus domesticis, quasi plura polliceretur quam praestare posset, non oportere ait quemquam a sermone principis tristem discedere; atque etiam recordatus quondam super cenam, quod nihil cuiquam toto die praestitisset, memorabilem illam meritoque laudatam vocem edidit: "Amici, diem perdidi"'. (Loeb translation).
126 'Anecdotes as historical evidence for the Principate', *G & R* 2nd ser. 27 (1980), 69ff.

Patronal language and ideology permeated Roman society, and there appears to be little justification for the hypothesis that the language can be dismissed as a 'jargon of bureaucrats'. The remaining chapters will be devoted to an analysis of patronal behavior at various levels of society. Before proceeding, we should perhaps ask what sort of general relationship between patronal ideology and behavior is to be expected, and how important a function the ideology fulfilled.

It is reasonable to suppose that the ideology exercised some influence on behavior. For instance, the existence of a patronal, instead of a universalist, ideology in the realm of administration meant that Roman officials were not restrained by concepts of the impropriety of all favoritism, and they were relatively free to indulge in the natural human propensity to use their official positions to aid family and friends.[127] Behavior, however, is rarely a simple reflection of the reigning ideology. Sydel Silverman has recently suggested that three distinctions of behavior and thought ought to be made in analyses of patronage.[128] First, there is the ideology of patronage — i.e., the ideals of how patrons and clients are supposed to act. These ideals are frequently reflected in anecdotes, such as the story about Titus. But, as Silverman points out, clients are aware that patrons do not live up to the ideal, and so the second distinction to be made is what the patrons and clients thought their relationships were really like. Silverman's fieldwork suggests that even this does not provide an accurate assessment of what was happening and so a third distinction must be added: the observer's description of the actual flow of goods and services between patron and client. Silverman further suggests that one of the most interesting questions arising from these distinctions is how the three levels influenced each other — for example, what is the function of the ideology in relation to behavior. This last question is as difficult as it is interesting. Indeed, it is impossible even to begin to reach an answer with the ancient evidence alone: we do not know of a single patron-client relationship from the Principate for which a complete balance-sheet of the exchange of goods and services can be drawn up. The best that can be offered is an outline of two possible, though hardly conclusive, answers suggested by modern studies.

The first stands in the tradition of anthropological functionalism. It suggests that in societies with great differences of wealth and prestige, patron-client bonds, cemented in accordance with the reciprocity ethic, provide cohesion between different class and status groups. Utilizing the patronal ideology, the weak attempt to turn their encounters with the strong into a moral

127 There were some constraints on favoritism, especially in judicial matters (below, p.56). The universality of the propensity seems to be demonstrated by its continued existence in communist societies despite the highly developed egalitarian ideology. See G. Ionescu, 'Patronage under Communism', in *Patrons and Clients*, ed. Gellner and Waterbury, 97ff.
128 'Patronage as myth', in *Patrons and Clients*, ed. Gellner and Waterbury, 7ff.

patron-client relationship so that they may lay some claim to the protection and favors of the strong. In return, the clients lend prestige to their patrons by their deference and perhaps also provide labor from time to time — both being commodities which they possess in ample supply. In short, the weak have an interest in propagating the patronal ideology which they then can manipulate as an instrument of survival.

Recently Marxists have ventured a critique of these functionalist ideas and suggested a different perspective. In their view, the patronal ideology and the concept of social cohesion have served to distract attention from the basic class structure. Despite patron-client relations cutting across class divisions, in the final analysis the patrons stand together to protect their class interests. M. Gilsenan suggests that 'the cross-cutting comes in the realm of the local model and ideology which does indeed speak of the face-to-face, individual relations, and which is significant in the class and status consciousness of both rulers and dependents. It also comes into the sociologists' model of consensus to which the notion of a patronage glue is fundamental'. By celebrating the integrative effect, the sociologist, in Gilsenan's view, covers up the structures.[129] In other words, the patronal ideology represents a false consciousness for the client and helps the patron maintain his superiority. Gilsenan's argument receives some support from Silverman's observations in Italy: although clients are aware that patrons do not meet the ideal, they still overestimate the goods and services which the patrons distribute.[130] Perhaps the ideology does encourage an overly optimistic view on the part of the clients, helping the patron to maintain his position at a minimal cost.

To choose between the functionalist and the Marxist views may not be necessary. From different perspectives both ask the same question and come up with much the same answer. The question is: what provides stability in societies with enormous centrifugal pressures (including unequal distribution of goods and services amongst various classes) pulling them apart? The answer for both is patronage and the patronal ideology. The Marxists, assuming the injustice and instability of the structure, view the ideology as a means of hiding from the weak their own true interests. The functionalists, on the other hand, do not assume that the clients are deluded as to their interests or would benefit from instability, and so they view the ideology as one part of the client's strategy for survival.

Neither assumption can be adequately tested for the Roman empire. Nor can a brief, general assertion be made about the indispensability of the patronal ideology to the stability of the empire. But we should keep in mind the question about the function of the ideology, and throughout the remainder of

---

129 'Against patron-client relations', in *Patrons and Clients*, ed. Gellner and Waterbury, 182.
130 'Patronage as myth', in *Patrons and Clients*, ed. Gellner and Waterbury, 11.

the study seek to identify the many specific social locations (e.g., between the emperor and leading senators) where the ideology and acts of patronage did provide some cohesion.

2

The emperor and his court

The *principes* of the late Republic were, first and foremost, great patrons—patrons of armies, of the urban masses, of foreign kings and provincial cities, of senators and *equites*. After Octavian eliminated his rivals, the *princeps'* role continued to be defined in terms of a patronal ideology. In the previous chapter arguments were adduced to suggest that this ideology was not an anachronistic survival from the Republic and that the patronal language was not sterile jargon. In this chapter the patronal aspects of the emperor's position will be explored in greater detail in an attempt to elucidate the reality which lay behind the ideology. First, a list of the *beneficia* at the emperor's disposal can be drawn up. This should help to define the range of imperial activities in which patronage was a factor. Next, the core of the chapter will approach the questions of who was able to secure the *beneficia* and in what contexts. Finally, after considering how the recipients fulfilled their reciprocal obligations, attention will be turned to the broad implications and significance of these exchange relationships.[1]

IMPERIAL BENEFICIA

The word *beneficium* occurs frequently in Pliny's *Panegyricus*, suggesting an important theme in the aristocrats' ideology of the good emperor.[2] The ideology clearly made an impression on the minds of the emperors themselves. Though the Suetonian anecdote about Titus may not be accepted as historically accurate, we possess documentary evidence of the imperial viewpoint.[3] In an edict preserved in a letter of Pliny, Nerva wrote that he had abandoned his *quies* and assumed responsibility for the empire 'in order that I might confer new *beneficia* and preserve those already granted by my predecessors'.[4]

1 This chapter owes a great deal to Fergus Millar's *The Emperor in the Roman World* for ideas and especially its collection of evidence.
2 *Beneficium* appears fifteen times in the *Panegyricus*.
3 See above, p.36.
4 *Ep.* 10.58.7-9: 'ut et nova beneficia conferrem et ante me concessa servarem'.

In the *Panegyricus* Pliny uses the word *beneficium* with reference to consulates, an emergency grain shipment to Egypt, the establishment of courts more sympathetic to the people, citizenship grants, and an extension of immunity from the inheritance tax.[5] In other sources of the period we find *beneficium* used to describe the grant of senatorial magistracies and governorships, equestrian procuratorships and *militiae*, priesthoods, and staff positions in the imperial household.[6] Citizenship was one of the several legal statuses granted as favors; freedman status, the *ius anulorum*, and the *ius ingenuitatis* were also called *beneficia*.[7] In addition, a wide variety of gifts, privileges and immunities were labelled *beneficia*, including monetary gifts, the *ius trium liberorum*, private use of the *cursus publicus*, the right to tap an aqueduct and permission to return from exile.[8]

The foregoing list of *beneficia* is by no means comprehensive, but it gives a preliminary indication of the scope of imperial favors.[9] We cannot be satisfied, however, with a mere list derived from a word study of *beneficium*, because 'beneficium imperatoris' can mean 'an administrative decision of the emperor' as well as 'a personal favor of the emperor'. It is necessary first to search through the sources to discover what the emperors distributed, and then to scrutinize the contexts of the grants to show that they were in fact personal favors.

Most prominent in the emperor's storehouse of *beneficia* were senatorial and equestrian offices. Appointments to the pre-quaestorial posts in the senatorial *cursus* (legionary tribunates and the posts of the vigintivirate) seem to have been made exclusively by the emperor.[10] Very little evidence is available to indicate what criteria the emperors may have applied when granting them, but patronage was undoubtedly a factor: Didius Iulianus received his appointment through the *suffragium* of Marcus Aurelius' mother, Domitia Lucilla, in whose house he was raised from childhood.[11] In the

5 *Paneg.* 91, 31.6, 36.5, 37.3, 39.3.
6 Magistracies: Suetonius, *Vesp.* 14; Seneca, *De Ben.* 1.5.1; 1.11.5; 2.9.1. Governorships: Seneca, *De Ben.* 1.5.1. Procuratorships: Fronto, *Ad Pium* 9. *Militiae: CIL* VI.2131. Priesthoods: Seneca, *De Ben.* 1.5.1. Staff positions: Vitruvius, *De Arch.* 1.pr.3.
7 Citizenship: Pliny, *Ep.* 10.5.1, 10.6.2, *Paneg.* 37.3-4; Seneca, *De Ben.* 3.9.2; *CIL* VIII.20682 (= *ILS* 6875). Freedman status: *Dig.* 48.19.8.12. *Ius Anulorum: Dig.* 27.1.44.2; 40.10.1-2. *Ius ingenuitatis: Dig.* 40.11.3.
8 Aqueduct: Frontinus, *Aq.*, *passim*, e.g., 72. Money: Suetonius, *Nero* 24.2. *Ius trium liberorum*: Pliny, *Ep.* 10.94.3; *Sent. Pauli* 4.9.9. *Cursus publicus*: Pliny, *Ep.* 10.120.2. Return from exile: Seneca, *De Ben.* 2.25.1; Tacitus, *Ann.* 12.8.
9 This list does not include the various imperial grants to cities which were also labelled *beneficia*—e.g., Nero's grant of freedom to the Greek cities (Suetonius, *Nero* 24.2).
10 Millar, *Emperor*, 300-13.
11 H. A., *Iul.* 1.4. Professor E. Birley suggests an alternative to patronage. Noting that *III viri capitales* and *IV viri monetales* show a better rate of success in their future careers, he argues that 'grading for posts in the vigintivirate, when candidates were still in their teens, took into account their aptitude for service in key appointments in another ten or twenty years' time...' ('Senators in the emperor's service', *PBA* (1953), 202). There is no literary

absence of elections or formal institutions for bringing candidates to the attention of the emperor, such *suffragatores* with access to the emperor would normally have been indispensable at this stage of the career.

The traditional Republican senatorial magistracies continued to be filled and continued to represent sought-after honors throughout the Principate. Though the emperor's role in the selection was less straightforward than in direct appointments to the pre-quaestorial posts, it is at least better documented. From the beginning of Tiberius' reign magistrates were elected by the senate.[12] The emperor could play a more or less dominating part: for quaestorships, tribunates, aedileships and praetorships he accepted or rejected candidatures.[13] In addition, he could commend as many candidates (*candidati Caesaris*) as he liked, thus ensuring their election.[14] At some point before the end of the first century consulates came to be exclusively at the disposal of the emperor, as is implied in Pliny's statement that after holding the praetorship a senator no longer required help with canvassing among senators for magistracies.[15] Precisely when and how the consulate became differentiated from the lower magistracies in this respect are matters of dispute. In any case, the emperor's *auctoritas* even in the early reigns was sufficient to ensure the election of those given his support.[16]

Amicitia Caesaris was assumed by contemporaries to carry with it *honores et auctoritas*[17] — an assumption which numerous examples from throughout the Principate confirm. In Tacitus' view, it was by *amicitia principum* that Poppaeus Sabinus (cos. 9 A.D.) moved through all of the senatorial magistracies and held governorships of great provinces.[18] Tiberius' favor ensured that Curtius Rufus would obtain a praetorship despite his low birth and competition from patrician candidates.[19] More than a century later the importance of the emperor's personal favor remained unaltered for new men. In the *Historia Augusta* Marcus Aurelius' enthusiasm for education is

testimony for this view, nor is it easy to see what means the emperor would have had for testing the aptitudes of boys in their early and middle teens. The statistical correlation can be explained in other ways: for example, those with effective patronage in their early careers often had sufficient influence to carry them to consulates and army commands. See Ch. 3 for a full discussion of career structure and merit or aptitude.

12 Tacitus, *Ann.* 1.15.1.
13 Millar, *Emperor*, 303, citing Pliny, *Ep.* 2.9.2 concerning the tribunate.
14 Millar, *Emperor*, 303f.
15 Pliny, *Ep.* 1.14.7.
16 Millar seems to date imperial control of the selection of consuls to the reign of Tiberius (*Emperor*, 307). In Levick's view ('Imperial control of the elections under the early Principate: *commendatio, suffragatio,* and "*nominatio*"', *Historia* 16 (1967), 226f.), the situation was less clear-cut. The precise nature and chronology of the evolution is far from clear. Dio 58.20.2 and Tacitus *Ann.* 1.81 do indicate that Tiberius was already playing a dominant role.
17 Fronto, *Ad Pium* 3.
18 *Ann.* 6.39.
19 Tacitus, *Ann.* 11.21.

demonstrated by the public offices and money which he bestowed on his teachers and fellow students. For instance, Eutychius Proculus, his *grammaticus Latinus*, was promoted by Marcus through a senatorial career to a proconsulship.[20] The tastes of Marcus' successors were not so intellectual. Until his death, Geta quarrelled with Caracalla over whose friends should be given offices.[21] The contemporary observer, Cassius Dio, tells of favors showered on Macedonians by the new Alexander, Caracalla: a military tribune Antigonus, son of Philip, was promoted *inter praetorios* on account of his Macedonian origin.[22]

Senatorial magistracies at all levels could be secured not only through direct, personal friendship with the emperor, but also through the patronage (or bribery) of those among the emperor's *amici* and entourage possessing *gratia*. Pliny indicated in a letter to a friend that he secured the emperor's support for Erucius Clarus in his candidature for the quaestorship,[23] and in another letter Pliny is found requesting from Trajan a praetorship for his friend Attius Sura (the success of the petition is not known).[24] For explicit testimony concerning consulates we have Dio's report that Iulius Ursus was protected from Domitian's anger and received a consulship through the favor of the emperor's niece Iulia.[25] Among those most famed for the sale of patronal support for office we should include Messallina, Vespasian's mistress Caenis, and Cleander.[26]

In addition to the traditional Republican magistracies and promagistracies, a number of new civilian and military posts were established in the Principate and available to senators only through imperial appointment. Some of these, especially provincial posts, could be profitable and so were valuable *beneficia* to be sought through patronage. The example of Poppaeus Sabinus, governor for twenty-four years owing to his *amicitia principum*, has been noted. The distribution of military posts through patronage can also be documented for later periods. Vespasian was said to have received his legionary legateship *Narcissi gratia* and more than a century later the influence of Aemilius Laetus, Commodus' praetorian prefect, secured a Danubian command for Septimius Severus (despite Severus' limited military experience).[27] With respect to civilian posts Epictetus assumed that appointments depended on patronage: in a discussion with a Roman senator Maximus, who was about to take up the

20 *Marc.* 2.5 and 3.8-9; see below, p.184.
21 Herodian 4.4.1.
22 Dio 77.8.
23 *Ep.* 2.9.2.
24 *Ep.* 10.12. For another example concerning a praetorship, Tacitus, *Ann.* 12.8.2.
25 Dio 67.4.2; see R. Syme, *Tacitus*, App. 7.
26 Dio 60.17.8, 66.14.3 and 72.10.2.
27 H. A., *Sev.* 4.4; see M. Hammond, 'Septimius Severus, Roman bureaucrat', *HSPh* 51 (1940), 164.

office of curator of the free cities of Greece, the philosopher asked whose hand
the senator had to kiss, before whose bedroom door he had to sleep, and to
whom he sent gifts in order to win the office.[28]

Finally, we may note that emperors also distributed senatorial *ornamenta*
and priesthoods as *beneficia*. Marcus Aurelius took advantage of his imperial
position to honor *omnes propinqui* with the *ornamenta* of various offices — a
praiseworthy display of *benignitas*.[29] A letter of Pliny to Trajan supplies an
excellent example of how the emperor distributed priesthoods: 'since I know,
Sir, that to be adorned with an honor by the decision of a good emperor is a sign
of praise of my character, I request that you add to the *dignitas* to which you
have promoted me by deeming me worthy to be an augur or septemvir...'[30] The
priesthood represents an honor to Pliny in part because it was an indication of
the emperor's personal favor.

To summarize, all senatorial magistracies, offices and honors were at the
disposal of the emperor. We possess examples which show that all were used—
either directly by the emperor or indirectly by those close to him — as *beneficia*
in patronal exchange relationships. Unfortunately, these scattered examples
cannot by themselves reveal whether patronage was a normal or an
exceptional factor in distribution. Several further considerations suggest that
patronage was in fact unexceptional and taken for granted. First, the exercise
of *gratia* draws remarks about its impropriety only when it is used either on
behalf of or by someone of unsuitably low station in life. Thus Tacitus clearly
disapproved of the *suffragium* of Tiberius on behalf of Curtius Rufus at the
expense of patrician candidates.[31] More intense discontent was expressed by
various aristocratic authors at the humiliations suffered by senators who had to
seek the *gratia* of imperial women, freedmen and slaves in order to advance
their careers. But no hint of discontent survives concerning Marcus' favoritism
towards his kin and teachers (with the exception of that enjoyed by
philosophers). On the contrary, he was praised for his generosity, in part
because he bestowed *honores* only on friends of suitable station, while those of
lower station were rewarded with money.[32]

Not only was patronage in the right circumstances proper, it was also
assumed to be the usual method by which new men in particular secured
advancement in a senatorial career. Epictetus sneered at those who sought
senior magistracies, on the grounds that achieving them required influence
won at the expense of kissing the hands of imperial slaves. Epictetus' view of

28 *Diss.* 3.7.31; see Millar, 'Epictetus and the imperial court', *JRS* 55 (1965), 145.
29 H. A., *Marc.* 16.1.
30 *Ep.* 10.13: 'cum sciam, domine, ad testimonium laudemque morum meorum pertinere tam
    boni principis iudicio exornari, rogo dignitati, ad quam me provexit indulgentia tua, vel
    auguratum vel septemviratum, quia vacant, adicere digneris...'
31 *Ann.* 11.21.
32 H. A., *Marc.* 3.9.

life at the imperial court was certainly something of a caricature, but the assumed need for patronage is confirmed elsewhere.[33] Extended descriptions of the rise of new senatorial families over several generations are rarely found outside imperial biographies. In these accounts of the emperors' lives the role of patronage is apparent. Of the four contenders for the throne in 69, three were from families which had entered the senate in the imperial period. For all three Suetonius describes the patronage which helped them along the way.[34] It would surely not be too rash to suggest that if we possessed similar accounts of the rise of all new families, patronal influence would be a factor in nearly all of them.

One last consideration arises from Pliny's letters. For Pliny, requests of senatorial offices and honors seem to have been an ordinary part of senatorial life. Pliny was not a special favorite of Trajan and yet his letters requesting a priesthood for himself and a praetorship for a friend show no hint of embarrassment or shyness which might point to their being unusual or improper. Indeed, in the letter concerning the praetorship Pliny reminds Trajan that he has had to make the same request previously: 'I know, Sir, that our requests do not escape your memory which is most anxious to confer benefits. Since you have granted me such requests before, I remind you and ask again urgently that you honor Attius Sura with a praetorship...'[35] The tone of the letter suggests that such requests for imperial *indulgentia* were sufficiently commonplace to arouse Pliny's expectation that they would be acted upon. Trajan's initial delay in fulfilling the request also serves as a reminder that the emperor's supply of senatorial and equestrian appointments was very limited. It was in the emperor's interest not to be forced to create illwill by refusals, but how the number of requests was restricted in practice is a question which cannot be answered with confidence.

One of the most characteristic developments in the early Empire was the growth of an equestrian administration. Throughout the period an increasing number of posts became available to *equites* solely by imperial appointment. It can be shown that these offices at all levels and in all periods could be treated as imperial *beneficia* and distributed through patronage.

Most equestrians pursuing careers began them by serving in one or more

---

33 *Diss.* 4.1.148; see Millar, 'Epictetus', 147. C. Starr, 'Epictetus and the tyrant', *CPh* 44 (1949), 20, points out that Epictetus' views grew out of his experience in Domitian's and Nero's courts.

34 Suetonius, *Otho* 1-3, *Vit.* 2-3, *Vesp.* 1-4. For a detailed discussion of Vespasian's career and support, J. Nicols, *Vespasian and the Partes Flavianae*, Historia Einzelschriften 28, 12.

35 *Ep.* 10.12; for an evaluation of the language, Sherwin-White, *Letters of Pliny*, 578. 'Scio, domine, memoriae tuae, quae est bene faciendi tenacissima, preces nostras inhaerere. quia tamen in hoc quoque indulsisti, admoneo simul et impense rogo, ut Attium Suram praetura exornare digneris, cum locus vacet.'

equestrian *militiae.*[36](At no point did the series of three *militiae* — *praefectus cohortis, tribunus militum* and *praefectus alae* — become so regularized that the majority of those serving went through all three.)[37]

Some of these appointments were left, at least *de facto*, to the senatorial commanders in the provinces, while other *militiae* were filled by the emperor. Pliny wrote to Trajan on behalf of Nymphidius Lupus, the son of his friend and assessor of the same name. Pliny says that he counts his assessor's relatives as his own and requests a second *militia* for the younger Lupus as a personal favor.[38] The use of equestrian military posts as *beneficia* is even clearer in the case of Martial: among the marks of favor which the poet boasts of having received from the emperor is an equestrian tribunate.[39] Several later examples have also survived and others may be surmised from careful study of the epigraphic evidence.[40]

After serving as officers some *equites* sought procuratorships, while others entered procuratorial careers from non-military backgrounds.[41] At this level all appointments seem to have been made directly by the emperor. In his Maecenas speech Dio recommends that such appointments be distributed as profitable rewards for ἀρετή.[42] The significance of ἀρετή will be considered in the next chapter; here we should take note of the numerous examples which show that procuratorships were treated as patronal favors.

A procuratorial career could bring with it riches, but the title alone was an honor worth pursuing through a patron. Fronto in a petition addressed to Pius indicates that the emperor had earlier bestowed two procuratorships upon the orator's friend, Sextus Calpurnius, who declined them with his *dignitas* enhanced by the offer. In this same letter (*Ad Pium* 9), Fronto requests for a third time a similar *beneficium* for Appian, promising that Appian would show similar *modestia*. Pius' initial refusals point once again to a scarcity and competition for offices, though in this case Fronto gives us an idea about how the number of requests to be seriously considered was restricted. Pius apparently excluded Greek advocates from consideration for these appointments as a matter of policy in order to avoid a flood of petitions from such men.[43]

---

36 Millar, *Emperor*, 284ff.; for a fuller treatment, E. Birley, *Roman Britain and the Roman Army*, 133ff. See below, p.131 ff.

37 See Table I in the next chapter.

38 *Ep.* 10.87.

39 *Epig.* 3.95.9.

40 Other examples include Pertinax (Dio 74.3.1), Aemilius Pardalas (*ILS* 4929 = *CIL* VI.2131) and L. Tusidius Campester (*ILS* 2735 = *CIL* XI.5632).

41 Pflaum, *Les procurateurs équestres sous le Haut-Empire romain*, deuxième partie, chs. 2, 4.

42 Dio 52.25.4-5. For the profitability of an equestrian career, see Tacitus, *Ann.* 16.17 and Epictetus, *Diss.* 1.10.5; also Pflaum, *Procurateurs*, 165ff.

43 See E. J. Champlin, *Fronto and Antonine Rome*, 41-2 and 98-100. For the scarcity of equestrian appointments, see note 57 below.

Men who took up their offices benefited in ways more tangible than an increase in *dignitas*. Claudius rewarded Iulius Paelignus for his companionship by appointing him procurator of Cappadocia.[44] Similarly, a century later the personal favor of the emperor enabled Nicomedes, *libertus* and *educator* of Lucius Verus, to pursue a remarkably successful equestrian career despite his servile origin: he was promoted rapidly through the sexagenariate and centenariate levels to the important ducenariate post of *procurator summarum rationum*.[45] Owing to the biographical data preserved by Philostratus, we know of several Greek sophists who were rewarded with procuratorships: Dionysius of Miletus secured several *beneficia* from Hadrian including a procuratorship of an unnamed province, and later Caracalla conceived a liking for Heliodorus, upon whom he bestowed the ducenariate post of *fisci advocatus* in Rome.[46]

As with senatorial magistracies, one need not have been a personal *cliens* of the emperor to enjoy his favor in the form of procuratorships. Gessius Florus is said to have been made procurator of Judaea by Nero as a result of the friendship which Florus' wife enjoyed with Poppaea Sabina.[47] Inscriptions supply several other explicit cases of patronage and numerous instances where patronage can be inferred. We possess three third-century dedications to patrons by whose *suffragium* three procurators secured sexagenariate and centenariate appointments.[48] The career of Sextus Attius Suburanus Aemilianus is one where patronal influence can be plausibly inferred. Suburanus began his career as a *praefectus fabrum*, and Pflaum suggests that he may have made a useful senatorial friend in this office. However that may be, after serving as *praefectus alae* he became an *adiutor* for Vibius Crispus in Hispania Citerior and then of Iulius Ursus in Rome and Egypt. Both of these men are known to have been prominent during the Flavian era, and their influence is likely to have aided Suburanus' procuratorial career, as Syme and Pflaum suggest.[49] More vaguely, Seneca ascribed the worldly success of his

44 Tacitus, *Ann.* 12.49; note also the example of L. Tusidius Campester favored by Hadrian (*ILS* 2735 = *CIL* XI. 5632).
45 *ILS* 1740 and H. A., *Verus* 2.9.
46 Philostratus, *V.S.* 524 and 626.
47 Josephus, *Ant. J.* 20.11.1.
48 *ILS* 1191 (= *CIL* VI. 1532), *ILS* 2941 (= *CIL* VI. 1418), *ILS* 4928 (= *CIL* VI. 2132).
49 *PIR²* I.630 for Ursus; Syme, *Tacitus*, 100f. for Crispus. For Suburanus' career see *AE* (1939), 60; Pflaum, *Les carrières procuratoriennes équestres sous le Haut-Empire romain*, 128f. For the significance of the staff positions of *adiutores* and *praefecti fabrum*, see below p.132f. Other probable examples of patronage include the following: (1) L. Cammius Secundus, *procurator Augusti*, who dedicated a stone to his *amicus*, the praetorian prefect M. Gavius Maximus (*CIL* III.5328; Pflaum, *Carrières*, 259); (2) T. Appalius Alfinus Secundus, who pursued a successful procuratorial career also with patronal support from M. Gavius Maximus who came from the same town (Firmum Piceni) and adopted Appalius' son (Pflaum, *Carrières*, 341f.); (3) C. Censorius Niger, who held senior procuratorships in Noricum and Mauretania Tingitana: a letter of Fronto informs us that he enjoyed the *amicitia* of Marcius Turbo and Erucius Clarus (*Ad Pium* 3; Pflaum, *Carrières*, 226f.).

procuratorial friend Lucilius to 'vigor ingenii, scriptorum elegantia, clarae et nobiles amicitiae' ('vigor of spirit, elegance of writing, and distinguished and noble friends').[50]

We began the discussion of procuratorships with Dio's suggestion that the emperor use these offices as rewards. We can conclude with a remark from Plutarch which reveals the assumption of those seeking procuratorships about how they were distributed. In his *Praecepta Gerendae Reipublicae* Plutarch says that most provincials used whatever influence they could muster in the great houses of Rome to secure governorships and procuratorships.[51] Influential *amicitiae* must have been a normal factor contributing to the rise of equestrian families, just as in the case of their senatorial counterparts.

During the later first century and in the second century the emperor increasingly filled the Palatine *officia* with equestrians, often those who had held procuratorships. Philostratus provides evidence that the *ab epistulis Graecis* position was sometimes treated as an honor to be bestowed upon favorite Greek sophists. The clearest case is that of Hadrian of Tyre who was honored with the post of *ab epistulis* on his deathbed by Commodus.[52]

At the top of the equestrian career hierarchy were the four great prefectures: of the vigiles, the annona, Egypt, and the Praetorian Guard. Tacitus' narrative of the Julio-Claudian era described these appointments as subject to patronal influences: Sejanus' rise began with his friendship with Gaius Caesar and then reached its peak in the praetorian prefecture, won through the favor of Tiberius; in Nero's reign Faenius Rufus was appointed *praefectus annonae*, Balbillus *praefectus Aegypti*, and Sextus Afranius Burrus praetorian prefect, all three appointed thanks to Agrippina.[53] For this same period Philo's account of Aulus Avillus Flaccus' career suggests that patronal support was needed not only to secure, but also to remain in these important jobs. One of Tiberius' *amici*, Flaccus was appointed to the Egyptian prefecture when the freedman Hiberus died in 32. Beginning with Tiberius' death in 37, Flaccus' support at court dwindled as Gemellus and then Flaccus' friend Macro were executed by Gaius. It is to the loss of these friends at court that Philo attributes the beginning of the sequence of events which culminated in Flaccus' downfall and exile.[54]

Numerous examples, then, indicate that the emperor distributed equestrian

50 *Ep. ad Luc.* 19.3 (see Ch. 3, note 26); one of Lucilius' *amici* named by Seneca was the senator Cn. Cornelius Lentulus Gaetulicus who was executed by Caligula. Seneca names as one of Lucilius' virtues his willingness to remain faithful to friends in times of danger (*Q.N.* IVA. praef. 15). During Nero's reign Seneca's influence must have aided Lucilius' career; see M. Griffin, *Seneca*, 91.

51 *Moralia* 814D; R. Syme, 'Pliny the Procurator', *HSPh* 73 (1969), 209f., stresses patronage instead of bureaucratic criteria for procuratorships.

52 Philostratus, *V.S.* 590; Millar, *Emperor*, 91f.

53 Tacitus, *Ann.* 4.1; 13.20-22.

54 *In Flaccum* 2, 11f.

posts at all levels to his own friends and to friends of those friends. The passage from Plutarch shows that provincials thought patronal influence to be the natural path to procuratorships. This passage together with the examples cited is suggestive, but the overall significance attached to patronage will depend in part on what alternative criteria existed as factors in making appointments. The analysis of equestrian *cursus* and related literary evidence in the next chapter seems to show that considerations of seniority and efficiency or 'merit' in a modern sense did not hamper the influence of patrons, as is traditionally argued.

Though the scope of this study is generally restricted to the aristocracies of the empire, it is perhaps worthwhile to give a few brief illustrations which show that patronage can be found throughout the emperor's administration. Vitruvius dedicated his *De Architectura* to Augustus, to whom he was obligated by the *beneficium* of his position in charge of construction and repair of *ballistae* and *scorpiones*. More interestingly, Vitruvius says that he continued his job through the *commendatio* of Augustus' sister Octavia: here, if anywhere in the administration, one might have expected considerations of technical competence to outweigh patronage.[55] Suetonius reports that the money for Otho's bribery of the Praetorian Guard was extorted from an imperial slave for whom Otho secured the apparently very profitable post of *dispensator*.[56]

The fact that the imperial slave reportedly paid Otho 1,000,000 sesterces for the *dispensatio* once again underlines how valuable many offices at the emperor's disposal could be as *beneficia*. Of course, this group of *beneficia* was relatively limited in number.[57] The emperor perhaps made something on the order of a hundred senatorial and equestrian appointments each year — a minute number in relation to the total population of the empire. Other *beneficia* in the emperor's stock were not so limited. In a society highly conscious of status, grants of status such as the *equus publicus* and citizenship were valued by the recipients but could be distributed widely by the emperor without cost. In this section consideration will be devoted to the main status grants: the *latus clavus*, the *equus publicus* and membership on the equestrian juries, and citizenship.

The *latus clavus*, a broad purple stripe on the toga, symbolized membership in the senatorial order and could be worn by senators and their sons. At some point in the early Principate (during the reign of Caligula or before) emperors

55 *De Arch.* 1. pr. 2-3.

56 Suetonius, *Otho* 5.2. For an anecdotal example, *Vesp.* 23.2.

57 We can come no closer in our guesses than rough order of magnitude, since the proportion of senatorial magistracies and *militiae* filled by the emperor is unknown and probably varied. The number of equestrian procuratorial appointments gives an indication of the smallness of the numbers: if the average tenure of each procuratorship was three years, only thirty procurators at the end of the first century and sixty in the early third century were appointed each year.

began to grant the *latus clavus* as a *beneficium* to equestrians desiring to pursue senatorial careers.[58] That it was treated as a mark of favor from the emperor is clear from the fact that some men included the grant in their *cursus* in inscriptions even though it was implicit in the fact of their elections to quaestorships.[59] The prestige derived from signs of the emperor's favor is underlined by an inscription dedicated to a local notable in Gaul: Q. Valerius Macedo lists among his achievements the offer from Hadrian of the *latus clavus* and quaestorship as well as his refusal of the honors.[60] Pliny's letters provide the clearest evidence of how the *latus clavus* was distributed: he indicates that it was through his patronage that his protégés, Sextus Erucius Clarus and Iunius Avitus, secured the *latus clavus* from the emperor.[61] Later in the second century Septimius Severus is said to have received ths *beneficium* from Marcus Aurelius through the support of his uncle.[62] Just how sought-after the *latus clavus* was is difficult to know. The reluctance of some to enter the senatorial order is attested.[63] On the other hand, the need for patronal support in other periods suggests that the demand exceeded the supply. As far as we know, direct contact with the emperor and patronal influence were the only ways of acquiring the *latus clavus*.

Inscriptions attesting imperial grants of equestrian status are found throughout the empire. Difficulties arise, however, when we try to decide just what was granted and what constitutes evidence of a grant. There seems to be general agreement that, on the one hand, a census of 400,000 sesterces was a

---

58 For discussion of the *latus clavus*, see Millar, *Emperor*, 290f. and A. Chastagnol, '"Latus clavus" et "adlectio" ', *RD* 53 (1975), 375 and 'Le laticlave de Vespasien', *Historia* 25 (1976), 253. Chastagnol argues from Suetonius, *Aug.* 38.2 and Dio 59.9.5 that Augustus restricted the wearing of the *latus clavus* to senators and their sons, with the result that *novi homines* only assumed the *latus clavus* with their quaestorship until Caligula began allowing *ad hominem* grants to new men pursuing a senatorial career. The argument appears doubtful: (1) the Suetonius passage says only that Augustus permitted sons of senators to wear the *latus clavus* and attend the curia as a matter of course so that they would become familiar with public business—nothing to suggest that other young men were excluded from wearing the *latus clavus* by special permission; (2) Dio does say that before Caligula's reign only senators and their sons had this right, but Dio seems uncertain and it is quite possible that he drew the wrong implication from a statement such as Suetonius', just as Chastagnol did (a parallel would be Dio's statement that Augustus *permitted* non-senators to marry freedmen, while in fact Augustus *forbade* senators to do so (54.16.2; cf. *Dig.* 23.2.44 together with S. Treggiari, *Roman Freedmen during the Late Republic* (Oxford, 1969), 82ff.)). Vespasian's *latus clavus* is problematic for Chastagnol, being granted in Tiberius' reign. Chastagnol argues that Vespasian only acquired the *latus clavus* when he took up the quaestorship, but this is to make nonsense of Suetonius' story (*Vesp.* 2), since Vespasian would have been eligible for the quaestorship only in 34 and actually held it in 35 or 36—how to explain Suetonius' comment that Vespasian refused to seek the *latus clavus* 'diu'?

59 Chastagnol, '"Latus clavus"', 387, lists examples.

60 *ILS* 6998 (=*CIL* XII. 1783).

61 *Ep.* 2.9 and 8.23.

62 H. A., *Sev.* 1.5.

63 Suetonius, *Claud.* 24.1.

prerequisite for equestrian status, and, on the other, the *equus publicus* was an *ad hominem* grant made by the emperor. The problem is this: was the census of 400,000 sesterces (together with the requisite free birth) a sufficient condition for being an *eques Romanus*? Or did that title, being synonymous with *exornatus equo publico*, require a special grant from the emperor? Since our sources provide no direct evidence about the nature of the grant, we are left to circumstantial epigraphic evidence. In favor of the view that *eques Romanus* was used loosely for all men of sufficient wealth, it has been pointed out that only inscriptions concerning the *equus publicus* mention imperial grants, which are not found in association with the title *eques Romanus*.[64] Moreover, there exist examples of men designated 'natus eques Romanus' in inscriptions — examples which are difficult to explain if all *equites Romani* required a special imperial grant.[65] But unfortunately the view that the title *eques Romanus* was used by all citizens meeting the census requirement cannot account for all of the evidence. The single known example of the status being the result of a formal grant ('eques Romanus ex inquisitione allectus') might somehow be explained away.[66] Other evidence, however, is less easily dismissed: a study of datable North African equestrian inscriptions has shown that the two titles, *exornatus equo publico* and *eques Romanus*, were not used in the same period for two different but overlapping status groups.[67] Rather, the former is found on inscriptions from the period up through the reign of Severus Alexander but not thereafter, while the latter is found almost exclusively on stones inscribed after the reign of Caracalla.[68] In an unpublished study a similar pattern has been found in equestrian inscriptions from Italy, though in this case there was a period of overlap when both *equus publicus* and *eques Romanus* were inscribed.[69] The obvious explanation for these patterns of change in usage would seem to be that *exornatus equo publico* was replaced by *eques Romanus* as the normal designation of equestrian status granted by the emperor. In the end it is probably impossible to reconcile the various circumstantial evidence in a single, neat explanation.[70] Though it seems likely

---

64 Millar, *Emperor*, 280.

65 E.g., M. Valerius Amerimnianus in *ILS* 1318 (= *CIL* VI. 1632).

66 *ILAlg.* I. 2145. For Millar's comment see *Emperor*, 281, n. 15.

67 Duncan-Jones, 'Equestrian rank in the cities of the African provinces under the Principate: an epigraphic study', *PBSR* 35 (1967), 149f.

68 *Ibid.*, 185.

69 My warmest thanks to Richard Duncan-Jones for discussing the matter with me, for sharing the results of his study of the Italian evidence, and for pointing out its consequences.

70 See also T. P. Wiseman, 'The definition of "eques romanus" in the late Republic and early Empire', *Historia* 19 (1970), 67-83. Wiseman suggests a change between the reigns of Vespasian and Hadrian from the situation postulated by Millar to that postulated by Duncan-Jones when censorial powers became inherent in the position of Princeps. His justification is not clear to me: some sort of equestrian rank continued to be granted by the emperor himself after Hadrian's reign (the implication being that it was more than just a

that the title *eques Romanus* was on occasion used loosely of any freeborn man with 400,000 sesterces, in most cases it probably indicates that a man received an imperial grant which in an earlier period was called the *equus publicus*.

In all of the numerous inscriptions recording the equestrian status there is no clear indication of how it was distributed.[71] Nor do we possess any *commendationes* concerning the *equus publicus* or membership in the *quinque decuriae*. A reference in Suetonius makes it clear that the latter was sought by patrons for their friends, and the letters of Pliny to Romatius Firmus suggest (though not explicitly) that Firmus was selected for the *quinque decuriae* as a result of Pliny's patronage.[72] As Duncan-Jones suggests, it is highly probable that both of these honors were obtained through the recommendation of patrons in the same way as the *latus clavus*.

Although special grants of citizenship to free peregrines, like the *latus clavus* and the *equus publicus*, were in the hands of the emperor alone, consideration of citizenship grants is best left to a later chapter about provincial patrons. It is worth pointing out in the Roman context, however, that such a grant constituted an honor and *beneficium* not only for the recipient, but also for the Roman patron who secured it. Pliny's gratitude and obligation to Trajan for the grant of citizenship to his *iatraliptes* have already been pointed out.[73] We may also note here Martial's pride in having procured citizenship for clients. In an epigram to his rival Naevolus (3.95) Martial boasted of his success as measured by the *praemia* received from Domitian: through the poet's requests a number of men received citizenship by the *munus* of the emperor. Claudius had a reputation for cheapening citizenship by distributing it too freely, but Domitian did not: the fact that a minor figure at the periphery of the court circles like Martial could obtain many grants for friends gives some indication of how often emperors bestowed this *beneficium*.[74]

In addition to the statuses granted to freeborn men, the emperor could grant other statuses to those of servile background. We know nothing about grants of freedom to slaves, the *ius anuli aurei* or the *ius ingenuitatis*, beyond the facts that they were called *beneficia* and were bestowed on imperial favorites such as Pallas, Asiaticus and the father of Claudius Etruscus.[75] Clearly these grants were matters of patronal favoritism. Whether they were often sought is a question that cannot be answered from our evidence.

   result of census-taking) and there is no reason to suppose that the loose usage of *eques Romanus* would have disappeared at that time.

71 Millar, *Emperor,* 282.
72 *Ep.* 1.19 and 4.29; Sherwin-White, *Letters of Pliny,* 129f. Despite Duncan-Jones' assertion, neither of these letters explicitly says that Pliny secured anything from the emperor for Firmus, though it may be a reasonable inference. Suetonius, *Tib.,* 51.1.
73 See above, p.35.
74 Dio 60.17.5f.
75 For a full discussion and a list of known instances of the grants, A. M. Duff, *Freedmen in the Roman Empire,* 85f.

For all of the above statuses except citizenship and freedom the only means of acquisition was by an *ad hominem* grant of the emperor. The emperor could also manipulate the administrative system and laws to deliver favors. We have already noted one example, the grants of access to aqueducts which Martial requested and Statius received.[76] Perhaps owing to the importance of inheritance of wealth in the ancient world the most frequently mentioned *beneficium* of this category was the *ius trium liberorum*. Augustan legislation had provided for special privileges for those with children and had specified certain penalties for those without (especially, limitation on rights of inheritance). Initially the senate granted the privileges to the childless, but at some point in the first century emperors themselves began to treat the *ius trium liberorum* as a favor for those not meeting the legal requirements.[77] One of Martial's epigrams was written as a request for this *ius* and two other poems acknowledge that he received it.[78] The letters of Pliny indicate that he too received the *ius* through the *preces* of his consular friend Iulius Servianus, and Pliny, in turn, secured it for his protégés, Voconius Romanus and Suetonius — all despite Trajan's claim that he bestowed this type of *beneficium* 'parce'.[79] Of additional interest is the fact that this *beneficium* was institutionalized in the sense that Trajan received the senate's approval for the bestowal of a certain number of grants.[80] The allotment of a number of exemptions from the law for distribution by the emperor is as clear a reflection as any of the patronal aspect of the regime.

We have no reason to think that other types of privileges and immunities were regulated by senatorial approval. For instance, the use of the *cursus publicus* was normally restricted to those on official business. When the grandfather of Pliny's wife died, Pliny sent her back to Italy hurriedly by the *cursus publicus* and then asked the emperor for the *beneficium* of belated approval.[81] Trajan approved in this case and is also known to have given the Greek sophist Polemo the right of free use of the *cursus publicus* among other marks of favor.[82] The casual nature of Trajan's response to Pliny's petition suggests that this *beneficium* was not limited by senatorial approval.

The above privileges are the principal ones for which evidence of imperial distribution survives. We know of others, mainly in relation to the sophists, teachers and philosophers of the East. Philostratus reports grants of dining rights at the Museum in Alexandria and immunity from local *munera*. These have been discussed at length elsewhere and there is no need to review the evidence here since these grants are not of great importance for the

---

76 See above, p.35. 77 Dio 55.2.6., 78 *Epig.* 2.91, 92, 3.95 79 *Ep.* 10.2.1; 2.13.8; 10.94; 10.95. Cf. Sherwin-White, *Letters of Pliny*, 558. 80 Pliny, *Ep.* 10.95. 81 Pliny, *Ep.* 10.120, 82 *Ep.* 10.121.

understanding of the emperor's relationship with his court and the senatorial and equestrian aristocracies.[83]

The *beneficia* discussed up to this point cost the emperor little or nothing in real terms. This was not true of another category of favors: gifts of estates and money. As Millar has pointed out, such gifts were thought to be a natural result of personal contact with the emperor.[84] Pliny, for instance, served as an assessor on Trajan's *consilium* at Centum Cellae and after several days of hearing cases left the villa, having received *xenia* from the emperor.[85] Several sources indicate that emperors participated in the traditional exchange of gifts during the Saturnalia.[86] That gift-giving was not only natural but expected of the emperor is evident from the complaint of Fabius Maximus about the meanness of Augustus' gifts to his *amici*.[87] Clearly, the imperial virtue of *liberalitas* applied to *ad hominem* gifts as well as to mass grants to the urban plebs.

One particular form of this type of *beneficium* comprised imperial subventions to senators, which can be traced to the reign of Augustus. Seneca in his *De Beneficiis* argued that Tiberius' subventions were not true *beneficia* because he humiliated the recipients in the process.[88] A story from Epictetus shows how impoverished senators sought supporters in the emperor's court for their requests: during the reign of Nero an unnamed senator is said to have begged the imperial freedman Epaphroditus for a subvention from the emperor.[89] Individual examples indicate that these gifts could be quite substantial, but no figures are available to satisfy our curiosity as to the total imperial expenditure on this form of *beneficium* (especially those bestowed on members of the imperial aristocracy). If such figures were available, we might be in a better position to evaluate the hypothesis that systematic impoverishment was an important factor in the high turnover of senatorial families in the Principate.[90]

Offices, statuses, privileges, immunities and money were expected to be used by the emperor as *beneficia* for his friends. Patronal influence could also

83 Bowersock, *Greek Sophists in the Roman Empire*, ch.3, and Millar, *Emperor*, 438-9, 499f.; for a discussion of immunity, see V. Nutton, 'Two notes on immunities: Digest 27.1.6.10 and 11', *JRS* 61 (1971), 52-63.

84 *Emperor*, 138, 496f.; see also Kloft, *Liberalitas Principis*, chs.3, 4 for a thorough treatment of the evidence.

85 *Ep.* 6.31.14.

86 Suetonius, *Aug.* 75; Martial, *Epig.* 5.49.

87 Quintilian, *Inst.* 6.3.52. The justice of this charge by Maximus may be doubted if we believe Pliny the Elder that Augustus bestowed 100,000,000 sesterces on L. Tarius Rufus (*N.H.* 18.37).

88 *De Ben.* 2.8; Millar, *Emperor*, 298f. for imperial subventions.

89 *Diss.* 1.26.11-12.

90 M. K. Hopkins, review of Millar, *Emperor*, *JRS* 68 (1978), 184.

be an important factor in the emperor's judicial decisions, but this kind of favor presents more complex issues. Millar treats the judicial activities of the emperor at length and notes 'the indivisibility of the giving of justice and of *beneficia*... it is possible to discern the essential fact that at least a large area of the emperor's jurisdiction was seen as a form of granting aid and succour to individuals and groups, and to take this as continuous with the related activities of hearing complaints, solving problems, conferring or affirming rights or privileges or making actual gifts'.[91] It should be added that in one respect judicial activity was different from the emperor's other *beneficia*. The latter were distributed as *ad hominem* favors without any restraining ideology of fairness or equality for all. People might object that the emperor was showing favoritism to the wrong people, but they never objected in principle to favoritism. The same cannot be said for the emperor's judicial decisions. Aelius Aristides, for instance, praised the emperor from whose attention no just claim escaped and who provided equal justice for the rich and poor alike.[92]

However unrealistic Aristides may have been — in fact inequality was institutionalized in the system at this time — his statement nevertheless points to the possibility of a conflict of ideology which was non-existent for the other imperial *beneficia*. The conflict took a concrete form in the two trials relating to Herodes Atticus, an *amicus* of Marcus Aurelius. The date and circumstances of the first, in which Fronto spoke against Herodes in defense of Demostratus, are extremely ambiguous: what is clear from Fronto's and Marcus' letters is that the request for Fronto to restrain his invective created a tension between the pursuit of justice (in the form of a vigorous defense) and patronal influence.[93] The second trial is more relevant here because it took place before Marcus after he had assumed the purple. Apparently Herodes undertook a prosecution of Demostratus and his allies before a provincial official. Demostratus fled to Marcus at Sirmium and levelled accusations against Herodes. Philostratus reports that Demostratus' oration was a masterpiece and that Marcus was torn by the account of the misdeeds and was left in tears. Faced with a choice between his obligation to justice and his obligation to *amicitia*, the emperor's final solution was to assign the blame to Herodes' freedmen and to punish them.[94] Quite how this constituted a decision

---

91 *Emperor*, 466ff.; for discussions of appeals, criminal and civil cases, 507-37. De Ste Croix, 'Suffragium', 42f. discusses the use of influence.

92 Εἰς Ῥώμην 38f. For the whole issue of inequality before the law, both in theory and in practice, P. Garnsey, *Social Status and Legal Privilege in the Roman Empire*. Millar, *Emperor*, 516f., notes the conflict between the emperor's roles as dispenser of justice and dispenser of *clementia*—the latter not being precisely identical with the personal patronal role.

93 Fronto, *Ad M. Caes.* 3.2-6; I follow the reconstruction of events by Bowersock, *Greek Sophists*, 92-100. For dating the trial, see also E. J. Champlin, 'The chronology of Fronto', *JRS* 64 (1974), 142.

94 *V.S.* 559ff., esp. 561. In addition to their appeal for justice, the Athenians also drew support

'worthy of a philosopher' is not at all apparent, but the conflict between *amicitia* and justice is clear — a conflict which does not arise in the accounts of distributions of other favors to Greek sophists.

A number of other examples are available to show the influence exerted by patronage on judicial decisions. Cotta Messallinus went so far as to speak in the senate of the protection he enjoyed by virtue of his friendship with Tiberius.[95] Messallina and Claudius' freedmen are said to have sold acquittals to the guilty; and in the next reign Nero prolonged the trial of his procurator in Asia, P. Celer, until he died a natural death.[96] The example of Herodes proves that such influence was not confined to the reigns of the so-called bad emperors. Pliny reports another interesting case in one of his letters: the heirs named in the will of one Iulius Tiro wanted to charge a Roman knight and an imperial freedman before the emperor with forgery of the will. The emperor agreed to hear the case, but then some of the heirs decided to drop the charge out of *reverentia* for the freedman procurator. Trajan resented the implication of influence, but seems to have been unable to persuade the heirs to press the charge.[97] Once again the conflict between justice and influence is evident, as is the assumption of the litigants that influence would be decisive. In this case, however, Trajan, unlike Marcus, announced that he would not be swayed by patronal considerations.

In the judicial matters so far discussed the cases were contested by two parties. Other judicial matters concerned only one party and for these Millar's comment about the connection between *beneficium* and jurisdiction can be accepted without reservation. For instance, permission to return from exile was thought a *beneficium* and such *clementia* was encouraged as an imperial virtue. We know of several instances where this *beneficium* was secured through patronal influence, the best known being the case of Seneca, who attemped to secure his restoration from Claudius through the intervention of the imperial freedman Polybius and then finally received it through Agrippina's *gratia*.[98] We know of other cases of restoration from other periods.[99] It should be noted that, unlike other *beneficia* which could be petitioned directly from the emperor, requests for restoration could never be submitted in person and always required a patronal mediator.

It is beyond the scope of this study to pursue the issues of legal ideology and the emperor's judicial role in detail. Moreover, it is impossible to determine from the evidence available the overall importance of patronage in the legal

from Marcus' wife and daughter.
95 Tacitus, *Ann.* 6.5.
96 Dio 60.16.2; Tacitus, *Ann.* 13.33.1.
97 *Ep.* 6.31.7.
98 *Cons. ad Polyb.*; Tacitus, *Ann.* 12.8.
99 Garnsey, *Social Status*, 36ff. and Millar, *Emperor*, 539f.; Seneca, *De Ben.* 2.25.1 may be another instance.

processes. We shall have to be content with the general conclusion that the emperor's judicial role provided opportunities for the distribution of favors.

Altogether, it is clear that the emperor possessed an abundant storehouse of *beneficia* on which he could draw: he played a dominant part in distributing Roman offices and statuses, and could alter men's fortunes with gifts of privileges, immunities and money. What is less clear is the actual frequency of distribution. Perhaps one very rough indicator can be used. As suggested above, Pliny's position was probably 'not untypical of that of reasonably well-placed senators as a whole'.[100] During a tenure of less than two years as governor of Bithynia we have a record of six patronal requests submitted by Pliny to the emperor — for an unspecified senatorial post, a staff appointment, an equestrian *militia*, citizenship, the *ius trium liberorum*, and approval for private use of the *cursus publicus*.[101] These requests may well represent a typical cross-section. If Pliny's rate of petitioning was at all normal, the emperor must have received hundreds of requests each year from consulars alone, most of which, to judge from Pliny's successes, seem to have met with positive responses.[102] Indeed, these requests were such common, everyday occurrences that they rarely deserved any mention in the historical narratives: the author of the *Historia Augusta* dismissed the emperor's appointments and promotions as trivial and worthy of no more notice than his diet and clothing.[103]

ACCESS TO IMPERIAL BENEFICIA

The preceding discussion produced a long list of names of recipients of imperial *beneficia* and their patrons. It is now time to analyze these names in order to discover what kinds of people could approach and petition the emperor, and in what circumstances. In short, we want to discover who possessed *gratia*. Of course, the answer will vary to some extent with the emperor, but much depended on structural features of the court which remained unchanged throughout the Principate.

100 Millar, *Emperor*, 114.
101 *Ep.* 10.26, 51, 87, 94, 104, and 120. The second, fourth, fifth and sixth of these are known to have been successful, while the outcome of the request on behalf of Geminus is uncertain (Syme, 'Pliny's less successful friends', *Historia* 9 (1960), 368f.).
102 The average life expectancy for a senator after holding the consulship may have been approximately fifteen years. If something like eight new consuls were appointed each year, then about 120 consulars were living at any given time. If each of these was sending three petitions per year like Pliny, then the emperor received an average of one each day. If anything, this probably underestimates the rate of petitioning. In 10.94 Pliny implies that important requests such as for the *ius trium liberorum* would not normally be made in writing, but in person. It should be added that the success rate depended on the *beneficium* requested: we know of no failures of senators to secure citizenship, an abundant *beneficium*, for clients, while failures are known for senatorial and equestrian offices.
103 H. A., *Macrinus* 1.4.

The group perhaps closest to the emperor and with unchallenged claim on his favors were the male members of his immediate family. Not all emperors had adult sons or grandsons (natural or by adoption), but when sons or grandsons existed, they and their friends were always natural candidates for the emperor's beneficence. Tacitus notes that Sejanus initially attached himself to Augustus' grandsons and then to Tiberius.[104] Sejanus was not the only equestrian to do so: Philo has Flaccus on his way into exile lament his fall in contrast with his promising beginnings as a schoolmate and companion of Augustus' grandsons and then as a friend of Tiberius.[105]

In the letters of Fronto we find much more specific evidence of the circumstances in which the emperor might be petitioned by his son. There survive two *commendationes* which Fronto sent to Marcus, requesting help in securing *beneficia* from Pius for clients. In one case, Fronto asks that Marcus extend his *benignitas* to a *conductor IIII publicorum Africae* whose accounts were about to be reviewed by Pius.[106] In the second letter Marcus is asked to use his influence with Pius to secure a procuratorship for Fronto's client, the imperial freedman Aridelus.[107] At other times Fronto is known to have written to and petitioned Pius directly.[108] The choice of alternative paths to the emperor for petitions perhaps depended on the nature of the request and the warmth of the various personal relationships involved. A man like Fronto with numerous and close contacts at court must have had alternative methods of forwarding requests to the emperor, and so was able to select the one judged to be most effective at any given time. It is interesting to note that after Marcus became emperor Fronto began to use Lucius Verus to forward his requests to Marcus himself.[109] Direct access to Marcus may have become more difficult, and members of the family were able to press requests in more intimate contexts.

In the Republic a man's life chances were determined in large part by the power and influence of his *amici*. This remained true in the Principate and of course the emperor became the most effective *amicus* available. The *amici Caesaris* constituted an amorphous group including senators, *equites* and others who had access to the emperor.[110] The friendships might be strictly

---

104 *Ann.* 4.1. It is worth noting that in the same period Ovid, after failing to secure return from exile through other avenues, began to cultivate friends of Germanicus as an indirect (and unsuccessful) method of winning the emperor's favor. Ovid's assumption clearly was that the emperor could be reached through his stepson (R. Syme, *History in Ovid*, ch. 9).

105 *In Flaccum* 158.

106 *Ad M. Caes.* 5.34.

107 *Ad M. Caes.* 5.37.

108 *Ad Pium* 9.

109 *Ad Verum Imp.* 2.8.

110 J. Crook, *Consilium Principis*, ch.3; Millar, *Emperor*, 110-22; Alföldy, *Römische Sozialgeschichte*, 105f.; W. Eck, 'Zu den prokonsularen Legationen in der Kaiserzeit', *Epigraphische Studien* 9 (1972), 32.

formal or warm and personal.

Some indication of the variety can be found in the letters of Pliny and Fronto. Pliny enjoyed a friendly, but not intimate relationship with Trajan. His *commendationes* are relatively formal and to the point, containing few personal or intimate details. Pliny often gives as a reason for venturing his requests the emperor's past *indulgentia*.[111] Fronto seems to have enjoyed the same sort of relationship with Pius and the *commendatio* addressed to him has the same characteristics as Pliny's.[112] Fronto's friendships with his pupils, Marcus and Lucius, on the other hand, were more intimate. In letters to them the language of *indulgentia* is replaced by the language of *amor;* Fronto's entire family is seen to be on friendly terms with the imperial family, particularly Marcus' mother Domitia Lucilla, with whom he exchanges letters. Expressions of affection between the families even find their way into letters intended as recommendations.[113] Altogether, we can distinguish Pliny's formal friendship with Trajan, typical of the exchange relationship enjoyed by prominent senators, from Fronto's exchanges with Marcus, which were embedded in a web of close family relationships.

Whether warmly personal or formal, *amicitia* with the emperor was an enormously important fact in an aristocrat's life. As suggested above, an *amicus* could expect *honores* for himself, and also *auctoritas* derived from his ability to influence decisions and secure *beneficia* for friends. The *auctoritas* was felt at Rome and throughout the empire. Pliny expressed concern about contesting a legal case with *amici Caesaris*.[114] More telling is an early third-century papyrus from Egypt in which the *strategoi* of Arsinoe are warned to behave with restraint toward a certain Titanianus on the grounds that he was known to be esteemed by Caracalla.[115]

An *amicus'* access to the emperor could be through personal contact or written communication. We have already discussed the latter with regard to Fronto and Pliny. It should be added that written communication was probably the less desirable method of approach. In a *commendatio* from Bithynia Pliny indicates that he would normally make such requests in person before the emperor.[116] The reason is not difficult to understand. We may suspect that a request made in person was less easy to refuse; it was certainly more difficult to

111 *Ep.* 10.4, 11-13, 26, 94, 120.
112 *Ad Pium* 9 on behalf of Appian. In *Ad M. Caes.* 2.1 Fronto describes the difference between his relationship with Hadrian and Pius. The former Fronto tried to propitiate as he would a god, but could not love because of a lack of *fiducia* and *familiaritas*. By contrast, Fronto says that he loves Pius.
113 The *amor* theme runs throughout the letters; see especially *Epist. Graec.* 7 and *Ad M. Caes.* 1.3; see p.13 above. Letters illustrating the relations between the two families include *Epist. Graec.* 1, *Ad M. Caes.* 2.8 and 4.6.
114 *Ep.* 1.18.3.
115 *P.Gen.* 1; Millar, *Emperor*, 114. Note also Epictetus, *Diss.* 4.1.95.
116 *Ep.* 10.94.

defer. Philo says that when the Jews of Alexandria were told by the prefect of Egypt Flaccus that he would send on to Rome their decree of honors for Gaius, they rejoiced because everything sent to the emperor by governors received immediate attention.[117] The implication of Philo's statement is that other written communication sent to the emperor was not necessarily dealt with as quickly. This is not surprising, given the mass of petitions and letters which the emperor was expected to read and answer personally.[118]

Thus face-to-face contact with the emperor was of special importance, even for *amici Caesaris*. Among Trajan's virtues Pliny emphasized his openness to the 'flower of the senatorial and equestrian orders' — in contrast to past emperors who 'were attended by a *manus satellitum*'. In other words, access to the emperor could not be taken for granted by leading members of the senatorial and equestrian orders. A *cubicularius*, for instance, might lock a man out of the emperor's presence and deprive him of the opportunity to govern a province.[119] In a discussion with an equestrian exile returning to Rome, Epictetus used admission to Caesar's court as the symbol of participation in Roman political life and access to office.[120] The significance of personal contact is more clearly illustrated by a letter of Fronto to the emperor Lucius Verus. Fronto describes the marks of esteem which Verus displayed towards himself — kisses of greeting, physical support while walking, and long conversations. These actions Fronto explicitly interprets as signs of favor which encourage petitions for *beneficia*, and they must also have given Fronto opportunities for expressing his wishes in person.[121]

Most *amici* cannot have been on such intimate terms with the emperor. They probably enjoyed most face-to-face contact in two basic settings: morning salutations and dinner parties. We know that morning *salutationes* provided the setting for daily contact between Pliny the Elder and Vespasian.[122] Other *amici* may have attended less regularly. Whether division of the *amici* into three *cohortes* on the Republican model described by Seneca was a constant feature of the *salutatio* throughout the Principate has been questioned.[123] Whenever they were divided, we would expect those in the second and especially the smaller and most select first cohort to be in a more advantageous

---

117 *In Flaccum* 100.
118 Millar, *Emperor*, 203-28. Note also Marcus' letter to Fronto (*Ad Anton. Imp.* 2.3) where Marcus indicates that he is overworked and has had to postpone reading material sent to him by Fronto.
119 *Paneg.* 23.3: 'neque enim stipatus satellitum manu, sed circumfusus undique nunc senatus, nunc equestris ordinis flore...'
120 *Diss.* 1.10.2-6.
121 *Ad Verum Imp.* 2.8.
122 Pliny, *Ep.* 3.5.9.
123 Compare Crook, *Consilium*, 23f. and Millar, *Emperor*, 111. The problem of formal categories is not of great importance here: the division or lack of it would not alter the fact that some *amici* were closer to the emperor than others.

position to press their requests. What cannot be doubted is that the morning meetings provided an occasion to deliver petitions.[124]

Like attendance at the *salutatio*, dining with the emperor was at once an honor and an opportunity. Vespasian is reported to have thanked Caligula for the honor of an invitation in a speech before the senate.[125] During the three days which Pliny spent at Centum Cellae as an assessor he dined with the emperor. After the meal the guests were entertained by recitations or joined in pleasant conversations.[126] Trajan must have been open to informal requests and suggestions at this time. Indeed, it may well be to such a context that we should assign the conversation between Pliny's patron Corellius Rufus and Nerva about Pliny's praiseworthy character.[127] When Epictetus wanted to highlight the hardships and worries endured by an *amicus Caesaris*, he singled out lack of sleep owing to the early morning *salutationes* and the humiliations of dining at the emperor's table as a social inferior — that is, the two standard contexts in which the emperor met his friends.[128] Other Romans without philosophical axes to grind would no doubt have emphasized these settings rather as opportunities to exercise patronal influence.

In addition to these relatively formal and structured meetings, a few *amici*, especially the equestrian secretaries and the praetorian prefect, worked beside the emperor. We would expect these men to have enjoyed some special opportunities for influencing imperial decisions. It is possible to show that on occasion the bureau secretaries obtained *beneficia*. Pliny praised Titinius Capito, Nerva's *ab epistulis*, for using his *amicitia principis* to secure permission to erect a statue of L. Iunius Silvanus Torquatus (executed by Nero) in the forum.[129] The evidence for praetorian prefects is more extensive, allowing us to document their patronage throughout the Principate: the influence of Sejanus, Burrus, Iulius Ursus, Septicius Clarus, Gavius Maximus, Aemilius Laetus and Plautianus is explicitly attested or can be surmised with some confidence.[130] While the impact of the imperial secretaries on decisions is difficult to gauge, it cannot be doubted that praetorian prefects, whose very appointments testified to the emperor's confidence in their loyalty and friendship, were among the most influential figures in imperial circles.

124 Millar, *Emperor*, 241f.
125 Suetonius, *Vesp.* 2.3.
126 *Ep.* 6.31.13.
127 *Ep.* 4.17.7; see below, p.109f.
128 *Diss.* 4.1.47f.
129 *Ep.* 1.17; see Millar, *Emperor*, 83-110 and also below, p.190 for an evaluation of Millar's remarks concerning the importance of educated provincials in secretarial posts channelling imperial *beneficia*.
130 Tacitus, *Ann.* 4.74 for Sejanus; for Burrus' patronage, Syme, *Tacitus*, 591, and also 55f. and 501 for the influence of Ursus and Clarus; for the patronage of Gavius Maximus, see above note 49 and below p.183; for Aemilius Laetus, above, note 27; for Plautianus, see below, p.129 and p.179. For a discussion of emperors and their prefects, Millar, *Emperor*, 122-31.

So far we have analyzed those people around the emperor who were on a nearly equal social footing with him. This near equality enabled them to communicate with the emperor by letter.[131] More importantly, they could approach the emperor in person — the more intimate the context, the better. This latter principle is underlined by the role of the emperor's male relatives. Because of their very close personal relationships with the emperor, men like Fronto often preferred to submit petitions through them, even when the petitions could have been submitted directly but in more formal circumstances. In other words, proximity (physical and emotional) was a critical factor in determining the channels through which imperial *beneficia* flowed. This will be a recurrent theme as we now turn our attention to groups of lower social status surrounding the emperor.

The first group in this category includes those who had access to the emperor on account of their literary or oratorical talents. Such men appear in our sources throughout the Principate, submitting their literary efforts or delivering orations to the emperor. Their names recurred often in the preceding section. They won *beneficia* not only for themselves, but also for those connected with them, cities and individuals. Hadrian of Tyre, for instance, held the chair of rhetoric in Athens and owing to his reputation got the opportunity to speak before Marcus Aurelius. The orator was so successful that he received the right to dine at public expense, a seat of honor at the games, immunity from taxation, priesthoods and 'as many other things as make men illustrious', including gold, silver, horses and slaves. These signs of wealth Marcus gave to Hadrian and his family as well.[132] Those especially favored by the emperor could hope to be appointed as imperial secretaries with all of the concomitant advantages.[133]

A second and related group consists of those educated men who served emperors as teachers and doctors. They enjoyed close personal proximity and benefited accordingly. Marcus Aurelius' teachers are best known: not all of them were initially of low social status, but one at least, Eutychius Proculus, required financial support for his senatorial career and so seems not to have been born into a wealthy aristocratic family.[134] Marcus' interest in learning was such that he continued to correspond with his teachers about learned questions after he assumed the purple in 161; the corollary is that his teachers continued to have Marcus' ear from time to time.[135] This access of teachers to *beneficia* can be traced back to the beginning of Augustus' rule: Areus, Octavian's tutor and companion during his entry into Alexandria in 30 B.C., was said to have

131 Millar, *Emperor*, 469f.
132 Philostratus, *V.S.* 589. For a fuller account, Millar, *Emperor*, 91f. and 491-506, and Bowersock, *Greek Sophists*, ch.3.
133 Philostratus, *V.S.* 592 concerning Diogenes of Amastris.
134 H. A., *Marc.* 2.5; see note 194 of ch. 5 below.
135 E.g., Fronto, *Ad Anton. Imp.* 1.2, 2.4.

been instrumental in saving Alexandria from punishment. Later Areus was appointed procurator of Sicily by Augustus.[136]

Similarly, the access of doctors can be documented beginning in Augustus' reign in the person of Antonius Musa.[137] The few fragments of evidence show that this group was able to channel benefits to themselves, their cities and their families. The doctors of Claudius and (probably) Caracalla, C. Stertinius Xenophon and L. Gellius Maximus, received important equestrian offices, while T. Statilius Criton, Trajan's doctor, probably furthered the procuratorial career of his Antiochene relative, T. Statilius Apollinarius. Perhaps owing to the low social prestige of medicine, none of these physicians reached the senatorial order themselves, but Maximus' son of the same name is found as legate of *legio IV Scythia* when its revolt against Elagabalus was crushed in 219.[138] Altogether, doctors and teachers, though of lower social status, were in very special positions in that they were able to provide emperors with personal services which were interpreted as *beneficia*.[139] Few other Romans had a similar ability to bestow *beneficia* upon the emperor and earn his *gratia* which was expressed in the form of gifts of offices and money.

The social status of litterateurs, doctors and teachers seems to have been sufficiently high for their influence not to have been resented by the imperial aristocracy. The opposite was true for two other groups at court: women, and imperial slaves and freedmen. The influence of women is recorded, in one form or another, for nearly every reign (not always with disapproval). Two important categories should be noted: the emperor's female relatives and the Vestal Virgins. The latter came into contact with the emperor in the performance of rituals, one result of which can be seen in several third-century inscriptions dedicated to Vestals.[140] Campia Severina figures in two such inscriptions: she is thanked in one by Q. Veturius Callistratus for her *suffragium* in securing a procuratorial appointment and in the other by Aemilius Pardalas for providing the necessary patronage to obtain two equestrian *militiae*.[141] Unfortunately, the other dedications are less specific, but they may relate to *beneficia* procured from the emperor: Flavia Mamilia, for instance, was thanked for her outstanding *pietas* by her nephews who were appointed to *militiae*, and other dedications mention *honores*.[142]

The emperor's female relatives were surely a more influential group. When

---

136 Plutarch, *Moralia* 207 Af.; see Millar, *Emperor*, 9, 85.
137 Millar, *Emperor*, 491f.
138 V. Nutton, 'L. Gellius Maximus, physician and procurator', *CQ* n.s. 21 (1971), 262-72. For Statilius Apollinarius, Pflaum, *Carrières*, 298. See Millar, *Emperor*, 85f., 491f.
139 Seneca, *De Ben.* 3.3.4 and 6.16.
140 Inez Scott Ryberg, *Rites of the State Religion in Roman Art* (Memoirs of the American Academy at Rome, 1955), 43, 51.
141 *ILS* 4928 and 4929 (= *CIL* VI 2132 and 2131).
142 *CIL* VI.2133. Others: *CIL* VI.2130, 2134, 32414 (= *ILS* 4930), 32415 (= *ILS* 4932) 32416 (= *ILS* 4931), 32417, 32418 (= *ILS* 4933).

Livia died, the senate voted an arch in her honor because, as Dio says, 'she had saved not a few of them and she had helped rear the children of many and had helped many provide dowries for daughters' — in short, because she had been a great patroness.[143] Some of her patronal resources probably derived from her own wealth, but her ability to deliver certain favors must have been a result of her influence on Augustus and Tiberius, as the letter from Ovid requesting restoration and the notorious case of Urgulania prove.[144] Dio neglects to mention one other patronal resource which must also have derived from Livia's influence on the emperor: support for career advancement. The senatorial career of Otho's grandfather received its start *per gratiam Liviae Augustae*. Other women in Augustus' household also enjoyed *gratia*: Vitruvius thanked his sister Octavia for the continuation of his appointment.[145]

This aspect of patronage was hardly unique to Augustus' and Tiberius' reigns. One of the notorious features of Claudius' reign was the influence of his wives and freedmen, who were alleged to have sold offices, honors and verdicts.[146] The general accusations may in part be attributed to exaggeration. But some of the evidence, especially Seneca's request for return from exile addressed to the freedman Polybius, cannot be dismissed.[147] Specific instances of Agrippina's *gratia* have been recounted above. What should be emphasized here is that Claudius' reign differed from others not in the fact of female influence, but in the quantity and kinds of favors granted. Imperial women are also alleged to have exercised patronage in the reigns of Nero, Vespasian, Domitian, Trajan, Marcus Aurelius and Caracalla.[148] We should take note especially of the evidence for Trajan's wife Plotina and Marcus' mother Domitia Lucilla. In a letter to Voconius Romanus, Pliny promised to deliver his letter to Plotina; the need for Pliny to deliver the letter indicates that Romanus was not a regular correspondent of Plotina and the most plausible suggestion as to the contents of the letter is a petition of some sort.[149] The testimony concerning Domitia Lucilla comes from the relatively reliable *Life of Didius Iulianus* in the *Historia Augusta* where she is said to have raised

143 Dio 58.2.3: καὶ προσέτι καὶ ἁψῖδα αὐτῇ, ὃ μηδεμιᾷ ἄλλῃ γυναικί, ἐψηφίσαντο, ὅτι τε οὐκ ὀλίγους σφῶν ἐσεσώκει, καὶ ὅτι παῖδας πολλῶν ἐτετρόφει κόρας τε πολλοῖς συνεξεδεδώκει. For Roman women, Balsdon, *Roman Women* and Finley, 'The silent women of Rome' in *Aspects of Antiquity*, 127–42. Balsdon's book provides little help in understanding the structural importance of women in the imperial court. Finley's essay is suggestive as to why the influence of women, when it surfaced, took such a vicious form (141f.).
144 Ovid, *Ep.* 3.1.131; Tacitus, *Ann.* 2.34.
145 *De Arch.* 1. pr. 2.
146 Suetonius, *Claudius* 25.5 and 29; Dio 60.17.8.
147 *Cons. ad Polyb.*
148 Poppaea Sabina under Nero: Josephus, *Ant. J.* 20.11.1; Caenis under Vespasian: Dio 66.14.3; Iulia under Domitian: Dio 67.4.2; Plotina under Trajan and Domitia Lucilla under Marcus, see below; Iulia Domna under Caracalla: Philostratus, *V.S.* 622.
149 Pliny, *Ep.* 9.28; Sherwin-White, *Letters of Pliny*, 510.

Iulianus and secured a vigintivirate post for him.[150] The significance of these two examples is that they occurred in the reigns of so-called good emperors who kept their households under control.

If the influence of imperial women illustrates the importance of proximity to the emperor, imperial freedmen and slaves make the point more strongly. The imperial bureaucracy initially grew out of the emperor's household administration and so under the Julio-Claudians freedmen were left in charge of the bureaux concerned with financial accounts, petitions and correspondence. Some of these freedmen achieved positions of power thought to be completely unsuitable to their low birth, providing a major source of irritation between the emperor and the aristocracy.[151] As early as the reign of Tiberius, Agrippa I is found lavishing gifts upon the emperor's freedmen in the hope of winning their support.[152] In the next three reigns the power of freedmen was more pronounced, as figures such as Callistus, Polybius, Narcissus, Pallas and Epaphroditus channelled *beneficia* in the form of offices, money and protection from prosecution to senators and others.

As is often noted, the power of these freedmen resulted not from any official positions, but from their personal contact and influence with the emperor. Though this has been denied, it seems to me to be the only sound conclusion in view of the nature of the senatorial complaints.[153] Callistus' protection of Domitius Afer, Narcissus' acquisition of a legionary legateship for Vespasian, his protection of Iunius Cilo, his lethal attack on Appius Silanus, Pallas' protection of Felix, and the sale of acquittals and citizenship were all a result of *gratia*, not of official responsibilities. Indeed, senatorial writers do not seem to have voiced any resentment about the official powers given to freedmen in their bureaux.[154] Rather the tension arose from the inversion of social roles in which senators had to accept the humiliation of approaching (and bribing) freedmen for patronal favors in order to advance their careers. Epictetus, who was a slave of Epaphroditus at Nero's court, described the source of resentment best when he wrote that senators, forced to cultivate such patrons, became δοῦλοι δούλων ('slaves of slaves').[155]

150 H. A., *Iul.* 1.3-4; for reliability, see Syme, *Emperors and Biography*, 42.
151 S. I. Oost, 'The career of M. Antonius Pallas', *AJPh* 79 (1958), 113-39; P. R. C. Weaver, *Familia Caesaris*; G. Boulvert, *Esclaves et affranchis impériaux sous le Haut-Empire romain: rôle politique et administratif*; Millar, *Emperor*, 69-83 and 'Epictetus'; M. K. Hopkins, 'Eunuchs in politics in the later Roman Empire', *PCPhS* n.s.9 (1963), 62-80.
152 Josephus, *Ant. J.* 18.6.1 (145).
153 Oost, 'Pallas', 125. Those stressing informal influence and proximity include Pflaum, *Procurateurs*, 198ff.; Millar, 'Emperors at work', *JRS* 57 (1967), 18; and Boulvert, *Esclaves et affranchis*, 371.
154 Dio 59.19.5f.; Suetonius, *Vespasian* 4; Dio 60.33.6; Dio 60.14.2-3 and Suetonius, *Claud.* 37; Tacitus, *Ann.* 12.54; Dio 60.16.2; Suetonius, *Claud.* 29.
155 *Diss.* 4.1.148; other passages describe the humiliation of begging freedmen for support: *Diss.* 3.7.31, 4.7.19f.; see Millar, 'Epictetus'.

Aristocratic reaction against the influence of freedmen was strong, and to the basic elements in the ideology of the good emperor was added his control of imperial freedmen. It can be found in Pliny's *Panegyricus:* 'Most emperors, though they were masters of their subjects, were slaves of their freedmen, ruled by their counsels and nods... You, however, have the highest esteem for your freedmen, but only as freedmen... for you know that the principal indication of a weak emperor is the greatness of his freedmen.'[156] Pius was also praised for maintaining control of his *liberti* and preventing the sale of 'smoke'.[157] Perhaps owing to the impact of this ideology on emperors, freedmen do not appear prominently in accounts of the Flavian or Antonine periods until the reign of Commodus. Nevertheless, because personal contact with the emperor remained important, freedmen continued to exercise some influence. Though Domitian's reign was not characterized by the power of his freedmen, Statius and Martial found it useful to dedicate poetry to Abascantus, Entellus and Parthenius (*ab epistulis, a libellis* and *cubicularius* respectively).These freedmen were wealthy enough to be patrons in their own right, but they also had access to Domitian. One poem from Martial specifically requests Parthenius to deliver the poet's *libellus* of poems to Caesar at the most propitious moment: 'You know the time of Jove's serenity when he shines with that calm look, all his own, that is accustomed to deny nothing to petitioners'.[158] A fragmentary letter of Fronto suggests a similar point about the importance of information about the emperor's mood and schedule. In 161 Lucius wrote to Fronto, gently scolding him for having failed to arrange a meeting at the Palace after four months' separation. Fronto replied that the fault was not his own. Most of the explanation is lost, but it is clear that Fronto wrote to Charilas, an imperial freedman, to enquire about Marcus and Lucius, asking, 'Is it convenient for me to come to them today? Please tell me as a man of sense and a friend.'[159] Although freedmen were never able to control access to the emperor in the Principate to the extent that eunuch chamberlains did in the later Empire, nevertheless, in every reign freedmen constituted one of the personal communication links to the court and so retained some of the influence which they enjoyed in the Julio-Claudian era.[160]

---

156 *Paneg.* 88.1-2: 'Plerique principes, cum essent civium domini, libertorum erant servi: horum consiliis horum nutu regebantur...tu libertis tuis summum quidem honorem, sed tamquam libertis habes...scis enim praecipuum esse iudicium non magni principis magnos libertos.'
157 H. A., *Pius* 6.4, 11.1.
158 Statius, *Silv.* 5; Martial, *Epig.* 8.68; quotation from *Epig.* 5.6.9-11:
   nosti tempora tu Iovis sereni,
   cum fulget placido suoque vultu,
   quo nil supplicibus solet negare.
159 *Ad Verum Imp.* 1.3-4: Ἆρα σήμερον εὔκαιρόν ἐστιν ἀφικέσθαι με πρὸς αὐτούς; σύ μοι δήλωσον ὡσανεὶ ἔμφρων κἀμοὶ φίλος· κἀμοί σε...
160 Hopkins, 'Eunuchs', esp. 66, 77.

The significance of the frequent and close contacts which gave imperial women and freedmen their *gratia* is best highlighted by a brief glance at the condition of other low-status groups. First, within the urban plebs there seems to have been a special group which constituted the emperor's *clientela*. According to Suetonius, Augustus did not normally interfere with trials, but he did appear at the trials of his *clientes*.[161] A century later Pliny, in his praise of Trajan's open reception of his subjects, spoke of four groups: senators, *equites, clientes* and the mass of spectators.[162] Quite possibly this clientèle was a carry-over from the time before he assumed the purple when he would have had a following among the urban plebs like other aristocrats.[163] Its precise size and composition we cannot even guess. Nor do we know exactly what the relationship involved. Perhaps it was to his *clientes* that Domitian sent *prandia* during the Saturnalia.[164] Finally, we do not know whether this special group of Romans continued to exist throughout the Principate.

In addition to these *clientes*, every inhabitant of the empire was a potential recipient of the emperor's *beneficia*. Millar has stressed that ideally the emperor was available to listen to all petitions. But for the unprivileged masses who were not on letter-writing terms the only means of petitioning seems to have been the delivery of a *libellus* either in person or through an agent. The requirement of being where the emperor was meant that most of the empire was *de facto* unable to enjoy the emperor's special patronage.[165] Moreover, even those within the vicinity of the emperor might face serious obstacles in the delivery of their requests. Tiberius made himself inaccessible on the island of Capri in the later part of his reign, and earlier during his Campanian trip he had ordered the road on which he intended to travel cleared with the intention of avoiding petitions. For the same reason, Tiberius is also said to have delayed embassies from provincial cities.[166] As one indication of Claudius' quickness to anger, Suetonius notes that he pushed away with his own hand those trying to approach him.[167] The implication of Pliny's praise of Trajan's openness is that

---

161 *Aug.* 56.
162 *Paneg.* 23.1f. The common view equates the emperor's *clientes* with the *plebs urbana* (recently J. Gérard, *Juvenal et la réalité contemporaine*, 202, following D. Van Berchem, *Les distributions de blé et d'argent à la plèbe romaine sous l'Empire*, 56f.). Van Berchem's view relies on several inscriptions including the word *clientes* and this passage from Pliny. All but one of the inscriptions certainly have nothing to do with imperial *clientelae*, while *CIL* VI.32098f (= *ILS* 5654f) is a fragment from a step in the amphitheater with *CLIENT* on it, providing no indication of what group the *clientes* comprised. With regard to the Pliny passage, if the emperor's clients included the entire *plebs urbana* it is difficult to see how Trajan could have 'displayed of his own accord certain signs of familiarity to his *salutatis clientibus*' who were distinct from the 'crowd of onlookers'.
163 See below, p.128f.
164 Martial, *Epig.* 5.49.
165 Millar, *Emperor*, chs. 1 and 8, esp. p. 3 for the ideology and pp. 475f. for the *de facto* limitations.
166 Suetonius, *Tib.* 40; Josephus, *Ant. J.* 18.6.5 (170-1).
167 *Claud.* 38.2.

his predecessors were not always so accessible — hence the significance of the proximity enjoyed by imperial women and freedmen.

We have found that throughout the Principate the structure of the imperial court put certain groups in positions to channel imperial *beneficia* to themselves and their friends and clients. The common characteristic of all these groups was proximity. The relative success of each group varied with each emperor (hence no discernible, permanent hierarchy of influence), but in no period did the structure of the court or the nature of the patronal network change sufficiently to eliminate the role of any group altogether. Even in the 'Golden Age' of the Antonines freedmen received favors and imperial women enjoyed *gratia*. Unfortunately, we are not in a good position to chart the shifts in each group's fortunes. No Roman was interested in a comprehensive study of such trivial matters as the means by which people received imperial appointments, and so their general statements about the influence of women and freedmen probably derive as much from stereotypes as from precise and trustworthy sources. Indeed, the stereotyped literary evidence for Caligula and Claudius is not nearly as valuable as are the casual references in the letters of Pliny and Fronto to the emperor's relatives, *amici* and freedmen. The latter show that manipulation of networks emanating from the emperor was a normal and essential part of court life, even for an aging senator such as Fronto who had completed his senatorial *cursus*.

RECIPROCITY AND SOCIAL COHESION

For an appreciation of the importance of imperial distribution of *beneficia*, we should place the foregoing description in the context of the reciprocity ethic described in the first chapter. Emperor and subject alike believed that an imperial *beneficium*, like any other, created a debt which could be repaid in gratitude and in more concrete forms. Upon assuming the purple, Nerva issued an edict claiming that one of his purposes in so doing was to grant *beneficia*. He reassured his subjects that he would not do this by nullifying the grants of past emperors in order to be able to grant them again and so oblige the beneficiaries to himself.[168] The idea that emperors could manipulate *beneficia* in order to put people in their debt is also implicit in a remark of Pliny about Trajan. In the *Panegyricus* Trajan is praised for a blanket extension of an exemption from the inheritance tax (in place of the *ad hominem* grants of the past) because he thereby selflessly forfeited 'tot beneficiorum occasiones, tam numerosam obligandi imputandique materiam' ('so many opportunities for giving *beneficia*, so much material for obligating and holding people accountable').[169] That subjects accepted this reciprocal obligation vis-à-vis the emperor is clear

168 Pliny, *Ep.* 10.58.7f.
169 *Paneg.* 39.3. Similarly, Seneca, *De Ben.* 6.19.2.

from Tacitus' famous remark at the beginning of the *Histories*. The historian says that he can be expected to write about Galba, Otho and Vitellius impartially since he did not receive *beneficia* nor suffer *iniuria* at their hands; moreover, he aimed to write about the Flavians without *amor* or *odium* despite the fact that his career began and owed its promotion to Vespasian and his sons. Clearly, Tacitus' readers would have assumed that the *beneficia* received in the course of a public career created obligations.[170]

The exchange relationship between the emperor and his subjects could hardly be on equal terms, given the disproportionate resources of the former. As Seneca points out, emperors 'are placed by Fortune in a position in which they are able to bestow many favors but will receive very few and inadequate gifts in return'.[171] Subjects, then, are left to acknowledge their gratitude and inability to repay in kind — in other words, to accept and acknowledge their inferior position. Tension could arise if subjects refused to accept their roles in the exchange and attempted to turn the tables. In Tacitus' view, Tiberius attacked C. Silius because Silius boasted at length that he held his troops on the Rhine loyal to the emperor while others mutinied. 'Caesar judged that his position was undermined by such comments and was unequal to repay such a service. For *beneficia* are welcome so long as they seem to be able to be requited: when they far exceed that, hatred replaces gratitude.'[172]

Normally the emperor's superiority in this respect was unquestioned, and subjects were left to express their *gratia* as best they could. First and foremost, this *gratia* was expected to take the form of loyalty (as Tacitus' preface to the *Histories* implies). Thus, Seneca wrote: 'an emperor, protected by his own *beneficium*, has no need of guards; he keeps arms for decoration'.[173] This idea of winning loyalty through *beneficia* underlies an anecdote about Vespasian. He was told to beware of Mettius Pompusianus on the grounds that he had an imperial horoscope. Rather than having him executed, Vespasian bestowed on him a consulship so that Pompusianus 'would one day be mindful of the *beneficium*'.[174] Whether the anecdote is true or not, it expresses a view found elsewhere about the connection between imperial *beneficia* and the goodwill of subjects.[175]

Recipients of the emperor's favors could give outward expression to their

---

170 *Hist.* 1.1.
171 *De Ben.* 5.4.2: Principes 'eo loco fortuna posuit, ex quo largiri multa possent pauca admodum et imparia datis recepturi'.
172 *Ann.* 4.18: 'destrui per haec fortunam suam Caesar inparemque tanto merito rebatur. nam beneficia eo usque laeta sunt, dum videntur exsolvi posse: ubi multum antevenere, pro gratia odium redditur.'
173 *De Clem.* 1.13.5: 'Hic princeps suo beneficio tutus nihil praesidiis eget, arma ornamenti causa habet.'
174 Suetonius, *Vesp.* 14: 'spondens quandoque beneficii memorem futurum'.
175 E.g., Philo, *Leg. ad Gaium* 268, 283f., 328; Pliny, *Paneg.* 85.8.

gratia in several ways. First and most simply, a Roman could dedicate a stone to the emperor, as he might to any other patron. The empire was littered with inscriptions such as the one M. Asinius Sabinianus, *vir clarissimus*, dedicated to Caracalla 'ob insignem indulgentiam beneficiaque eius erga se'.[176] Apparently a need was felt to exceed the expressions of gratitude used for ordinary patrons, and so religion came to play a role in the exchange. After Caelius Clemens, Pliny's kinsman, was transferred to Pliny's staff in Bithynia, Pliny acknowledged his debt to Trajan 'to whom I do not even dare to return *gratiam parem*, try as I might. And so I have recourse to *vota* and beseech the gods that I may not be judged unworthy of the favors which you are continually bestowing on me.'[177] Pliny's *vota* amount to a public and sacred expression of gratitude and loyalty, and as such were of symbolic importance in a situation in which even a wealthy senator could not hope to reciprocate adequately in real terms. As A. R. Hands explains, the ruler's beneficence, beyond the capacity of his subjects to return and thus superhuman, naturally deserved reciprocation appropriate to the superhuman.[178] And so the imperial cult performed a useful function in the exchange relationship. In a Narbonne inscription the plebs of the city, carrying out a promise to dedicate an altar to the *numen Caesaris Augusti*, added: 'if anyone wishes to clean, decorate or restore [this altar], because he has received a *beneficium*, let it be *ius fasque*'.[179] This seems to suggest an expectation that gratitude for the emperor's favor might be displayed through spending for the improvement of the altar to his *numen.*

Finally, there was a more worldly method of repaying the emperor's favors. From the reign of Augustus it was customary for imperial *amici* and beneficiaries to name the emperor in their wills. It has been suggested recently that legacies made a significant contribution to the imperial income.[180] In addition, they had an important symbolic value as final attempts of subjects to repay their debts to emperors. While some emperors attempted to widen the group of those expected to leave them legacies, many refused to accept bequests from subjects whom they did not know, using legacies as a barometer of the goodwill of their friends. According to Pliny, Trajan re-established the

---

176 *CIL* VI.1067 dated to 214.
177 *Ep.* 10.51: 'cui referre gratiam parem ne audeo quidem, quamvis maxime possim. Itaque ad vota confugio deosque precor, ut iis, quae in me adsidue confers, non indignus existimer.'
178 *Charities and Social Aid*, 55.
179 *CIL* XII 4333 (= *ILS* 112): 'si quis tergere, ornare, reficere volet, quod beneficii causa fiat, ius fasque esto'. It is not explicitly indicated that the *beneficium* is from the emperor, but this seems the natural interpretation, since the altar was first built out of gratitude for an imperial *beneficium.* ˙
180 Millar, *Emperor*, 154f. (M. K. Hopkins has pointed out in seminar that there is an error in Millar's calculations: the income from inheritances [accepting Suetonius' figures] amounts to 70,000,000 sesterces—nearly equal to the income from Gaul and Egypt rather than nearly twice the income from the provinces, as Millar suggests.)

freedom of people to name whom they pleased in their wills; the result was that his *amici* named him for his *merita* while strangers passed him over.[181] A number of specific examples of legacies are recorded for the reigns of Augustus and Tiberius, neither of whom would accept legacies from strangers or friends with children.[182] When Gaius Fufius Geminus was charged with *maiestas* against Tiberius, Dio records, he took his will to the senate and read it out. The fact that Tiberius was named as a co-heir was apparently intended as proof of Geminus' loyalty and goodwill.[183] The case of T. Marius Urbinas reflects the same idea: he 'was raised by the favors (*beneficia*) of Augustus from a low rank in the army to the highest military offices and was made rich by the abundant profits from them. Not only for the remainder of his life did he say publicly that he would leave his fortune to the one from whom he received it, but the day before his death he said the same thing to Augustus himself, although he had not even mentioned Augustus' name in his will.'[184] What is interesting about this passage is not only that Marius was thought to have displayed ingratitude by omitting Augustus in his will, but also that to include the imperial benefactor was a matter of public knowledge and honor.

In sum, there was a particular group of Romans who enjoyed an exchange relationship with the emperor and were in his debt. Gaudemet notes that all those known to have named Augustus or Tiberius in their wills had profited from imperial largesse or *clementia*. Some later emperors, notably Gaius and Nero, attempted to widen this circle and to compel certain groups (*primipilares*, imperial freedmen and *amici*) to leave legacies on the grounds that they also were in the emperor's debt.[185] At no point did any emperor attempt to extend the compulsion to the whole population of the empire. Thus, the view that every imperial act was good simply by association with the emperor who thus became a benefactor of the whole empire does not seem satisfactory.[186] There was a defined group of beneficiaries and, judging by the volume of legacies left to Augustus, the number of the emperor's personal

---

181 *Paneg.* 43.1f.
182 J. Gaudemet, 'Testamenta ingrata et pietas Augusti', *Studi Arangio-Ruiz* vol. 3, 115 for evidence concerning emperors' refusals to accept legacies under certain conditions. See also R. S. Rogers, 'The Roman emperors as heirs and legatees', *TAPhA* 78 (1947), 140.
183 Dio 58.4.5.
184 Valerius Maximus 7.8.6: 'Neque aliis dignus fuit T. Marius Urbinas, qui ab infimo militiae loco beneficiis divi Augusti imperatoris ad summos castrensis honores perductus eorumque uberrimis quaestibus locuples factus, non solum ceteris vitae temporibus ei se fortunas suas relinquere, a quo acceperat, praedicavit, sed etiam pridie quam expiraret idem istud ipsi Augusto dixit, cum interim ne nomen quidem eius tabulis testamenti adiecit.'
185 Gaudemet, 'Testamenta', 131ff.
186 Veyne, *Le pain*, 659. Gaudemet further argues in his article that some emperors did not limit the circle from whom they would accept legacies on the grounds that all of their subjects owed them *pietas*. But there was still a special group of subjects who could be said to be *ingrati* if they neglected the emperor in their wills.

friends and clients must have been substantial.[187]

Finally we must address ourselves to the issue of the functional significance of imperial patronage in the regime established by Augustus. We may take as a starting point Seneca's statement that an emperor could be protected by the loyalty established by his *beneficia*. The history of the Principate confirms Weber's observation that a patrimonial ruler depends on the goodwill of his subjects: a ruler relying solely on armed compulsion makes himself precariously dependent on the army.[188] Premerstein and Syme in the 1930s developed Seneca's statement, suggesting that the emperor's position rested not so much on any legal or constitutional basis as on the social bonds of patronage.[189] Premerstein's basic argument was that Augustus and his successors usurped the patronal resources and the clientèles of the great senatorial houses of the Republic. The emperor's patronage relationships were cemented by an oath taken annually by his soldiers and subjects. As the patronal resources of senatorial families were usurped, senators were pressed into the background, while their senatorial and especially their equestrian protégés and clients were bound instead to the emperor by imperial *beneficia* in the form of offices and honors.[190] Others have taken the argument further and have suggested that emperors, in order to bypass the senatorial order, developed an administration of *equites* dependent solely upon imperial patronage for advancement, and hence loyal only to the emperor.[191]

Recently Premerstein's basic position has been challenged with a variety of objections. It is said that Premerstein attributes far too much importance to the oath of loyalty sworn annually to the emperor. Moreover, it is unrealistic to think of the emperor as the patron of the entire population of the empire. In fact, it is suggested, the epigraphic and papyrological evidence demonstrates that the dozens of millions of subjects 'obeyed the emperor in the same way as all subjects of all states of the world: as to a chief of state'.[192] Now the validity of certain of these criticisms should be admitted. The whole empire did not constitute a personal clientèle; indeed, we have seen that there was a specific, defined group of *amici* and *clientes* who enjoyed the personal favor of the emperor and were personally bound to him. Further, scepticism is warranted with regard to the binding force of the oath alone. It is impossible to judge its

---

187 Veyne's remarks about the insignificance of imperial beneficence (*Le pain*, 659) seem untenable in view of this evidence.
188 *Economy and Society*, 1020.
189 A. von Premerstein, *Vom Werden*; Syme, *Roman Revolution*.
190 *Vom Werden*, esp. 113 for the conclusion. Syme (*History in Ovid*, 199) appears to take a similar position: 'the 'domus regnatrix' annexed [senators'] *clientelae* at Rome and throughout Italy'.
191 See below, p.112.
192 Veyne, *Le pain*, 620.

precise effect on Romans, but to place too much emphasis on an oath is to return to a quasi-legalistic interpretation in which it is thought that because an oath existed it must have been adhered to. Finally, we may agree that the relationship between the emperor and the mass of provincial subjects was one of anonymity and obedience.

Premerstein's central thesis, however, remains worthy of consideration, and an important issue is trivialized by the assertion that Romans obeyed the emperor as a magistrate just as subjects in all ages obey heads of state — that, in other words, obedience and loyalty to the emperor do not require explanation, and Premerstein is pursuing a non-question. Surely, Premerstein's basic supposition is correct: after a century of civil wars and the murder of Julius Caesar, the stability of the regime introduced by Augustus does require explanation — obedience of the Roman aristocracy and the army could not be taken for granted by the emperor and should not be taken for granted by modern historians.

The history of the Principate shows that emperors faced two threats built into the structure of the administration and the court: first, conspiracies of those in close physical proximity, and secondly, rebellions by those with military commands. In order to maintain his position the emperor need not have had the empire for his personal clientèle; he needed only to secure the loyalty of these two critical groups with his patronal resources. This was a realistic possibility in a way that patronage of the entire empire was not, and the previous sections have shown that the emperor did in fact distribute *beneficia* individually to virtually all leading members of the imperial aristocracy and to his household staff. These men owed their positions and the profits derived from them ultimately to the emperor. Marius Urbinas was thought to have insulted Augustus personally when, having enriched himself through imperial appointments, he did not return any of the profits in his will.

Premerstein's model of patronage, however, is inaccurate in one major respect. While it is true that the emperor usurped the most important patronal resources, we cannot agree with him that senatorial families were pressed very far into the background or that senators ceased to be important patrons.

If senators were not excluded from power in the new regime, we must ask how they were included in the new structure in a way which provided relative stability in comparison with the late Republic. The question can best be answered by utilizing an expanded model of patronage recently outlined by anthropologists. Jeremy Boissevain has suggested a distinction between two categories of patronal resources:

The first are resources, such as land, jobs, [etc.]... which [the patron] controls directly. The second are strategic contacts with other people who control such resources directly or have access to such persons. The former may be called *first order resources*, the latter *second order resources*. Persons who dispence first order resources may be called patrons. Those who dispense second order resources are brokers.[193]

Given the fact that in most of the examples of exchange cited in the first section the *beneficia* were secured from the emperor by third parties, this expanded model seems promising. Indeed, the distinction between patron and broker supplies just the concept needed to enable us to accept Premerstein's indisputable statement that the Princeps usurped many of the (previously senatorial) first-order resources without following his conclusion that the senatorial order was therefore cast into the background. By permitting senators to remain important as brokers, the emperor accomplished two things. First, he greatly enlarged the group of those who received his personal favors and owed personal loyalty to him in return: by using senators and *equites* as brokers to distribute his *beneficia* throughout Italy and the empire, the emperor found the mediators needed to bind to himself through a chain of personal bonds numerous municipal aristocrats and provincials with whom he had no personal contact.[194] Perhaps more importantly, by allowing senators and leading *equites* to maintain their power as his brokers, the emperor bestowed on them a *beneficium* which deserved *gratia* in the form of loyalty in return.

Attention to the exchange relationship which Pliny enjoyed with Trajan illustrates the explanatory value of this model. Premerstein, Syme and others have noted that emperors won the loyalty of senators and *equites* with offices and priesthoods. This is certainly correct, but more in evidence in Pliny's letters is the fact that Trajan secured Pliny's gratitude by granting favors for Pliny's relatives and clients. Book X includes evidence of ten requests for others, including five during his stay in Bithynia.[195] While an emperor might be in a position to grant a senator like Pliny an office or honor for himself only once every few years, the exchange on behalf of a senator's clients could be much more frequent, almost continuous.

Trajan allowed Pliny to act as his broker in distributing *beneficia*; in return, Pliny expressed his gratitude as emphatically as possible, as is shown in the letter concerning the transfer of Caelius Clemens to Bithynia. In other letters Pliny gives two reasons for his gratitude. First, it is only with Trajan's help that he can maintain his position as patron-broker. One letter opens with an explicit admission of this: 'My recent illness, Sir, has put me in debt to my doctor Postumius Marinus. I am able to repay his services adequately by your favor (*beneficium*), if you will indulge my wishes in accordance with your

---

193 *Friends of Friends*, 147f.

194 See de Ste Croix, 'Suffragium', 38. That the mediators would have received the credit and gratitude from the ultimate recipient of the favor is clear from the last sentence of Pliny, *Ep.* 3.8, where Pliny secures a tribunate for Suetonius who passes it on to a relative, with the result that the relative is indebted to Suetonius who is in turn indebted to Pliny.

195 *Ep.* 10.4-6, 11, 12, 26, 51, 87, 94, 104.

characteristic benevolence.'[196] The favor in question is a grant of citizenship. Secondly, as in the Republic, favors for another man's clients were used as tokens of esteem for the man himself. Pliny certainly interpreted Trajan's approval of requests in this way and treated them as contributions to his own public prestige. Pliny concluded his petition for senatorial rank for Voconius Romanus thus: 'therefore, I ask, Sir, that you make me a participant in my most hoped-for joy and fulfill my worthy desires, so that I am able to be proud of your recognition not only of me, but of my friend'.[197] The end of another request on behalf of Rosianus Geminus is more to the point: 'I ask, Sir, that you delight me by increasing the *dignitas* of my former quaestor — that is to say, my *dignitas* through him — as soon as is convenient.'[198] In short, these imperial grants not only helped Pliny put his clients and protégés in his debt, but they also served as public proof that Pliny, being in the emperor's favor, was a man of some importance. The significance of this latter aspect is underlined in one other letter. Pliny boasted to his friend Priscus of his influence with the source of beneficence: on behalf of Romanus 'I recently sought from the *optimus Princeps* the *ius trium liberorum* which, although he gives it sparingly and with discrimination, he nevertheless granted at my request, as if he had made the selection himself.'[199] Pliny's sincerity in the other letters addressed to Trajan could be called into question, but this letter was sent to a friend and shows with unmistakable clarity the pride which Pliny took in securing imperial *beneficia* for protégés. It would be perverse to deny that they helped to maintain Pliny's goodwill and loyalty.

Pliny is the broker whose relationship with an emperor can be most fully delineated, but there is no reason to think it unusual. In the first section of this chapter numerous other instances of brokerage were presented. Fronto, for example, played the role of a mediator for requests from a *conductor IIII publicorum Africae*, an imperial freedman, several equestrians and a junior senator.[200] In a passage quoted above, Plutarch indicates that this phenomenon was customary: when provincials went to Rome seeking

---

196 *Ep.* 10.11: 'proxima infirmitas mea, domine, obligavit me Postumio Marino medico; cui parem gratiam referre beneficio tuo possum, si precibus meis ex consuetudine bonitatis tuae indulseris'.

197 *Ep.* 10.4.6: 'rogo ergo, domine, ut me exoptatissimae mihi gratulationis compotem facias et honestis, ut spero, adfectibus meis praestes, ut non in me tantum verum et in amico gloriari iudiciis tuis possim'. The best single Republican expression of this can be found in Cicero's letter to C. Antonius, governor of Macedonia (*Ad fam.* 5.5): in the letter Cicero expresses his intense annoyance at Antonius' insults and lack of esteem, suggesting that Antonius could make amends by being of service to Atticus ('si quid in te residet amoris erga me, id omne in Pomponi negotio ostendas').

198 *Ep.* 10.26.3: 'teque, domine, rogo, gaudere me exornata quaestoris mei dignitate, id est per illum mea, quam maturissime velis.' Millar briefly makes a similar point (*Emperor*, 286).

199 *Ep.* 2.13.8: 'nuper ab optimo principe trium liberorum ius impetravi; quod quamquam parce et cum delectu daret, mihi tamen tamquam eligeret indulsit'.

200 *Ad M. Caes.* 5.34, 37; *Ad Pium* 9; *Ad Verum Imp.* 2.7.

procuratorships or governorships, they were expected to go not directly to the emperor, but to the houses of the great Roman aristocrats who possessed *gratia*.[201] It is noteworthy that even after holding a praetorship, Pliny did not feel that he was in a position to petition for the *ius trium liberorum* directly; Iulius Servianus mediated the request.[202] Unlike Pliny, Servianus was a consular commander of a large army. Pliny's loyalty to Trajan may not have been vital, but if similar goodwill was inspired by *beneficia* distributed through such men as Servianus, the importance of patronage to any emperor becomes clear. Seneca's statement that an emperor was 'suo beneficio tutus' was not an exaggeration.

The discussion of patronage and brokerage has emphasized the social cohesion developed by imperial favors. Some analyses of the emperor's position have in the past emphasized instead the divisive policy of emperors: it has been claimed that the emperor bound the lower orders directly to himself by his patronage and used them in administration to diminish the power of the senatorial order. The evidence for brokerage has a direct bearing on this argument. Clearly, emperors did not as a matter of policy distribute equestrian and freedmen offices and honors only in a direct fashion (as Premerstein supposed); rather they frequently bestowed them through *senatorial* brokers. In so doing, far from manipulating any alleged antipathy between orders, they positively encouraged 'vertical' bonds of patronage between senators and administrators of lower orders.

Marcus Aurelius had a reputation for encouraging harmony and cohesion within the aristocracy.[203] By contrast, certain other emperors, perhaps feeling threatened, pursued a strategy which produced division and conflict (though not between the orders, as we shall see).[204] Here we should note briefly that manipulation of *beneficia* played an important part in the strategy. The emperor could encourage rivalry in the aristocracy by channelling his *beneficia* through men like Sejanus or Vibius Crispus, thus making them powerful.[205] Tacitus describes the senatorial and equestrian clientèle which Sejanus built up and attributes it to public knowledge of the emperor's favor.[206] The *eques* Marcus Terentius is supposed to have said in defense of his friendship with Sejanus after his fall: 'I will confess both that I was a friend of Sejanus and that I rejoiced at having been taken into his *amicitia*... His relatives by blood and by marriage were honored by offices; as one was close to Sejanus, so one's friendship with Caesar was strong. On the other hand, those towards whom he

201 *Moralia* 814D.
202 Pliny, *Ep.* 10.2; for Servianus, see Syme, *Tacitus*, 17 and App. 7.
203 Fronto, *Ad M. Caes.* 4.1, and also *Ad M. Caes.* 1.6 and *Epist. Graec.* 3 for Marcus encouraging Fronto's friendship with Herodes Atticus.
204 See below, p.138f.
205 See Syme, *Tacitus*, 4f. and 100f.
206 *Ann.* 4.74

was hostile were tormented by danger and suppliants' garments.'[207] Whether intentionally or not, through his patronage Tiberius enabled Sejanus to build a faction which produced enormous tensions within the aristocracy.

An emperor could create divisions most effectively by encouraging *delatores* with rewards of offices and honors.[208] When this policy was followed, *amicitiae* with the emperor and with other aristocrats became dangerous as friendships were used as grounds for prosecution and persecution.[209] To take one instance, according to Seneca many men in the era of Sejanus' power were ruined on account of their *amicitia Asinii Galli*.[210] Later Seneca himself met his death on a charge of *amicitia* with the conspirator Piso.[211] Roman authors emphasize that in such circumstances the *fides* necessary for *amicitia* dissolved as emperors created an atmosphere in which everyone selfishly pursued his own interests.[212] Two points should be made about this policy of creating dissension. First, it should again be repeated that the struggling factions did not divide along class or *ordo* lines: senators and *equites* cooperated in prosecutions. Secondly, it should be emphasized that the strategy of manipulating *beneficia* to encourage tensions and divisions within the aristocracy was not, on the whole, a good one for ensuring survival, as the fates of Gaius, Nero, Galba, Domitian, Commodus and Caracalla indicate.

The most successful emperors were those who, like Augustus, were able to utilize skillfully the offices, honors, statuses and administrative decisions at their disposal to produce cohesion in a web of personal exchange relationships extending from themselves. Awareness of this led Seneca, Dio of Prusa and others to point out to emperors that it was not merely a part of their role but in their self-interest to act as good patrons distributing *beneficia*.[213] I have argued that it would be an oversimplification to imagine the emperor patronizing each individual in the web directly. Rather it is more accurate to think that the emperor ensured the loyalty of an inner circle of friends with his *beneficia* and then granted them the resources to build their own clientèles whose loyalty was thus indirectly secured.

---

207 *Ann.* 6.8: 'fatebor et fuisse me Seiano amicum et ut essem expetisse et postquam adeptus eram laetatum... illius propinqui et adfines honoribus augebantur; ut quisque Seiano intimus, ita ad Caesaris amicitiam validus; contra quibus infensus esset, metu ac sordibus conflictabantur.'

208 Dio notes that Domitian and Caracalla encouraged informers in this way (67.1.4 and 78.21.5). See Syme, *Tacitus*, 100f.

209 Pliny recounts the danger which he faced by visiting the philosopher Artemidorus who was abandoned by his other *amici* (*Ep.* 3.11). See also Seager, 'Amicitia in Tacitus and Juvenal'.

210 *Ep. ad Luc.* 55.3.

211 Tacitus, *Ann.* 15.60.

212 Pliny, *Paneg.* 42.2 and Tacitus, *Hist.* 1.2.

213 Seneca, *De Clementia*; Dio of Prusa, *On Kingship* 1.30 and 3.86f.

3

Seniority and merit: alternatives to patronage?

It has been suggested that official posts were among the most important *beneficia* which the emperor bestowed upon Roman aristocrats. But it need not be the case that, simply because the emperor made the appointments, they were treated as personal gifts or favors. Those scholars who view the emperor primarily as a rational administrator have assumed or argued that the appointments were made on the basis of relatively impersonal bureaucratic criteria, in particular, seniority and/or merit. If this view is accurate, the emperor would have been restrained from treating appointments as purely personal favors to be granted on the basis of friendship and loyalty. Indeed, those who have taken this argument to its logical conclusion have minimized the role of patronage in the Principate, labelling it an aberration, significant only in the reigns of bad emperors.[1]

The position taken on this question has broad implications for the historian's conception of Roman imperial government. Modern 'rational-legal' bureaucracies are characterized in part by the objective of appointing and promoting in accordance with the impersonal criteria of seniority and merit. Though it may not be achieved, the objective is at least pursued through bureaucratic regulations and institutions (e.g., the Civil Service Examination). By contrast, in a patrimonial government there is little regulation: appointments depend on the discretion of the ruler who is apt to select on the basis of personal loyalty and friendship. Augustus' administration, made up of his household and friends, can be characterized as 'patrimonial'. The question is then: to what extent did appointment and promotion come to be regulated in the following two centuries? In answering this question, we shall also be offering a partial answer to the more general question of how far Roman imperial government was 'rationalized' in the Principate.[2]

---

1 Pflaum, who labels patronage 'un mal' in his discussion of the influence of the great functionaries on behalf of their protégés, concludes: 'l'influence de ces derniers ne l'emportait pas sur la *forma* toute-puissante'. He then qualifies these words by suggesting that under bad emperors certain coteries could monopolize access to office (*Procurateurs*, 206).

2 These two extremes are in accord with the ideal types worked out by Max Weber, *Theory of Social and Economic Organization*, 334. That it is possible to devise systems of evaluation of

In the first two sections of this chapter the evidence for the influence of the principles of seniority and merit will be set out. The evidence will not permit completely compelling conclusions, but it does indicate that the role of a seniority principle cannot have been great. Further, the Roman concept of merit is not identical with that of a developed, modern bureaucracy in that it did not emphasize impersonal assessment in a way which might exclude patronage.

Finally, because some historians' have drawn on the Chinese bureaucracy as a model to explain the significance of seniority and merit in the Roman administration, an appendix will be devoted to a brief comparison of the two. The Chinese example will illustrate how far appointment and promotion could be rationalized in a premodern bureaucracy. Its elaborate organization and rules underline how fundamentally traditional and patronal the Roman administration remained.

SENIORITY

In varying degrees modern historians have credited seniority with being a factor in promotion in senatorial and equestrian careers. Professor Eric Birley has argued with regard to the senatorial *cursus* that three different groups of senators can be distinguished, each having a characteristic type of career structure.[3] Developing this view further, Professor Eck has recently concluded 'dass gerade durch die relativ straff gewordenen Beförderungsregeln, durch eine Art "Objektivierung" des Cursus, eine gewisse Automatik sich entwickelt hatte, die es dem Kaiser nicht erlaubte, ganz nach Willkür mit den Senatoren zu verfahren'.[4] Concerning the equestrian bureaucracy M. K. Hopkins has suggested that the emperors 'might have liked to promote by merit but this would have opened the way to subjective (that is nepotistic or patronal) and therefore uncontrollable estimates of talent by subordinates. By and large, therefore, emperors favoured seniority as the principle of promotion...'[5] T. F. Carney, advocating a similar view, has spoken of procuratorial promotion as a 'long grim, grey haul step by step upwards within the bureaucracy'.[6]

officials which eliminate most of the subjective element is clear from studies of American agencies where the evaluation of employees' performance became so objective in the use of quantitative data as to run the risk of destroying the supervisor's authority, because he was no longer able to influence his subordinates' promotion by his subjective judgements. See Peter M. Blau, *The Dynamics of Bureaucracy*, 21f., 36, 44. To suggest that the attempt to place Roman government in the continuum from patrimonial to rational-legal is misguided because all bureaucracies are a mixture seems to me to overlook the vast differences in objectives and institutions.

3 'Senators', 197-214.

4 W. Eck, 'Beförderungskriterien innerhalb der senatorischen Laufbahn, dargestellt an der Zeit von 69 bis 138 n. Chr.', *Aufstieg und Niedergang der römischen Welt* II.1, 226.

5 'Elite mobility in the Roman Empire', *P&P* 32 (Dec. 1965), 22f.

6 *Bureaucracy in Traditional Society*, 18.

In Professor Birley's view, senatorial careers can be divided into three groups: first, those senators who never entered the emperor's service, holding only senatorial magistracies including perhaps a proconsulate in a senatorial province; secondly, those 'who from the outset sought, and obtained, appointments in the emperor's service'; thirdly, those who began their careers in the second group but then changed course and held senatorial magistracies. The first group has attracted little attention; the third group is by definition heterogeneous; and so it is to the second group that historians have devoted their energies in the search for career patterns, which seemed readily identifiable. It was argued that senatorial candidates for the emperor's service were evaluated in their teens with regard to their military aptitude and at that point their careers were planned. 'The ablest candidates might reasonably be expected to secure the most rapid passage to the consulate, which qualified them for those major commands.' Thus, before his consular command, the promising *vir militaris* as a rule 'will have held only two praetorian posts, as legate of a legion and in some more senior appointment' (i.e., governor of a praetorian province or prefect of one of the two treasuries).[7]

Now if senatorial careers were as highly structured from an early age as this view suggests, the clear implication is that considerable limitations were placed on the emperor's discretion concerning appointments. The arguments related to the role of specialization will be examined in the next section. Here it is important to note that, although the age at which the Republican magistracies were held was fairly regular, appointment to the important posts in the emperor's service was not nearly as predictable as has been thought. A recent reconsideration of the evidence has indicated that considerable modification of the old view is required.[8] The names of the 73 men who held consular legateships between 70 and 235 A.D. and whose earlier careers are known in detail were collected. Of these only nine had careers conforming to the pattern of the *vir militaris* (i.e., holding only a legionary legateship and governorship of a praetorian province between their praetorship and consulate). Further, '43 out of the 73 hold 3 or more regular praetorian posts; several hold as many as 6'.[9]

The logic behind holding only two praetorian posts was supposed to be that talented military men were hurried through their consulate to make them eligible for the great commands in the prime of their lives. The evidence for this seems to be weak as well. Indications of age during the consulate can only be deduced for twenty-one men in the list: fourteen of these seem to hold the consulate at a normal age; four were older; and the younger consuls can be

7 Birley, 'Senators', 199ff.
8 Campbell, ' "Viri Militares" ', 11.
9 *Ibid.*, 12.

explained by other factors, such as membership in the patrician order.[10] In short, it seems that there was no particular career structure with special rules for select 'viri militares'.

In another recent important study a somewhat different argument for a highly structured senatorial *cursus* was advanced, and requires detailed consideration. The decisive point in a senator's career, in this view, came after the praetorship. At that time about half of the eighteen praetors were selected for praetorian posts in the emperor's service (legateships of legions, governorships of imperial provinces, curatorships of the roads, and prefects of the treasuries). The group of men who reached these offices could expect promotion at the appropriate time to a consulship and beyond by 'eine gewisse Automatik'.[11] The literary testimony supporting this view is limited to a comment in Tacitus' *Agricola* (9.1) that Agricola's appointment as *legatus pro praetore* for Aquitania was distinguished in part because it indicated that he was destined for a consulship. As additional support for the argument, figures are adduced to show that three-quarters of known praetorian governors of imperial provinces are also known to have reached consulships.

None of this evidence, however, demonstrates the existence of rules for automatic promotion. It is true that senior praetorian posts in the emperor's service carried with them great honor and the likelihood of appointment to a consulship (though not necessarily directly). But that there can have been *automatic* promotion in senatorial careers from the legionary legateship on seems improbable, if for no other reason than the variety in the order and number of praetorian and consular posts held.[12] Moreover, while career patterns indicate that men in certain prestigious posts were favored for further promotion, the diminishing number of openings available as the senatorial career progressed implies that selection by the emperor was necessary at most stages. Approximately half of the praetors could secure legionary legateships, and, in turn, only about half of the twenty-four legionary legates could be appointed to the twelve praetorian governorships of imperial provinces.[13]

10 *Ibid.*, 16f. Also J. Morris, 'Leges annales under the Principate', *LF* 87(1964), 336, n. 39.
11 Eck, 'Beförderungskriterien', 199 and 226 for proportion of praetorian governors reaching the consulship.
12 Campbell, ' "Viri Militares" ', 23.
13 Eck, 'Beförderungskriterien', 181ff. for numbers of posts available. G. Alföldy ('Consuls and Consulars under the Antonines; prosopography and history', *Anc Soc* 7 (1976), 277f.) offers an argument similar to Eck's for the reign of Antoninus Pius, but he does not believe that the career was completely structured as early as the legionary legateship. He produces figures to show that all men in senior praetorian offices in the emperor's service received consulships, and that this group, together with men of patrician families, was sufficiently numerous to take all but a very few of the consulships available — thus, promotion at this point was nearly automatic. The emperor, however, may have made more choices than Alföldy believes. He probably overestimates by 20% or so the number of senior ex-praetors in the emperor's service available for consulships each year by not allowing sufficiently for those who held two senior praetorian posts (e.g., almost half of the known curators of the Appian, Flaminian and

Since the tenure of these governorships was normally three years and since more than one such post rarely went to the same man, an average of four men would have been available for promotion from these especially distinguished offices each year. While there were enough consulships for distribution to each member of this small élite group, the same cannot be said for all those who held a praetorian post in the emperor's service. During the reigns of Trajan and Hadrian there were seven consulships on average available for first-time holders each year. Of these, slightly more than half appear to have gone to men who had held legionary legateships. Thus, only something like half of the eight to ten legionary legates appointed each year (on average) would have been able to reach the consulate. In view of this, it is not surprising that Tacitus singles out the governorship of Aquitania as the source of Agricola's expectation of a consulship, not his legionary legateship (as Eck's argument would lead us to believe).

The process of selection, moreover, must also have been a feature in consular appointments. Not even all of those who had been favored with appointments to imperial provinces after their praetorships could have advanced to the great consular commands. Although the numbers of such praetorian and consular governorships were nearly the same, consulars (unlike praetorians) frequently held several commands at this level. This, together with the fact that a substantial proportion of consular commands went to men who had not as praetorians been appointed *legati pro praetore*, meant that even those in the select group of praetorian *legati pro praetore* could not be sure of promotion to consular governorships. In sum, the observable career patterns exhibit regularities, but also enough variety to have left room for the exercise of *gratia* by influential men. At no point could promotion have been entirely automatic, nor was the emperor's discretion limited by rules other than a minimum age for the traditional magistracies.

The procuratorial bureaucracy perhaps offers a more interesting case for testing the hypothesis about the role of seniority. The senatorial *cursus* continued to be based on Republican institutions, but the equestrian bureaucracy grew up in the first and second centuries and is often thought to be the most characteristic part of the more rational governmental organization of the Principate. This traditional view provokes the question whether procurators really were recruited and promoted in a more rational way than senators. H.-G. Pflaum in his monumental work about procurators concluded that seniority was the 'grande règle' governing the movement of equestrians

Aemilian roads of this period and one-fifth of the prefects of the treasuries were not promoted directly to consulships but to other senior posts in the emperor's service). The calculations involve a certain amount of guesswork and are not secure, but there is reason to doubt that the sums are quite as tidy as Alföldy suggests. For a valuable collection of the relevant data, see his *Konsulat und Senatorenstand unter den Antoninen.*

through procuratorial careers.[14] Though it may be necessary to disagree with
this conclusion, Pflaum's catalogue of procurators provides an indispensable
tool facilitating studies such as the one presented here.[15]

Initially it must be asked what is meant by a seniority principle. Pflaum uses
the word 'ancienneté' in relation to both offices and officials. These two usages
should be clearly distinguished. The seniority of an office is defined by where it
stands in a hierarchy of offices. So the consulate had seniority over the
praetorship. The seniority of an official depends on how long he has served in
office. Promotion according to a principle of seniority means that the level of
an administrator's next appointment is based on the number of years he has
already served. The distinction is important because, while promotion
according to seniority presumes a hierarchy of offices, the latter does not imply
the former as an important criterion for promotion. So, for instance, though
the magistracies of the Republic were ranked according to seniority, the
magistrates were not selected in accordance with a seniority principle.

Pflaum's work, especially the fourth chapter of the Deuxième Partie of *Les
procurateurs équestres*, undoubtedly shows that there was a hierarchy of
procuratorships which was relatively stable from the beginning of the second
century.[16] But if this does not prove that promotion was necessarily governed
by a seniority principle, what evidence does so? The literary evidence is
confined to a single passage in Fronto's *commendatio* to Marcus Aurelius on
behalf of Aridelus, an imperial freedman. Fronto recommended Aridelus as a
'homo frugi et sobrius et acer et diligens. Petit nunc procurationem *ex forma
suo loco ac iu⟨st⟩o tempore*' ('an upright, sober, intelligent and diligent man.
He now seeks a procuratorship *ex forma suo loco ac iusto tempore*').[17] These
last words Pflaum translates: 'selon le texte du règlement conformément à son
rang et à son ancienneté'.[18] He then concludes his discussion of promotion: 'le
passage de Fronto *ex forma suo loco ac iusto tempore* s'est avéré comme la
grande règle de la hiérarchie romaine'.[19] Recently this interpretation has been
challenged, with the observation that the *ex forma* phrase may qualify not the
procuratorship, but the subject of the verb, Aridelus, in the act of petitioning.
So the passage can be translated: 'Aridelus is now petitioning in the proper
manner, on his own behalf, and at the proper time.'[20] In this interpretation the

---

14 *Procurateurs*, 295. A. N. Sherwin-White, 'Procurator Augusti', *PBSR* (1939), 25, similarly
   concludes that the equestrian bureaucracy became 'mechanical and regular' in the second
   century.
15 *Carrières*. For a more detailed discussion of this issue, see my 'Promotion and patronage in
   equestrian careers', *JRS* 70 (1980), 44-63.
16 Millar comes to this conclusion after suggesting modifications in his review of *Carrières* in *JRS*
   53 (1963), 198.
17 *Ad M. Caes.* 5.37.
18 *Procurateurs*, 210.
19 *Ibid.*, 295.
20 Champlin, *Fronto and Antonine Rome*, 102f. with notes 52 and 53.

emperor's patronal role as a receiver of petitions is stressed — a role thoroughly documented by Millar.[21] Both translations seem plausible, and so the passage is of limited value as evidence in an argument for a seniority principle. Furthermore, Aridelus was a freedman, and it is by no means clear that whatever rules (if any) governed careers in the *familia Caesaris* would have applied to equestrian procurators.[22]

Beyond Fronto's ambiguous words no literary evidence can be adduced in support of a seniority principle (for example, there are no remarks or complaints that a procurator was promoted before his turn). Moreover, one particular omission may be noted as significant. Cassius Dio inserted into his account of the reign of Augustus a debate between Agrippa and Maecenas about the vices and virtues of monarchy. Though the debate is set in 29 B.C., nearly all of the details and suggestions in Maecenas' speech are related to Dio's own time. 'The most important part of the speech concerns the recruitment, training, functions, and status of the two leading orders of the State.'[23] For senators Dio gives precise details of the *cursus*: enrollment as an *eques* at age eighteen, as a senator not younger than age twenty-five, appointment as praetor from age thirty.[24] With regard to *equites*, by contrast, in the several pages of discussion about the organization of the prefectures and procuratorships there is not even a hint of a formal *cursus* structure or a seniority principle. This is not because Dio neglects to mention criteria for appointment: praetorian prefects are to be appointed from the ἄριστοι of the order and procurators selected as a reward for ἀρετή.[25] This silence as late as the third century may not be conclusive, but surely it shifts the burden of proof onto those who think they can find patterns of promotion according to seniority in the equestrian career inscriptions.

In his work on procurators Pflaum explains the hierarchy of procuratorships in the following way: the rank of procurators depended on the level of pay; the salary was in turn attached to the official, not to the office; but particular offices were regularly held by men at a particular salary level; so despite some irregularities procuratorships can be classified in a hierarchy according to salary levels. Early in the Principate three salary levels existed: 60,000 sesterces, 100,000 sesterces and 200,000 sesterces. Under Marcus Aurelius

---

21 *Emperor.*
22 It has been argued that the age of an imperial slave or freedman may have had an influence on the level of office for which he was eligible (P. R. C. Weaver, *Familia Caesaris*, 224ff.). Though the evidence cited shows more of a pattern than any similar evidence for equestrian procurators, it is still less than compelling (G. Burton, 'Slaves, freedmen and monarchy' (review of Boulvert, *Esclaves et affranchis impériaux sous le Haut-Empire romain, rôle politique et administratif* and *Domestique et fonctionnaire sous le Haut-Empire romain: la condition de l'affranchi et de l'esclave du prince*), *JRS* 67 (1977), 162f.).
23 Millar, *A Study of Cassius Dio*, 104 and 111.
24 Dio 52.20; Morris, 'Leges annales'.
25 Dio 52.24-5.

another, 300,000 sesterces, was added. Since most procuratorships were
included in the first three levels and since the last applied primarily to Palatine
officia, attention will be focused on the first three. The 100,000 and 200,000
levels are further subdivided by Pflaum into two and four echelons
respectively.

Within this hierarchy, can sufficiently clear patterns of promotion be
distinguished to prove a seniority principle? Pflaum argued that it is possible
and illustrated various patterns with individual careers. But this method of
illustrating patterns with examples may have its pitfalls: surely it would be
better to suggest some hypothetical seniority principle and then test it against
all relevant careers. This Pflaum does not do, nor does he give any clear idea
about what he thinks a normal procuratorial career in accordance with 'la
grande règle' should be.

In the search for such a norm the first step is to sort out and map all of the
potentially useful evidence. This is done in Table I on the following pages.
Much of the evidence in Pflaum's catalogue of some 350 careers of *equites* can
be excluded for our purposes here. First, careers before the reign of Trajan
(falling in group A of Pflaum's tables) are not included since they come before
full development of the hierarchy and so should not be used as evidence of
irregularity. Secondly, only those from equestrian backgrounds (as opposed to
primipilares) are listed. Careers of those rising from the centurionate follow a
different pattern, according to Pflaum, but we do not possess enough clearly
complete careers even to attempt to demonstrate promotion through
procuratorships by seniority for them. (Only four from the second century and
one from the third century are known.) Finally, fragmented careers are
excluded; the table includes only those which are complete or complete up to a
point. Such strict selection is necessary in order to prevent circularity of
argument (using a presumed pattern to fill in or order fragmented careers, and
then adducing the same careers as evidence for the pattern).

An initial search through Table I indicates that there was no close
relationship between promotion patterns and the subdivisions within the
salary levels (nor does Pflaum claim any). No procurator moved up step by
step through all six echelons within the centenariate and ducenariate levels,
despite the fact that some held enough offices to have been able to do so.
Indeed, the irregularity is more noticeable than the regularity: a number of
equestrians skipped some echelons and then held three offices or more in the
same echelon (see nos. 168, 183, 193, 295 and 331 bis for the clearest cases).

Table I: Procuratorial careers

Career No.	NAME	Militiae	LX	C		CC				Palatine	Officia	Great Pref.
				Lower	Upper	1st	2nd	3rd	4th			
95	T. Haterius Nepos	3	x	x			xx			(x)		x
98	T. Flavius Macer	—	xx	x								
101	—— Rufus	3	x	x								
103	M. Aemilius Bassus	3	xx xx	x								
104	M. Vettius Latro	3	x	x	x		x					
106B	C. Iulius Celsus	—	xxx	x			xx	x		x		
110	Valerius Eudaemon	—		x	xx	xxx		x		x		x
112	A. Ofellius Maior Macedo	2		x		x				x		
113	L. Valerius Proculus	2	x		xx	xx	x		x	(x)		x
116	Aemilius Iuncus	4		x	x	x						
117	M. Petronius Honoratus	3		x			x	x		x		x
119	T. Statilius Optatus	4	xx	x			xx			x		x
120	M. Maenius Agrippa L. Tusidius Campester	3			x	x						
121	L. Baebius Iuncinus	3		x		x						
125	P. Aelius Marcianus	3	xx									
128	C. Lepidius Secundus	2	x									
131	...A...	3	x	x								
132	Annius Postumus	—	xxx	x								
134	C. Iunius Flavianus	1	x	x	x	x		x		x		x
136	M. Statius Priscus Licinius Italicus	5	x	Adlected into senate								
137	Sex. Cornelius Dexter	3	x	x	x	x		x				
139	T. Furius Victorinus	3		x	x	x	x	x		x		x
140	L. Domitius Rogatus	4	x	x	x							
141	L. Volusius Maecianus	1	xx	x			x			x		x
142	Sex. Caecilius Crescens Volusianus	—		x			x			x		
144	T. Appalius Alfinus Secundus	3	x	x	x		x					
145	P. Gavius Balbus	3	xx	x								
147	(Crepereius)	3	x									
150	M. Antonius Fabianus	—	x	x								
151	C. Antonius Rufus	—		x								
152	Q. Plotius Maximus Trebellius Pelidianus	2	x	x								
153	L. Faesellius Sabinianus	—	x	x								
156	T. Varius Clemens	4		x	x		xx	x	x			
157	M. Arruntius Frugi	3	x	x	x							
158	M. Claudius Restitutus	2	xx	x								

Table I, cont.

Career No.	NAME	Militiae	LX	C			CC			Palatine	Officia	Great Pref.
				Lower	Upper	1st	2nd	3rd	4th			
160	P. Fulcinius Vergilius Marcellus	2	xx									
160B	L. Vibius Apronianus	1	x			x						
163	L. Aurelius Nicomedes	—	x			x		x				
164B	Ti. Claudius Proculus Cornelianus	3	x		xx	xx	x(?)					
168	L. Marius Perpetuus	—	x			x		xxx	x			
169	— —	?		x				xxx	x			
170	— —	4			xx	x						
171	M. Campanius Marcellus	3	x	x								
174	T. Iulius Saturninus	2	x									
	AE (1962), 183											
	Q. Domitius Marsianus	1	x	x			x					
178	...ilius	—	x			x	xx	x	x		x	
180	T. Iulius Vehilius Gratus Iulianus	4		x	xx	x	x	x	x	x		x
181	M. Aurelius Papirius Dionysius	—	x	x			x				x	x
181B	M. Valerius Maximianus	4			xx	Adlected into senate						
183	T. Flavius Germanus	—	xxx			x		xxx	x			
184	P. Cominius Clemens	3	xx	x		x	x	xx	x			
185	Sex. Iulius Possessor	2	xx									
186	C. Cominius Bo... Agricola ..elius Aper	3	x									
187	M. Porcius Aper	1	x									
188	M. Macrinius Avitus Catonius Vindex	4			x	Adlected into senate						
193	M. Aurelius Mindius Matidianus Pollio	—					x	xxx				
198	Ti. Plautius Felix Ferruntianus	?	x									
201	Q. Petronius Melior	1	xx									
202	C. Annius Flavianus	3	x			xx						
203	Ti. Claudius Candidus	2	x	Adlected into senate								
204	C. Sextius Martialis	1	xx			x						
206	M. Flavi Marcianus Ilisus	—	x			xx						
207	M. Bassaeus Axius	1	x									
208	Q. Calpurnius Modestus	—	x			x						
209	M. Veserius Iucundianus	—	x									
212	T. Petronius Priscus	3	x			x						

Table I, cont.

				C			CC					
	NAME	Militiae	LX	Lower	Upper	1st	2nd	3rd	4th	Palatine	Officia	Great Pref.
217	L. Egnatuleius Sabinus	2	xx	x								
218T	T. Antonius Claudius Alfenus Arignotus	3		x(?)								
222	Ti. Claudius Xenophon	—	xx	x		xxx	x	x				
224	M. Rossius Vitulus	4	xxx	xx		x						
226	T. Cornasidius Sabinus	3	x		xx							
228	Ti. Claudius Zeno Ulpianus	3	xxx	xx								
231	P. Messius Saturninus	2		x		x				x		
235	L. Cominius Vipsanius Salutaris	—	xx	x	x	x				x		
236	P. Magnius Rufus Magonianus	4		x	x	x						
240	...ius Lollianus	2	xx									
			xx									
241	——	2		x	x							
242	Ti. Claudius Subatianus Proculus	3		x	Adlected into senate							
244	M. Iunius Punicus	—		x	x							
251	L. Baebius Aurelius Iuncinus	—	xx	x			xx	x				x
257	Ulpius Victor	2	xx	xx		xx						
258	C. Iulius [Ale]xianus	3		x	Adlected into senate							
262	P. Aelius Sempronius Lycinus	?		x		x	x	x				
264	Q. Cosconius Fronto	2	xx	x		x	x					
265	Q. Gabinius Barbarus	—			xxx		x	x				
268	T. Aurelius Calpurnianus Apollonides	2		x		xx	xx					
271	——	?	xxx		x		x			x		x
272	Ti. Antistius Marcianus	3	x									
274	M. Herennius Victor	—	xxx	x	x							
278	M. Pomponius Vitellianus	3		x	x							
280	C. Valerius Fuscus	—	xxx									
			xxx									
281	Sex. Cornelius Honoratus	?	x									
282	Q. Iulius Maximus Demetrianus	f.a.	xx									
291	Q. Acilius Fuscus	f.a.	xx									
295	L. Didius Marinus	. 1	xxx		xx			—?—		x		x
			xx									
312	——		xxx		x							

Table I, cont.

Career No.	NAME	Militiae	LX	C		CC				Palatine officia	Great Pref.
				Lower	Upper	1st	2nd	3rd	4th		
317	C. Furius Sabinius Aquila Timesitheus	1	x		x	xx	xx	x	x		x
318	P. Bassilius Crescens	1	xx								
319	L. Caecilius Athenaeus	?		x							
320	Pomponius L... Murianus	f.a.		x		x					
321	T. Caesius Anthianus	3	xxx								
327	C. Attius Alcimus Felicianus	f.a.	xx xx		xx	x	xx			x	x
328	Q. Axius Aelianus	—	xx xx	x							
329	P. Aelius Ammonius	3	x			x					
331	L. Iunius Septimius Verus Hermogenes	1	x								
331B	L. Titinius Clodianus	4		x		xxx xxx	xx				
346	...milius Victorinus	?	xx								
349	L. Musius Aemilianus	4	x	x			x				x
352	M. Aurelius Hermogenes	2	x	x							
355	——	2	x	x			x			x	(x)

Key: x   = office held in a particular echelon.

      (x) = office assumed to have been held in a particular echelon.

      x(?) = office of uncertain echelon held.

* Career numbers refer to Pflaum, *Carrières*.

Setting the subdivisions aside, can we discover any norm for the promotion of men from one salary level to the next? Table I would not seem to offer much hope. Consider, for example, the list in Table II of thirteen men from equestrian backgrounds reaching the Palatine *officia* whose careers are fully known. (Literary men reaching the office of *ab epistulis* are excluded on the grounds that they may represent a special class.)[26]

From this table one can say that some careers progressed more rapidly than others (as Pflaum does), but that would be true whatever criteria the emperor and his friends were using for promotion. It does not prove that the

26 Millar, *Emperor*, 102f.

Table II: Career patterns of procurators reaching Palatine *officia*

Name	Career Number	Number of posts held			
		LX	C	CC	Total
T. Haterius Nepos	95	1	1	2	4
A. Ofellius Maior Macedo	112	0	1	1	2
L. Valerius Proculus	113	1	2	4	7
M. Petronius Honoratus	117	0	1	2	3
T. Statilius Optatus	119	2	1	2	5
C. Iunius Flavianus	134	1	1	3	5
T. Furius Victorinus	139	0	1	4	5
T. Varius Clemens	156	0	1	4	5
L. Iulius Vehilius Gratus Iulianus	180	0	3	4	7
L. Cominius Vipsanius Salutaris	235	2	2	1	5
— —	271	3	1	1	5
C. Furius Sabinus Aquila Timesitheus	317	1	1	6	8
C. Attius Alcimus Felicianus	327	4	2	3	9

average was thought to be normal promotion by virtue of seniority. It is, of course, difficult to prove a negative generalization. But one can say that whatever might be picked out as a normal pattern of advancement according to rules of seniority, there will be more exceptions than regularities. A man could hold a centenariate post after none, one, two, three or four sexagenariate posts or a ducenariate after one, two or three centenariate posts. The variation in the number of ducenariate posts held before promotion to the Palatine *officia* is even greater.

Of course, Professor Pflaum recognizes that variation or a certain 'souplesse' existed within the system, and argues that, though an *eques* might move slowly through one level, he would be advanced more quickly at later stages by the seniority principle. Several examples of this can be discovered in the catalogue.[27] L. Domitius Rogatus (no. 140) held four *militiae,* and then passed through the procuratorships *ab epistulis* (60,000HS) and *moneta* (100,000HS) to reach the ducenariate post in Dalmatia. The rapidity of this allegedly normal career is attributed in part to Rogatus' prolonged military service. Other scholars have found the same principle to be applicable at a higher level: Ti. Claudius Xenophon (no. 222), after holding two sexagenariate posts in Rome and Egypt and four centenariate posts in the provinces and Rome, was promoted to the relatively important ducenariate procuratorship of Asia — 'cas exceptionnel, compensation peut-être à un

---

27 For comments about variation, *Carrières,* nos. 106 bis, 132; for the seniority principle, nos. 310, 312.

séjour particulièrement long dans l'echelon centenaire'.[28] No explanation, however, is offered in these studies as to why this principle is not universally applicable. T. Statilius Optatus (no. 119), like Rogatus, held four *militiae,* but nevertheless had to serve in two sexagenariate posts (one more than the average number of sexagenariate posts held in the second century), while men such as Valerius Eudaemon (no. 110) and Sex. Caecilius Crescens Volusianus (no. 142) skipped this level altogether despite their lack of military service.

In the final analysis, little progress is to be achieved through the citation of examples and counter-examples, none of which may be typical. The issue may be settled only by a somewhat more sophisticated statistical technique. If a seniority principle did in fact exercise an influence over the promotion of procurators, there should be a correlation between the length of past service and prospects for promotion. Or, to put the question in a form which can be tested, one may ask if there is a negative correlation between the number of offices a procurator had held in the past and the number of offices required at the man's current salary before promotion. Pflaum's thesis requires that the correlation coefficient be closer to -1 than zero. A coefficient near to zero would indicate that no significant relationship exists between the two. The coefficient can be easily calculated for each level from the data in Table I. Separate calculations have been made for the second century and the Severan period onwards, in order to assure that no major change occurred as the number of posts grew.

To begin, then, is it true that lengthy service in the *militiae* led to rapid promotion in later procuratorial service? Even without the statistician's formula this might seem doubtful, since in the second century the average number of sexagenariate posts held before promotion to a centenariate post was approximately one, regardless of whether zero, one, two, three or four *militiae* had been held previously ($N = 56$). Indeed, the correlation coefficient between *militiae* and sexagenariate posts held before promotion is -0.23, or close enough to zero to be insignificant. The corresponding coefficient for the third century is somewhat higher (-0.31), but the sample is small ($N = 29$) and the coefficient is of questionable significance.[29] Though the number of *militiae*

---

28 H. Pavis-d'Escurac, *La préfecture de l'annone, service administratif impérial d'Auguste à Constantin,* 392.

29 An examination of the individual cases from the third century suggests that, to the very limited extent that the emperor took *militiae* into consideration, he distinguished not between those who had held three *militiae* and those with fewer than three, but between those holding some *militiae* and those with none. For these calculations I have not included the careers of men who held various civilian posts (e.g., the four third-century *fisci advocati* in Table I) before their first sexagenariate posts, on the grounds that it is not clear how such offices would have counted in some hypothetical seniority scheme. Their inclusion would change the calculations very little. In the third-century sample, in the case of procurators whose *cursus* inscriptions mention no *militiae,* I have counted them as having held no *militiae.* There are indications that in this period *equites* became less concerned about giving full details about

held seems to have exercised little influence on the pace of the subsequent procuratorial career, perhaps a stronger correlation can be detected within the procuratorial *cursus* itself. If it is asked whether an *eques* holding more than the usual number of sexagenariate posts received special consideration at the centenariate level, the answer would again seem to be no. The correlation coefficient is -0.07 for the second century (the third-century sample is too small for a useful calculation).[30] Similarly, despite Mme Pavis-d'Escurac's example of Ti. Claudius Xenophon, the rapidity of promotion through the ducenariate level to the Palatine *officia* seems to have been unrelated to the number of posts held in the lower procuratorial ranks (R = -0.17), at least during the second century (for the third century the relevant careers are not sufficiently numerous to justify any statement).[31]

An objection might be raised against this argument on the grounds that the calculations have been based on numbers of posts rather than length of service. The objection cannot be fully satisfactorily answered. There can be little doubt that the length of tenure of office varied.[32] It is conceivable that behind what appears to be random variation in the numbers of posts lies a regular seniority system with years of service as the main criterion for promotion.[33] Only in a very few *cursus* are the appointments to, or tenure of, several offices datable; and these do not support the hypothesis of regularity. In the Trajanic period T. Haterius Nepos (no. 95) held a mere four procuratorships before taking up his Palatine post as a *libellis*: despite the fact that he held fewer posts than the average (five in the second century) before promotion to a Palatine bureau, he spent only a year or so in each procuratorship. By contrast, it took M. Vettius Latro (no. 104) 22 years to pass through three *militiae* and three procuratorships to reach the governorship of Mauretania Caesariensis in 128 (his service, however, may not have been continuous). Both M. Iulius Maximianus (no. 114) and Calvisius Faustinianus (no. 177) were appointed Idiologos in Egypt during the second century, the former some 21 years after a sexagenariate Egyptian post and the latter only thirteen years (and perhaps

their military service, and it is possible that they held *militiae* without including any hint of them on their *cursus* inscription. If the *cursus* without *militiae* were excluded from the sample as uncertain, the coefficient would again be changed little: R = -0.26 (N = 21). For the statistical methods, R. Floud, *An Introduction to Quantitative Methods for Historians*, ch. 7.

30 Based on 30 second-century and 17 third-century careers.
31 Based on twelve careers, a sample too small for firm conclusions.
32 Brunt, 'Administrators of Roman Egypt', 137, n. 58, found it impossible to draw conclusions from the few bits of data available.
33 Pflaum's comments seem to suggest that he may believe in such a hypothesis. E. g., with regard to P. Magnius Rufus Magonianus (no. 236), it is concluded: 'les postes se succèdent de telle sorte que chaque catégorie n'est représentée que par un seul emploi, prouvant la longue durée des fonctions, puisque rien ne nous permet de supposer une suite de promotions particulièrement rapide et brillante'. But the hypothesis about the longer tenure of fewer offices is never argued in detail, much less proven.

only ten) after serving in the third *militia*.[34] Though too scanty to be conclusive, this information does not suggest a system with a seniority principle based on years of service rather than number of offices.

In summary, the evidence for any sort of seniority principle regulating equestrian promotion seems to be weak. Clearly, a development in organization took place as procuratorships were sorted out into a hierarchy, and equestrian officials were usually required to hold one post at each level from the point of entry before advancing to the next level. Moreover, this hierarchy was integrated with the hierarchy of top centurionate posts, so that the *primipilares* and *primipilares bis* who were promoted regularly entered at certain levels.[35] Though this represented a considerable advance in bureaucratic organization, it provided only a minimal structure for procuratorial careers. The pace of advancement always varied greatly and was in the emperor's discretion, just as with senatorial careers. Thus, it is not surprising that Dio (52.19f.) treats the distribution of senatorial and equestrian posts in much the same way, the only distinction being that the former should be awarded to aristocrats of the first rank and the latter to those of the second rank, as judged by the aristocratic virtues of birth, excellence and wealth.

MERIT

The importance of merit as a criterion for appointment and promotion has also been variously estimated by modern historians. In a recent essay G. Alföldy has argued that two main, contrasting principles were operative in the selection of senators for high office: attention was given to birth and to 'the principle of ability in order to recruit the best-suited men for the vital tasks in the imperial administration'.[36] With regard to the equestrian administration, A. Stein suggested that though there were exceptions, promotion in the 'service aristocracy' normally was based on 'Verdienst und Tüchtigkeit'. Thus the Principate opened the way for the 'self-made man' who made his way 'durch eigene Kraft und Tüchtigkeit'.[37] E. Birley explained the mechanism for

---

34 Faustinianus is attested in the ducenariate office in 173, but Pflaum plausibly suggests that he may have gone out to Egypt with his friend the prefect in 170.

35 B. Dobson, 'The significance of the centurion and "Primipilaris" in the Roman army and administration', *Aufstieg und Niedergang der römischen Welt* II.1, 402.

36 'Consuls and consulars under the Antonines; prosopography and history', *Anc Soc* 7 (1976), 291. See also *Konsulat und Senatorenstand*, 95ff.

37 *Der römische Ritterstand*, 226, 229, 369 as examples. Lucilius, the friend of Seneca, is one of the examples. In a letter to him Seneca wrote: 'you are an *eques Romanus*, and to this *ordo* you have brought yourself by your own *industria*' (44.2). On the basis of this passage Lucilius has been called a 'self-made eques' who rose 'durch eigene Kraft und Tüchtigkeit zu prokuratorischen Ämtern' (Griffin, *Seneca*, 91 and Stein, *Ritterstand*, 369). Such a characterization with its modern individualist connotations is misleading, for elsewhere Seneca enlarges on what he meant: 'ingenii vigor, scriptorum elegantia, clarae et nobiles amicitiae' brought Lucilius into the midst of public life (*Ep. ad Luc.* 19.3).

evaluation: 'if an initial recommendation secured a first appointment, still more must a man's promotion have depended on the confidential reports by superior officers...'[38] In his *Tacitus* Syme has taken a broader view and pointed to the potential importance of various factors for equestrian promotion: 'the path [was] open for education, talent, and loyalty to rise under the patronage of the dynasty'.[39] By contrast, merit is allotted only a minimal role in the selection process by de Ste Croix and Hopkins.[40] As far as I know, no attempt has been made to evaluate and reconcile the arguments on behalf of these different positions.

Perhaps it should be admitted at the outset that the question of merit is more complex than that of seniority, and cannot be dealt with in a straightforward manner of counting offices in *cursus* inscriptions. Nevertheless, it is of importance to a patronage study to decide whether the Romans were interested in developing a system in which appointments were supposed to depend on an objective evaluation of a candidate's merit and to exclude personal factors such as patronage. That no system can entirely suppress the subjective element in selection is not important here: the issue is whether there were any attempts to do so, similar to attempts in other bureaucracies (see Appendix 3A). Two considerations seem relevant. First, it must be asked what qualities emperors were looking for in an official. Then, what institutional mechanisms were employed in the selection process.

Several sources are available which outline the Roman ideology of how and why a good emperor was supposed to allot offices. Essentially, the good emperor was to promote men of excellence to reward their excellence and to encourage their loyalty. In his *Panegyricus* Pliny contrasted Trajan's reign favorably with that of Domitian.

It is profitable for people to be good [now], since it is more than enough if it is not harmful; upon good men you bestow offices, priesthoods, provinces — they flourish by your friendship and judgement. Those like them are spurred on by this prize for integrity and industry, while those unlike them are attracted to their ways; for rewards for virtue and vice make men good or bad.[41]

Echoing this theme, Dio of Prusa devoted much space in his first and third discourses on kingship to the emperor's need for loyal friends of high moral qualities to help him govern the empire. Offices should be distributed to virtuous friends to demonstrate that friendship with and loyalty to the emperor

---

38 *Roman Britain*, 142.
39 P. 54. See now Syme's *History in Ovid*, 70.
40 'Suffragium'; Hopkins, 'Elite mobility', 22f.
41 *Paneg.* 44.7: 'Prodest bonos esse, cum sit satis abundeque, si non nocet; his honores, his sacerdotia, his provincias offers, hi amicitia tua, hi iudicio florent. Acuuntur isto integritatis et industriae pretio similes, dissimiles alliciuntur; nam praemia bonorum malorumque bonos ac malos faciunt.'

carry with them great rewards.[42] This holds especially for the emperor's kin.

For he considers his household and relatives as a part of his own soul, and he takes care not only so that they share in what is called his good fortune, but more importantly so that they seem worthy to take part in his rule, and above all he is eager that he be seen to honor them not on account of kinship, but on account of ἀρετή.[43]

Ideally, then, Roman offices were to be filled with men of excellence. It must then be asked what sort of excellence the Romans had in mind: the answer illustrates the divide separating Roman and modern bureaucratic ideology. In the line following the passage cited above, Dio indicates that by those with ἀρετή he means τοὺς ὀρθῶς ζῶντας. Likewise, Pliny's *boni* are characterized by *constantia, rectitudo, integritas* and *industria*. These ideal qualities are found not only in orations addressed to emperors. In praise of Agricola's governorship of Aquitania Tacitus attributes to him *iustitia, gravitas, severitas, misericordia, integritas,* and *abstinentia.*[44] Antoninus Pius was thought to have been adopted by Hadrian because during his governorship he showed himself to be *sanctum gravemque.*[45]

These characteristics, of course, are nothing other than a list of the ancient Republican *virtutes.* Cato the Younger, the paragon of the antique virtues, was praised by Sallust for his *eloquentia, integritas, constantia, modestia, severitas* and *abstinentia.* Caesar's somewhat different but nonetheless Republican virtues included *munificentia, misericordia, facilitas* and *labor.*[46] In short, far from developing any sort of new bureaucratic ideology based primarily on expertise, the Romans continued to think of the ideal qualities of the good official as those of the good aristocratic gentleman.

The most forceful single illustration of this is in Cassius Dio's political pamphlet. After a discussion of the structure of the senatorial and equestrian administrations, Dio outlines his ideas for the education and training of senators and *equites.*

While they are still children they should go regularly to schools, and when they have grown out of boyhood into youths, they should turn to horses and arms with publicly paid teachers for each skill. For in this way they will become more useful to you in each kind of activity by having learned and studied from childhood all the things which they

---

42 *Discourse on Kingship* 1.30 and 3.86f.
43 *Ibid.* 3.120: ὅς γε τοὺς οἰκείους καὶ τοὺς συγγενεῖς μέρος νενόμικε τῆς αὑτοῦ ψυχῆς, καὶ προνοεῖ γε οὐ μόνον ὅπως μετέχωσι τῆς λεγομένης εὐδαιμονίας, πολὺ δὲ μᾶλλον ὅπως ἄξιοι δοκῶσι κοινωνεῖν τῆς ἀρχῆς, καὶ τοῦτο ἐσπούδακεν ἐξ ἅπαντος, ὅπως μὴ διὰ τὴν συγγένειαν αὐτούς, ἀλλὰ διὰ τὴν ἀρετὴν φαίνηται προτιμῶν.
44 *Agric.* 9.
45 H. A., *Pius* 4.3. In the codicil of appointment to a ducenariate procuratorship sent by Marcus Aurelius to Q. Domitius Marsianus (*AE* (1962), 183), Marsianus is exhorted to maintain his moral qualities — *diligentia, innocentia* and *experientia.*
46 Sallust, *B.C.* 54.

must accomplish upon growing into manhood.[47]

Not only does Dio see no reason for specialist training, grouping senators and *equites* together, but as a senator with administrative experience from the third century, he is still seriously advocating horseriding and practice with arms as preparation for all types of careers. This was meant to inculcate precisely the good character and loyalty described above. 'Have no fear that anyone who has been raised and educated as I propose will ever attempt a rebellion.'[48] In Dio's view, then, the emperor ideally wants to select his officials on the basis of virtuous character inculcated by the traditionally aristocratic martial arts.

The call for officials with the traditional aristocratic virtues is perhaps not as much a simple platitude as might at first be suspected. The goals of Roman administration were relatively narrow. As Millar has forcefully demonstrated, the emperors were not interested in the promulgation of centrally directed reforms.[49] To the extent that reform might occur, it was thought to be the result of imitation of virtuous behavior. Ideally, the emperor's virtues were reflected in the conduct of officials who in turn set examples for the masses. This general principle of government is explained by Plutarch: 'it is necessary for the statesman already in power and trusted to try to train the character of the citizens...' For this purpose the confidence of the people in their leader's upstanding character is of great importance.[50] Aelius Aristides applies this principle specifically to Roman governors.

The governors sent out to the city-states and ethnic groups are each of them rulers of those under them, but in what concerns themselves and their relations to each other they are equally among the ruled, and in particular they differ from those under their rule in that it is they — one might assert — who first show how to be the right kind of subject.[51]

Dio of Prusa, in an oration addressed to the emperor, carries the point to its logical conclusion with respect to appointments and promotions. Just as the

47 52.26.1f. (for a discussion of the passage, Millar, *Cassius Dio*, 116): ἵνα ἕως τε ἔτι παῖδές εἰσιν, ἐς τὰ διδασκαλεῖα συμφοιτῶσι, καὶ ἐπειδὰν ἐς μειράκια ἐκβάλωσιν, ἐπί τε τοὺς ἵππους καὶ ἐπὶ τὰ ὅπλα τρέπωνται, διδασκάλους ἑκατέρων δημοσιεύοντας ἐμμίσθους ἔχοντες. οὕτω γὰρ εὐθὺς ἐκ παίδων πάνθ' ὅσα χρὴ ἄνδρας αὐτοὺς γενομένους ἐπιτελεῖν καὶ μαθόντες καὶ μελετήσαντες ἐπιτηδειότεροί σοι πρὸς πᾶν ἔργον γενήσονται.
48 Dio. 52.26.5: μήτ'αὖ δείσῃς ὅτι τραφείς τέ τις καὶ παιδευθεὶς ὡς ἐγὼ λέγω νεώτερόν τι τολμήσει.
49 *Emperor.*
50 *Moralia* 800Af.: τὸ μὲν οὖν τῶν πολιτῶν ἦθος ἰσχύοντα δεῖ καὶ πιστευόμενον ἤδη πειρᾶσθαι ῥυθμίζειν ἀτρέμα πρὸς τὸ βέλτιον ὑπάγοντα καὶ πράως μεταχειριζόμενον. (See also Vell. Pater. 2.126.4.)
51 *Εἰς Ῥώμην* 31: οἱ δὲ ἄρχοντες οἱ πεμπόμενοι ἐπὶ τὰς πόλεις τε καὶ τὰ ἔθνη τῶν μὲν ὑφ' ἑαυτοῖς ἕκαστοι ἄρχοντές εἰσι, τὰ δὲ πρὸς αὐτούς τε καὶ πρὸς ἀλλήλους ὁμοίως ἅπαντες ἀρχόμενοι, καὶ δὴ καὶ τούτῳ φαίη τις ἂν αὐτοὺς τῶν ἀρχομένων διαφέρειν, ὅτι πρῶτοι δεικνύουσιν ὅπως ἄρχεσθαι προσήκει.

emperor should imitate Zeus, so 'among generals and commanders of armies and of cities and of peoples, whoever especially imitates your manner and is seen to present himself in a way as similar as possible to your practices, this man would be among all men your closest and dearest companion. But if anyone becomes dissimilar and opposite to you, he would justly come upon censure and disgrace, and being quickly removed from his command, he would give way to better companions more able to administer.'[52]

From a more pragmatic standpoint, the emperor's basic objectives in day-to-day administration were to maintain law and order and to collect taxes. In order to accomplish these goals it was thought necessary for the emperor to have senatorial and equestrian officials with some general experience and competence, but not with specialist skills or especially high intelligence.[53] From his study of the careers of consular commanders Campbell concludes that 'in the context of Roman society, ideas of specialization and professionalism are largely anachronistic... The senatorial career was built around traditional Roman conceptions of office-holding and service of the state. The men who governed the great consular provinces were, in general, all-round amateurs...'[54] This conclusion is based on the findings that the consular commanders were not on the whole military specialists, nor were they specialized in any particular regions of the empire. For instance, of the 73 consular legates listed by Campbell, nearly two-thirds (46) held both civil and military praetorian posts; of the remainder fifteen held only military praetorian posts, while as many as nine held only civilian offices between their praetorship and consulate.[55]

P.A. Brunt draws a very similar conclusion for procuratorial careers on the

52 *Discourse on Kingship* 1.44: ὥσπερ οὖν ὅσοι στρατηγοί τε καὶ ἄρχοντες στρατοπέδων καὶ πόλεων καὶ ἐθνῶν, ὅστις ἂν τὸν σὸν μάλιστα μιμῆται τρόπον καὶ τοῖς σοῖς ἤθεσιν ὅμοιον αὑτὸν ὡς δυνατὸν φαίνηται παρέχων, οὗτος ἂν εἴη σοὶ πάντων ἑταιρότατος καὶ προσφιλέστατος · εἰ δέ τις ἐναντίος καὶ ἀνόμοιος γίγνοιτο, δικαίως ἂν τυγχάνοι μέμψεώς τε καὶ ἀτιμίας καὶ αὐτῆς γε τῆς ἀρχῆς ταχὺ παυθείς, παραχωρήσειεν ἑτέροις ἀμείνοσί τε καὶ ἄμεινον δυναμένοις διοικεῖν.

53 Emperors no doubt wished to avoid entrusting administrative offices to fools (though even fools need not have been disastrous if the freedman-slave infrastructure was working), but most aristocrats must have met this minimum qualification, with the result that greatest emphasis was placed on moral qualities. On occasion aristocratic officials are credited with 'ability' in a sense which moderns might use: Curtius Rufus, for example, is said to have possessed 'acre ingenium' (Tac. *Ann.* 11.21). But there is no evidence that the emperor specially selected his appointees for intelligence or technical knowledge, and indeed this seems unlikely in view of the absence of mention of such characteristics in *commendationes* (see below, pp. 107f.). Moreover, Tacitus implies that emperors might prefer to avoid appointing men of outstanding capabilities: Poppaeus Sabinus was said to be 'pars negotiis neque supra' (*Ann.* 6.39). In short, the requirements for competence were not such that the emperor felt compelled to suppress patronage in order to secure talent (as the British did in the nineteenth century, see n. 112 below). See also P. Stirling, 'Impartiality', 58f.

54 Campbell, '"Viri militares"', 27.

55 *Ibid.*, 17ff.

basis of his study of the Egyptian prefects. Egypt provides an especially good test case because, if any province had been felt to require administrators with specialist skills, it would have been Egypt. Brunt, however, finds that 'before taking office most prefects were unfamiliar with government in Egypt. They were seldom men of long military experience, and still more rarely jurists. They had usually held many financial posts, but this would hardly have prepared them for the peculiar complexities of the assessment and collection of taxes, and the maintenance of the irrigation system, in the Nile valley.'[56] Brunt concludes that the imperial freedmen and slaves were the true professional bureaucrats, providing whatever special skills were needed for the complex features of the administration.

A quite different conclusion was reached in a more recent study of the prefecture of the *annona:* 'compétence et expérience financières ou qualification juridique semblent avoir été les qualités plus particulièrement requises des *praefecti annonae...*'[57] The implication would seem to be that emperors were strongly influenced by qualifications of special expertise (though exceptions are acknowledged). A close examination of the relevant careers, however, would seem to reinforce Brunt's conclusion: the *praefecti annonae* do not seem to represent anything other than a cross-section of all procurators. Only one prefect had held a subordinate procuratorship in the prefecture of the *annona* in his earlier career.[58] Moreover, a study of the general distribution of various types of procuratorships to equestrians of different backgrounds would appear to indicate that emperors made no attempt to give their officials specialized experience: though emperors avoided giving the few procuratorships with military responsibilities to men

56 'Administrators of Roman Egypt', 141. Recently Ramsay MacMullen has reasserted the idea of regional specialization in *Roman Government's Response to Crisis*, 55. He claims that 'equestrians were more often than not stationed near their homes'. As evidence he first cites Jarrett, *Historia* 12 (1963), 223: Jarrett's statistics, however, concern equestrian *militiae* of Africans (not administrative offices) and show that far fewer than half of these Africans were stationed in Africa. MacMullen also cites four procuratorial careers from Pflaum's catalogue: out of the hundreds of known careers, this hardly amounts to an impressive pattern.

57 Pavis-d'Escurac, *La préfecture de l'annone*, 79. The assertion that the *praefecti annonae* were selected for financial expertise can be tested with two questions: were those who held financial procuratorships favored over those holding military procuratorships and were the secretaries *a rationibus* favored as is asserted (70)? The ratio of prefects with military background to those with civilian background is 1:2, but the same comparison for all those reaching Palatine officia or the great prefectures gives a ratio of 5:18 and for all procurators it is 25:86. So in fact those with military experience were proportionally overrepresented in the prefecture of the *annona*. As for the second question, it is true that most prefects were secretaries *a rationibus*, but it is also true that most men who reached the other great prefectures also held the office of *a rationibus*. In neither case can any special selection be demonstrated nor a group of financial specialists be singled out. Note that in Seneca's tendentious passage about the prefect's duties, he does not seem to think that they required any special mental skills and likens the work to that of plodding oxen (*De Brev. Vitae* 18).

58 *Ibid.*, 79.

with no military experience, the bulk of non-military offices were distributed to all types of *equites* regardless of background.[59]

One other consideration serves to underline the amateurish nature of the top levels of Roman imperial administration: the amount of his working capacity which an official devoted to his office.[60] That senators were amateurish in this regard is not usually doubted, but sometimes equestrians are thought to have been more professional.[61] Two considerations are relevant to the proportion of the procurator's working capacity which was devoted to official business: how many years of his life he was actually holding office, and how much of his day was devoted to duties while holding office. In answer to the first question, it may be noted that most procurators held only a few procuratorial offices during their lives. The fragmentation of our evidence makes a precise knowledge of years spent in office impossible, but several indicators are available. Of the 34 complete procuratorial careers listed in Table I, seventeen held three or fewer offices. This sample of careers, however, is not representative: most of those included in it (two-thirds) reached the Palatine offices or the great prefectures and this usually is the indicator which signals that the procuratorial career was complete. Thus the median of between three and four procuratorships per career must be an overestimate of the median for all procurators. This generalization can be confirmed in another way. By the reign of Hadrian the number of procuratorships in each of the three pay levels was roughly equal (34 ducenariate, 35 centenariate, 35 sexagenariate). This filling out of the bottom of the procuratorial hierarchy has been thought to be a development which permitted smooth promotion up through the ranks. The problem with such a view is that, while *equites* tended to hold an average of about one sexagenariate post and one centenariate post, at the ducenariate level they held nearly three offices on average (2.7). The clear corollary of this fact is that, unless tenure of the ducenariate posts was significantly shorter than lower posts, there simply were not enough ducenariate posts to allow many *equites* to pursue their careers beyond the centenariate level. Indeed, it looks as if somewhat more than half of the procurators during the second century and somewhat fewer than half during the third century could not have pursued

---

59 'Promotion and patronage', 52ff.

60 See M. Weber, *Economy and Society*, 958f.

61 M. Griffin, for example, in her recent book (*Seneca*, 356) suggests that '*De Tranquillitate Animi* and *De Otio*, like *De Brevitate Vitae*, envisage the life of *officia civilia* as full-time activity in public office...' A careful reading of these dialogues indicates that Seneca thought that *officia civilia* infringed on *otium*, as they did no doubt in the case of Pliny the Elder cited below. But that need not mean that the *officia* constituted full-time jobs in the modern sense, and Seneca does not say anything specific in support of such a conclusion. (One can note the example of the younger Pliny who complained about the burdensome private *officia* which kept him from his literary pursuits: these *officia* certainly did not constitute full-time jobs (*Ep.* 8.9.2).)

their careers beyond the centenariate rank.[62] This would usually have meant holding two or fewer offices. In other words, while some *equites* spent many years in procuratorships, many, perhaps most, held only one or two, devoting just a few years of their lives to the bureaucracy.

As for the second question about working capacity, while a satisfactory answer cannot be given, a few passages indicate that the offices were not very demanding. In a letter to Baebius Macer, Pliny the Younger explained how his uncle was able to write seven works comprising 102 books while enjoying the *amicitia* of the emperor and fulfilling *officia maxima*.[63] The answer lay in Pliny the Elder's daily routine: he awoke in the middle of the night and began his scholarly work by lamplight; before dawn he went to visit Vespasian and then to his official duties (perhaps as prefect of the Misenum fleet);[64] he then returned home to study; after a light meal he read while sunning himself; next a bath, a short sleep and more literary work until dinner during which he listened to a reader. Though the younger Pliny selected Rome as the setting for his uncle's normal day here, since many of the 102 books were written during his uncle's tour of duty in the provinces, Pliny must have intended the reader to understand that a similar daily routine made possible their production. It appears, then, that even for the conscientious elder Pliny a senior procuratorship took up only a few hours of his day and barely impinged on his studies. If volume of time is used as an indicator, Pliny was an aristocratic scholar, not a bureaucrat, despite the number of procuratorships he held.

Much the same thing can be said about Seneca's friend, the equestrian Lucilius, who is characterized as industrious. In the preface to the fourth book of his *Naturales Quaestiones,* Seneca wrote to Lucilius:

> To judge from what you write, my excellent Lucilius, you like Sicily and the duty of a leisurely procuratorship. And you will continue to like it, if you are willing to keep it within its own limits and not to make into *imperium* what is a procuratorship. I do not doubt that you will do this; I know how foreign ambition is to you and how familiar leisure and letters.[65]

Of course, not every procurator will have been as devoted to scholarship and literature as Pliny and Lucilius. But the point is that neither was thought to have been negligent: equestrian *officia* have to be placed within the context of a continuing aristocratic lifestyle.

If the senatorial and equestrian administrations were not specialized or

---

62 See Appendix 3B.
63 *Ep.* 3.5.
64 Pflaum, *Carrières,* 110; also see R. Syme, 'Pliny the Procurator', 201ff.
65 4.praef.1: 'Delectat te, quemadmodum scribis, Lucili virorum optime, Sicilia et officium procurationis otiosae delectabitque, si continere id intra fines suos volueris nec efficere imperium, quod est procuratio. Facturum hoc te non dubito. Scio, quam sis ambitioni alienus, quam familiaris otio et litteris.'

professional, then there is no reason to believe that the moral virtues which the sources claim to have been qualifications for office were mere platitudes behind which stood what we today would consider more important qualifications of technical competence.

Moreover, virtuous character was relevant to office-holding for very pragmatic reasons. First, virtuous character implied loyalty, and, in view of the continuing possibility of rebellion, loyalty of imperial officials was the foremost need of the emperor. Cassius Dio's proposed education of senators and *equites* was aimed at inculcating loyalty. Dio of Prusa asserted the king

protects his good fortune not so much by taxes, armies and other forms of power as by the loyalty of friends. For on the one hand no one man is sufficient to meet even one of his own needs; for kings, on the other hand, since it is incumbent upon them to carry on more and greater activities, they have need of fellow workers both greater in number and of greater goodwill. For he must either entrust to his companions the greatest and most weighty affairs or abandon them.[66]

Dio's assertion is probably not very controversial, but the connection between good character and loyalty ought to be underlined and set in the context of the ethic of reciprocity. As pointed out in the first chapter, the man of virtue responds to the grant of an office (a *beneficium*) with *gratia* expressed as loyalty.

Secondly, dispensation of justice in the provinces was thought to require good character more than legal expertise. As pointed out above, many senatorial and equestrian officials did not have special legal training. Tacitus points out that it was not necessary: though Agricola lacked the 'calliditatem fori', he was able to govern justly owing to his 'naturalis prudentia'. When dispensing justice he was 'gravis intentus severus et saepius misericors'. [67] In other words, a good aristocrat was *ipso facto* a good judge. A passage from Philo's *In Flaccum* makes much the same point. Before beginning his polemic against Flaccus, the prefect of Egypt, Philo praised him for his 'λαμπροτέραν καὶ βασιλικὴν φύσιν'. As features of this φύσις Philo cited the facts that 'he carried himself proudly (for to a ruler pomp is very advantageous), he judged important cases with those ἐν τέλει, put down the over-proud, prevented a motley mass of humanity from being organized to the danger of the peace', etc.[68] Clearly, in the ancient view aristocratic bearing and character were of

66 *Discourse on Kingship* 3.86f.: Φιλίαν γε μὴν ἁπάντων νενόμικε τῶν αὑτοῦ κτημάτων κάλλιστον καὶ ἱερώτατον. οὐ γὰρ οὕτως αἰσχρὸν εἶναι τοῖς βασιλεῦσιν οὐδὲ ἐπικίνδυνον χρημάτων ἀπορεῖν ὡς φίλων, οὐδ' ἂν οὕτως τῇ χορηγίᾳ καὶ τοῖς στρατοπέδοις καὶ τῇ ἄλλῃ δυνάμει διαφυλάττειν τὴν εὐδαιμονίαν ὡς τῇ πίστει τῶν φίλων. μόνος μὲν γὰρ οὐδεὶς πρὸς οὐδὲν οὐδὲ τῶν ἰδίων ἱκανός ἐστι· τοῖς δὲ βασιλεῦσιν ὅσῳ πλείω τε καὶ μείζω πράττειν ἀνάγκη, πλειόνων δεῖ καὶ τῶν συνεργούντων καὶ μετ' εὐνοίας πλείονος. ἀνάγκη γὰρ τὰ μέγιστα καὶ σπουδαιότατα τῶν πραγμάτων ἢ πιστεύειν ἑτέροις ἢ προΐεσθαι.
67 *Agric.* 9.
68 *In Flaccum* 4: οἷον σεμνότερον ἦγεν αὑτόν — ἄρχοντι δὲ λυσιτελέστατον ὁ τῦφος — ἐδίκαζε

direct importance to the first of the government's primary interests, law and the preservation of order.

To the second interest, collection of taxes, good character seems to have been relevant as well. As Brunt points out, few of the equestrian officials sent to Egypt, the most complex province financially, can have had much useful fiscal experience. The best that could be hoped for was that the equestrian official would be reasonably intelligent and honest, at least vis-à-vis the imperial government.[69] The implication of Philo's comments about Flaccus is that few prefects knew enough to control effectively the fiscal apparatus of Egypt. It seems to me indicative of Roman values that, while we rarely hear of a senator or equestrian praised for fiscal expertise and efficiency,[70] we hear of exorbitant praise for minor displays of honesty. In a letter to Maturus Arrianus, Pliny tells the tale of Egnatius Marcellinus' *gloria*. As quaestor,

he had in his possession a sum of money intended for the salary of the secretary allotted to him who had died before the day his salary was due; and, feeling strongly that he ought not retain this, he consulted the Emperor on his return, and with his permission the Senate, to know what was to be done with it. It was a small point but a genuine one.[71]

Though it may have been a 'small point', Pliny devoted a letter to publicizing it, and Marcellinus won the approbation of the emperor and the senate for his honesty. Praise of honesty might, of course, be found in almost any era, but in the Roman world good character seems to be given precedence over technical competence.

The answer to the question about what the emperor looked for in his officials, then, is that he wanted men with general experience and good character. Neither senatorial nor equestrian careers were designed to produce professionals. Of course, in an emergency on the frontiers an experienced general might be needed, but on the whole the daily duties of aristocratic administrators did not require any special technical skills. In short, neither the ideology nor the pragmatic needs would seem to have been of a nature to encourage the suppression of patronage and the development of formal, impersonal evaluations of official performance.

How then did the emperor select his senatorial and equestrian officials? What institutional mechanisms did he have at his disposal? It should be said at

τὰ μεγάλα μετὰ τῶν ἐν τέλει, τοὺς ὑπεραύχους καθῄρει, μιγάδων καὶ συγκλύδων ἀνθρώπων ὄχλον ἐκώλυεν ἐπισυνίστασθαι.

69 Brunt, 'Administrators of Roman Egypt', 142.

70 Flaccus is praised by Philo as an intelligent amateur, but even this intelligence was thought by Philo to be secondary to his kingly nature.

71 *Ep.* 4.12: 'Cum in provinciam quaestor exisset, scribamque qui sorte obtigerat ante legitimum salarii tempus amisisset, quod acceperat scribae daturus, intellexit et statuit subsidere apud se non oportere. Itaque reversus Caesarem, deinde Caesare auctore senatum consuluit, quid fieri de salario vellet. Parva quaestio sed tamen quaestio.' (Loeb translation.)

the outset that the evidence available to answer these questions is very fragmentary and so the conclusions will be tentative. Now the first point to be made is an obvious one: the emperor cannot usually have had first-hand experience of provincial administrators' performance of duties. So we must decide what sort of second-hand information was available and in what circumstances the emperor made his selection.

It has been suggested (and accepted by some historians) that once a year, during the annual appointments period, the emperor selected his officials on the basis of confidential files which the *ab epistulis* kept for every aristocrat in the emperor's service. If this suggestion is true, it carries important implications for both the significance of patronage and more generally the level of rationalization in the imperial government. It would mean, for example, that successful candidates would not have been certain of the specific source of their success in securing an appointment and hence less likely to attribute it to the patronage of any particular author of a *commendatio* on their behalf.

Evidence for an annual appointments period has been found in the following passage from Suetonius' *Life of Domitian*.[72]

Domitian continually gave splendid and expensive games, not only in the amphitheater but also in the circus, where in addition to the annual two-horse and four-horse chariot races he even staged a two-fold battle (on horseback and on foot), not to mention a naval battle in the amphitheater, hunts and gladiatorial fights, even in torchlight at night. The fights were not limited to men, but women also participated. Moreover, he always attended the Quaestorian Games, which he had revived... And throughout every gladiatorial show (*omne spectaculum*) a little boy clothed in scarlet with a monstrous head sat at his feet. He chatted with him at length, sometimes seriously. Indeed, he was heard to ask the boy if he knew why he had decided by his most recent appointment to have Mettius Rufus govern Egypt.[73]

From this anecdote the appointment of Mettius Rufus is dated to just before the Quaestorian Games and the annual appointments period is assigned to the month of November. But the passage seems to say nothing of an annual

72 Pflaum, *Procurateurs*, 204. In addition, Pflaum notes that Fronto unsuccessfully requested a procuratorship for Appian from Antoninus Pius twice in two years (*Ad Pium* 9) — a fact which can be explained in ways other than the assumption that the emperor only made appointments once each year.

73 *Dom.* 4: 'Spectacula assidue magnifica et sumptuosa edidit non in amphitheatro modo, verum et in circo, ubi praeter sollemnes bigarum quadrigarumque cursus proelium etiam duplex, equestre ac pedestre, commisit; at in amphitheatro navale quoque. Nam venationes gladiatoresque et noctibus ad lychnuchos, nec virorum modo pugnas, sed et feminarum. Praeterea quaestoriis muneribus, quae olim omissa revocaverat, ita semper interfuit... Ac per omne gladiatorum spectaculum ante pedes ei stabat puerulus coccinatus parvo portentosoque capite, cum quo plurimum fabulabatur, nonnumquam serio. Auditus est certe, dum ex eo quaerit, "ecquid sciret, cur sibi visum esset ordinatione proxima Aegypto praeficere Mettium Rufum" '.

appointments period, which is otherwise undocumented, nor does it imply that Mettius Rufus was appointed just before the Quaestorian Games. Suetonius lists the games which Domitian sponsored including the Quaestorian Games and then says that at all of these gladiatorial shows Domitian conversed with the grotesque child to whom he put the question about Mettius Rufus. Suetonius does not intend us to understand that the incident occurred at the Quaestorian games in particular.

The idea of a confidential file system supervised by the *ab epistulis*, as expressed by E. Birley, rests on a difficult passage from Statius' *Silvae*.[74] The poem is at this point praising and glorifying Abascantus, Domitian's *ab epistulis*. The emperor is said to have placed on Abascantus' shoulders an immense burden, one part of which was the following:

> praeterea, fidos dominus si dividat enses,
> pandere quis centum valeat frenare, maniplos
> inter missus eques, quis praecepisse cohorti,
> quem deceat clari praestantior ordo tribuni,
> quisnam frenigerae signum dare dignior alae.[75]

Adding this passage to several of Pliny's *commendationes* to Trajan (*Ep.* 10.85-87), Birley concludes that 'such reports [as Pliny's] would inevitably pass through the hands of the Emperor's secretary *ab epistulis*, and be filed by him; and that explains how in the military sense he came to act as Adjutant-General and Military Secretary, responsible — as we learn from a famous passage in Statius (*Silvae* 5.1.94f.) — for all military appointments, from direct commissions as centurions upwards...'[76] Birley is not explicit about how he would translate the passage, but his conclusion about the file system would suggest that he interprets it as does Millar (who does not necessarily accept all of Birley's argument): this passage shows the *ab epistulis* 'receiving news of events and, apparently, reports on individuals and making them known ("pandere")' — presumably to the emperor.[77]

This would seem to be a misinterpretation of the passage. The grammar permits, but does not compel this understanding: the subjunctive *valeat* can be an anticipatory subjunctive (i.e., the *ab epistulis* makes known, or advises, 'who would be capable of controlling a century'), but it can equally be a subjunctive in indirect question (i.e., he makes known, in publicizing the emperor's appointment, 'who has the power to control a century'). On the first hypothesis the emperor is the object to whom the information is made known; on the second, the understood object is the appointee and presumably any other interested party.

74 *Roman Britain*, 142.
75 *Silv.* 5.1.94f.
76 *Roman Britain*, 142.
77 'Emperors at work', 15.

Though the grammar is not compelling one way or the other, it seems to me
that the passage is better understood by adopting the second translation
(which the Budé edition accepts). Statius limits the appointments in which the
ab epistulis is involved to relatively minor equestrian *militiae* and
centurionates. Given the interest in glorifying Abascantus, the limitation to
minor posts demands some explanation, and no satisfactory answer can be
given on the hypothesis that Statius is referring to the receipt by the *ab epistulis*
of confidential reports concerning all officials, senior as well as junior. Birley
attempts to explain the limitation: 'Statius himself, indeed, seems to confine
such appointments to the centurionate and the three equestrian military
grades, but it will be recalled that Vespasian owed his command of II
Augusta... to the influence of Claudius' powerful *ab epistulis*, the freedman
Narcissus.'[78] The implication here is that Statius was simply being arbitrary in
his reference to junior military posts only, and that the *ab epistulis* was
responsible for files on men as important as legionary legates. But the passage
concerning Vespasian and Narcissus will not bear the weight of this argument.
It contains nothing about a file: Vespasian got the appointment 'Narcissi
gratia', just as Otho's grandfather reached the senate 'per gratiam Liviae
Augustae'[79], or Seneca received a praetorship by the influence of Agrippina.[80]
Personal proximity to the emperor in each case, not oversight of a confidential
file system, opened up avenues of influence. There is no reason to believe that
Statius arbitrarily avoided mention of senior offices, and so we are still left to
ask why he included only the group of four minor posts when his goal was the
glorification of Abascantus.

The second translation offers a solution to the problem. *Pandere* here
means 'make known' in the sense of 'rédaction et expédition des lettres de
nomination'[81] and has nothing to do with a file system. The reason for
including only minor posts is that, according to Vegetius, more senior
appointees were notified by codicil 'per epistulam sacram Imperatoris'.[82]

If personal files were kept for aristocratic administrators, our ignorance of
them is complete. It has been suggested that the files comprised confidential
reports such as Pliny's letters 85, 86a, 86b, and 87. Now the last lines of letters
85, 86a and 86b suggest that *commendationes* were regularly written by a
governor for subordinates, but the content does not reveal a serious evaluation
of performance and the suggestion that these *commendationes* were

---

78 *Roman Britain*, 143 with reference to Suetonius, *Vesp.* 4.1.

79 Suetonius, *Otho* 1.1.

80 Tacitus, *Ann.* 12.8.

81 Stace, *Silves* v.II, ed. H. Frère and transl. H. J. Izaac, notes to p.177.

82 Vegetius 2.7. Vegetius' comment is partially confirmed by the codicil from Marcus Aurelius
   to Q. Domitius Marsianus of Bulla Regia (*AE* (1962), 183). The codicil notified Marsianus of
   his appointment to a ducenariate procuratorship and seems to have come from the hand of the
   emperor (Pflaum, 'Une lettre de promotion', 357).

meaningful reports does not seem justified. In letter 85 Maximus, an imperial freedman, is recommended to Trajan as *probus, industrius, diligens* and *disciplinae tenacissimus*. In the next letter Gavius Bassus, the *praefectus orae Ponticae*, is said to be *integer, probus, industrius* and *reverentissimus mei*. Though there is some difficulty in reading the name, it is perhaps Fabius Valens who is described as possessing *iustitia* and *humanitas* in letter 86b. In letter 87 an appointment is requested for Nymphidius Lupus who is said to be *probus* and *industrius* and whose father was a friend of Pliny. On the surface, these letters would not seem to have the characteristics of confidential reports: nothing is said about performance of particular duties and it is difficult to see anything in the contents requiring secrecy. Indeed, given the banality of the adjectives and the complete absence of anything resembling a critical evaluation, it is impossible to imagine how an emperor, faced with a pile of such recommendations, could have made any appointment on the basis of objective merit. It has been argued, nevertheless, that these letters can be read as meaningful reports.

Pliny uses stock epithets, but qualifies or varies them, so that Trajan can read between the lines, as in Ep. 26.2. Maximus [the subject of the letter under examination] is accorded neither the *integritas* of Bassus (86a) and Rosianus Geminus (Ep. 26.2), nor the *reverentissimus mei* of the former, which quality Ep. 27 suggests that he lacked. But he is allowed other qualities. The younger Lupus, who had not served under Pliny, is given the minimum, Ep. 87.3. None of these are recommended as strongly as the subject of Ep. 86b.[83]

Such an attempt to transform these *commendationes* into meaningful reports does not carry conviction. If Trajan 'read between the lines', as suggested, then the implication is that every time a *commendatio* from Pliny came in, Trajan went to his files to find and compare all other recommendations from Pliny in order to judge what adjective was left out of the one under consideration (thus presupposing a fairly elaborate and otherwise unattested cross-reference system). Even had he undertaken such a comparison, it is not likely that Trajan would have derived a very clear idea of the relative merits of the various candidates from the few general moral virtues ascribed to each. In the argument cited above we find the assertion that the recommendation in Epistle 86b was the strongest, despite the fact that nothing is said of the man's honesty, industry or technical competence. It might well be suggested, on the contrary, that the letter on behalf of Nymphidius Lupus (87) was intended to carry the greatest weight with Trajan precisely because of its stress on Pliny's personal relationship with the candidate. Altogether, it seems doubtful whether Trajan would have been better able than modern readers to find a critical evaluation of merit in these letters.

83 Sherwin-White, *Letters of Pliny*, 681f.

In sum, it seems that none of the regular mechanisms postulated by historians for selection of meritorious candidates is securely attested. It may have been customary for governors to give their subordinates *commendationes* to carry to the emperor, but the content of Pliny's recommendations suggests that they were not designed to provide the emperor with a critical and discriminating report. Nor is there any reason to believe that his letters were edited in order to remove any more substantive content.[84] This is not to say that the letters were meaningless, but rather that they, like the information received from oral sources, must be understood in relation to the qualities sought and placed firmly in the context of a patronal society.

In the past, it seems to me, scholars have not always taken sufficient notice of the Republican tradition of recommendations on which Pliny was drawing. The language of Pliny's letters was descended directly from that found in the book of *commendationes* of Cicero. In different letters Cicero recommends men for *modestia, humanitas* and esteem for himself; or for *humanitas, observantia,* and *probitas;* or for *humanitas* and *probitas;* or for *probitas* and *modestia.*[85] These are but a few of the virtues which Cicero uses again and again undiscriminatingly throughout Book 13. No one would argue from these letters that *probitas* and *humanitas* here represent critical judgements of the client's objective merits; rather they are the common language of letters of patronage. So they are also in the *commendationes* of Pliny and those who came after him.[86] Perhaps the clearest illustration of this is the fact that the same virtues seem to be cited irrespective of the office, honor or privilege requested (except that in the case of senatorial offices extra attention is devoted to high birth).[87] The message in each case is the same: 'this man is a friend or client of mine and hence of worthy character'. Indeed, it is this link in Roman thinking between friendship and good character which enables us to make sense of recommendations, both written and oral.

In modern recommendations it seems that the author attempts to persuade the reader of his candidate's objective merit based on some universally recognized criteria. In Roman *commendationes,* by contrast, the personal relationship between patron and client is stressed and there is no attempt to appear impartial. This is because the aristocratic qualities sought were

---

84 *Ibid.,* 12.
85 *Ad Fam.* 13.15, 17, 33, 63.
86 For *industria, sobrius, acer, diligens, honestas, probitas, innocentia, castitas* in Fronto, see *Ad Amic.* 1.1-5, 8; *Ad Pium* 9; *Ad M. Caes.* 5.37; *Ad Verum Imp.* 2.7. The indiscriminate use of such adjectives is illustrated by a funerary dedication to a ten-year-old boy which includes the same language as that applied to officials (*AE* (1931), 43 from Africa).
87 Pliny, *Ep.* 10.94: a request for the *ius trium liberorum* in which Suetonius is described as *probissimus, honestissimus* and *eruditissimus,* while in *Ep.* 2.9 Sextus Erucius is recommended for the aedileship on the grounds that he is *probissimus, gravissimus,* and *eruditissimus.*

manifested largely in the context of friendship and patron-client relationships. In other words, the recommender illustrates his client's loyalty, integrity and industry by reference to his display of those qualities in their mutual friendship.

Evidence of this connection between friendship and virtuous character can be found scattered throughout the literature of the Principate. Perhaps the best illustration comes from the *commendationes* where, juxtaposed with the list of the protégé's virtues, is a description of the personal relationships between protégé and referee; frequently the description of the friendship overshadows the list of virtues. This leads one commentator to remark on what he considers to be the irrelevance of much of what is said in the *commendationes* to holding office.[88] But this may be to misunderstand Pliny's purpose: by his description of his friendship with Voconius Romanus or the loyalty displayed by Cornelius Minicianus, Pliny illustrates his protégés' good aristocratic character.[89]

Beyond what is actually expressed, the *commendatio* itself was an act of friendship and reflected on the protégé's character because in the Roman view a man's character was reflected in his friends. The clearest statement of this is in Pliny's letter to Minicius Fundanus on behalf of Asinius Bassus. Pliny asked Fundanus to take Bassus as his quaestor when elected consul. Bassus was recommended on the basis of his father's virtuous character, one reflection of which was the father's friendship with Pliny and Tacitus.

He is an outstanding man and most devoted to other good men, among whom why should I not count myself? He has also embraced Cornelius Tacitus (whose reputation you know) with a close bond of friendship. So, if you approve of both Tacitus and myself, you must feel the same about Rufus (the father), since likeness of character is perhaps the tightest bond for holding together friendships.[90]

In a context of belief in guilt and virtue by association, the very fact that a man possessed a recommendation associated him with the worth of its author.

One of the few pieces of evidence for oral recommendations to the emperor suggests that the same assumption may have been prevalent in these circumstances as well. Pliny wrote to Clusinius Gallus about his dead patron Corellius Rufus and his obligation to defend his daughter Corellia in court. Explaining his debt to Corellius, he wrote:

---

88 Sherwin-White, *Letters of Pliny*, 211.
89 *Ep.* 2.13: the *eloquentia* attributed to Romanus is also a mark of good aristocratic upbringing and is relevant to the quality of his companionship. Also see *Ep.* 7.22; 2.9.4-5; 3.2.1-3; 4.15.7; 6.6.3; 7.31.5.
90 *Ep.* 4.15.1-2: 'Est homo eximius et bonorum amantissimus. Cur enim non me quoque inter bonos numerem? Idem Cornelium Tacitum (scis quem virum) arta familiaritate complexus est. Proinde si utrumque nostrum probas, de Rufo quoque necesse est idem sentias, cum sit ad conectendas amicitias vel tenacissimum vinculum morum similitudo.'

What a reputation that man built for me at home and in public, even in the presence of the emperor. When a discussion about good young men happened to take place before Nerva, and many were speaking of me in praise, for a while Corellius kept his silence, which used to increase his authority greatly. Then, with the seriousness (which you know), he said, 'I must praise Pliny sparingly, since he does nothing except with my advice.' With these words he gave a compliment to me which I would have been immodest to request — that I always act with the greatest wisdom, since I do everything by the advice of the wisest of men.[91]

The connection between virtue and the patron-protégé relationship is explicit here: Pliny's virtue (and so promise for a good career) was a direct result of his loyalty toward and imitation of a patron who himself had a reputation for noble character.

Pliny's story suggests a second way in which the meaning of the recommendations depended on the patronal context. The emperor's evaluation of character references of such a general and subjective nature (being essentially testimonies of friendship) must have depended heavily on his own personal relationship with the referee. Corellius' judgement of Pliny carried weight precisely because he enjoyed the friendship and respect of Nerva. Further, the setting of Pliny's story suggests another way in which friendship between the emperor and the patron was important: *amici* such as Corellius had access to the emperor. As pointed out in the previous chapter, this was especially important, since important requests on behalf of protégés were normally made in person, not by letter.[92] This may well explain why only a few letters requesting appointments or promotions to senatorial and procuratorial posts survive: much of the discussion about the character and worth of men at this level must have gone on in the kind of setting depicted by Pliny — the emperor with a circle of friends discussing promising young men.

Altogether, it would seem that there is no reason to believe that the emperor did not treat equestrian and senatorial offices as gifts in his power to bestow. There is no strong evidence that any attempt was made in the Principate to transcend the particularistic criterion of patronage by the introduction of the universalistic and rational criteria of seniority and merit (in the modern sense). Though the emperor no doubt considered merit, the Roman conception of merit was not such as to encourage impartial evaluation. Indeed, both the

91 *Ep.* 4.17.7: 'Quantum ille famae meae domi in publico, quantum etiam apud principem adstruxit! Nam cum forte de bonis iuvenibus apud Nervam imperatorem sermo incidisset, et plerique me laudibus ferrent, paulisper se intra silentium tenuit, quod illi plurimum auctoritatis addebat; deinde gravitate quam noras: "Necesse est" inquit "parcius laudem Secundum, quia nihil nisi ex consilio meo facit". Qua voce tribuit mihi quantum petere voto immodicum erat, nihil me facere non sapientissime, cum omnia ex consilio sapientissimi viri facerem.'
92 *Ep.* 10.94

ideology and the mechanism of reporting, the *commendatio*, should be placed in the Republican tradition of patronage. The emperor sought officials who, in addition to general experience and energy, possessed the traditional qualities of good character. These characteristics were manifested in friendship and patron-client relationships, and so the *commendatio*, frequently little more than a testimony to loyal friendship, was an appropriate instrument for reporting in a patronal society despite the banality of its objective content to the modern eye.[93]

APPENDIX 3A

Comparative evidence from the Chinese bureaucracy

An examination of comparative evidence from China, though unusual in specialist studies in Roman history, is justified, I think, for several reasons. First, the Chinese example has been influential in the formulation of models to account for the structural significance of bureaucracies in pre-modern societies, including Rome. Secondly, the analysis in the previous sections of this chapter has, at least implicitly, measured the Roman system against an ideal type of a rational-legal bureaucracy. An objection might be raised that this is a meaningless comparison because even modern bureaucracies do not fully satisfy the criteria for this ideal type. It is hoped that the Chinese evidence might meet such an objection by illustrating how far appointment and promotion in a pre-modern administration might be rationalized. The contrast between it and the Roman system will then throw into relief the traditional character of the latter. Three aspects of this contrast will be discussed here: the general conditions giving rise to the bureaucracies; the specific organizational mechanisms involved in selection; and the bureaucratic ideology concerning promotion.

At the structural level much of China's past is interpreted as a struggle between the centripetal force of the emperor and the centrifugal force of the great landowning aristocracy. Basically, the emperor's interest was in centralization and the tapping of the resources of the whole empire, while the great landowners had an interest in withdrawing their lands from imperial exploitation. In this struggle one of the emperor's strengths lay in developing a highly structured and effective bureaucracy capable of compelling the great landowners to submit to the central administration. The effectiveness of the bureaucracy depended on recruiting able men and eliminating widespread patronage by which the great landowners could fill the ranks of the administration with their own people and hence enjoy immunity from government measures.[94]

93 I have not intended by this chapter to suggest that patronage was of exclusive importance in imperial appointments or that the emperor was unconcerned about the competence of his administrators. Rather the point has been that (1) patronage was indispensable to the system because no formal bureaucratic mechanisms existed for bringing candidates to the emperor's attention, and (2) because the Romans thought of the merit of officials in more general and moralistic terms than we do, the subjectivity in the evaluation of official conduct was correspondingly greater, and with it the latitude for acceptable patronage.
94 Edwin Reischauer and John Fairbank in their *East Asia: the Great Tradition* emphasize this struggle and the place of the bureaucracy in it (esp. 124).

This pattern of structural conflict has been abstracted and applied to 'historical bureaucratic empires' in general by S. N. Eisenstadt. Usually emerging from periods of unrest, turmoil, or dissolution of the existing political system,

> the rulers had to find allies, whether passive or active, who could enable them to achieve their goals in spite of these various aristocratic or patrician forces. They had to forge various instruments of power and policy with which to mobilize the various resources they needed — whether economic resources, manpower, or political support. They naturally tried to find their allies among the groups and strata whose interests were opposed to those of the more traditional and aristocratic groups, and who could benefit from their weakening and from the establishment of a more unified policy.[95]

One of those newly forged instruments of power was a bureaucracy characterized by (1) organization of administrative activities, (2) recruitment based increasingly on skill, wealth, achievement and loyalty, (3) development of internal bureaucratic organizational autonomy (centralization, hierarchy of authority, specialization, organizational rules), (4) professionalization of staff, (5) development of a professional or semi-professional ideology.[96]

This general pattern has, in turn, been applied to Rome. In the Principate the conflict between emperor and senate is said to have given rise to a bureaucratic organization. In staffing, 'emperors used men of lowly origin in key positions of administration because they were not identified with aristocratic interests, because their mobility made them more dependent upon, even grateful to the emperors, and because they might not be too easily assimilated to the aristocracy'. In order to limit the role of subjective judgement of merit in promotion through the organization, the emperor is said to have favored seniority as the guiding principle.[97] It seems that here we have clear echoes of the Chinese pattern.

The Chinese structural conflict, however, does not seem to be sufficiently analogous to the conditions of Rome of the Principate to make this general model useful. The situation of the later Empire may have been similar, when the great rural patrons struggled to secure *de facto* immunity from taxation and army recruiting for the land and clients under their protection.[98] But no one to my knowledge has suggested that this phenomenon occurred on a significant scale in the first two centuries A.D. As a result, the emperors of this period had no motivation to exclude substantial landowners from their administration. On the contrary, emperors continued to draw on senators even for the army commands and began increasingly to use equestrians — men who were by definition aristocratic landowners.

An examination of the mechanisms involved in the Chinese bureaucracy suggests that here too the differences between it and the Roman administration are more important than the similarities. The Chinese mechanisms of appointment and promotion evolved

95 *The Political Systems of Empires*, 14.
96 *Ibid.*, 21f.
97 'Elite mobility', 22f.
98 For rural patronage in the later Empire, L. Harmand, *Libanius: Discours sur les patronages.*

over a period of many centuries. The developed system of the Sung dynasty (960-1279 A.D.) can be outlined briefly. The civil service was made up of a hierarchy of nine grades. There were several avenues of entry into the system, the most famous being the examinations. By the time of the Sung dynasty the examinations leading to the *chin-shih* degree in letters had emerged from the variety of examinations (in law, history, rituals and the classics) as the most important, owing to its emphasis on 'originality and skill in reasoning and composition rather than on mere memory'.[99] From 1065 A.D. the examinations were held regularly every three years and accompanied by an elaborate ritual.

There were three levels of examinations. First came the examinations held by the individual prefectures or government schools. Scholars who passed these, reportedly varying between one and ten percent of the candidates, went on to an examination given by the central government at the capital. About ten percent of these were passed and were then subjected to a 'palace examination', which rejected a few more and ranked the remaining successful candidates.[100]

As the selectiveness suggests, the examinations were rigorous and required years of study. At the end of the twelfth century about 400 candidates received the *chin-shih* degree every three years.[101]

There is considerable controversy over the significance of the *chin-shih* degree in producing a bureaucracy based on merit. As a method of entry, some Chinese specialists prefer instead to emphasize the *yin* privilege of allowing officials to coopt relatives without examination into the civil service at a particular grade.[102] Though evaluation of the statistical data presented by the various sides differs, it seems to be generally accepted that in the top grades of the civil service *chin-shih* holders predominated. This is significant because, together with the fact that more than one-half of the degree holders in the period 1148-1256 had had no civil servants in the preceding three generations of the paternal line, it suggests that the examination system opened an important avenue of upward mobility.[103] (This is not to deny that access to the requisite education did not vary greatly with the candidate's class and geographical location.)

Elaborate mechanisms were also developed to regulate promotion, which depended on several factors: the length of tenure of office, a system of merit ratings, special examinations of specific assignments, and the sponsorship of higher officials.[104] With regard to the last of these, 'the Chinese had long recognized not only that patronage was inevitable, but that it offered actual advantages when practised with the interests of the state in mind'.[105] Complex mechanisms were established to regulate sponsorship. First,

99 Reischauer, *East Asia*, 202
100 *Ibid.*, 202.
101 K. Wittfogel, 'Public office in the Liao dynasty and the Chinese examination system', *Harvard Journal of Asiatic Studies* 10 (1947), 31.
102 *Ibid.*, 25.
103 The conclusion of studies by E. A. Kracke, Jr, 'Family vs. merit in the Chinese Civil Service examinations during the Empire', *Harvard Journal of Asiatic Studies* 10 (1947), 103ff. and Francis L. K. Hsu, 'Social mobility in China', *Amer. Soc. Rev.* 14 (1949), 764-71.
104 E. A. Kracke, Jr, *Civil Service in Early Sung China, 960-1067*, 84f.
105 *Ibid.*, 194.

the sponsor was not to recommend anyone related to himself. From 1010 A.D. court officials had the privilege and obligation to recommend one and only one man. The higher provincial commissioners were not so limited in numbers in order to help overcome the bias of the system against provincials and so draw in men experienced in local administration. Further, the sponsor took legal responsibility for the official conduct of his candidate and was liable to punishment in the case of misconduct. Thus the sponsorship mechanism was 'a remarkable and unique endeavor to increase responsibility in the civil service: responsibility in the act of appointing and promoting officials, and responsible conduct on the part of the officials appointed and promoted. The play of personal influence [was] brought into the open, and subjected to rules and standards.'[106] Just how effective these mechanisms were is problematic, but even a scholar stressing the *yin* privilege concedes that 'appointment to the empire's leading offices was determined in the main by considerations of personal qualification'.[107]

The Roman system was much more traditional, exhibiting few signs of conscious design. Though the *chin-shih* examination may not have tested candidates for the skills required of an official, it did represent a formal and impersonal method of initial selection. Through this mechanism it was possible for talented but unconnected commoners to enter the imperial service. Without connections few Romans could have hoped to have come to the emperor's attention at all, much less have their talents recognized. It might be argued that rhetoricians winning procuratorships from the emperor offer some parallel to the Chinese literati. But even between these two groups the differences are enormous. The number of rhetoricians in the Empire receiving hearings and winning procuratorships by oratorical display cannot have been large; the hearings given by the emperor were completely haphazard and far from impersonal. This is not to say that oratorical ability was not an impetus to certain Romans' careers, but only that its value needs to be understood in a patronal context. For example, one of the characters in the *Dialogus*, Aper, argues for the importance of oratory to worldly success not on the grounds that an impersonal examination of the skill wins one a place in the bureaucratic hierarchy, but on the grounds that use of the skill in court can win a man of common birth a clientèle of rich and powerful men.[108]

With regard to promotion through the bureaucracy, the Roman system possessed none of the Chinese regulative mechanisms: no merit ratings, no rules of seniority, no examinations and no restraints on sponsorship. While the Chinese argued about how to make sponsorship an institution to promote equal opportunity and merit, the Romans in the Principate did not conceive of patronage as a problem on the grounds that it offered unfair advantage to some. It has been claimed that, though emperors in the early Empire would have liked to promote on the basis of merit, they refrained because of the subjectivity thus introduced, but no evidence has been offered for the view.

Finally, brief consideration ought to be given to the ideology surrounding the Chinese system. It has been noted that 'if there was not equality in the examination system, there was a general belief in the "spirit of equality", and this belief together with the fact that some mobility did exist helped to stabilize the society and maintain the

106 *Ibid.*, 194.
107 Wittfogel, 'Public office', 28.
108 Tacitus, *Dial.* 6.2. and *passim*.

status quo.'[109] This 'spirit of equality' is reflected in proverbs such as 'overnight, the poor student becomes a somebody.'[110] It is also reflected in the debates over how best to select men of merit and to limit patronage, for example, the debate which went on over the mechanism of sponsorship — whether it in fact encouraged the rise of talented men or simply gave sponsors a means of favoring their personal preferences.[111]

As pointed out above, there is considerable controversy about how far the ideology reflected a real feature of Chinese society. We need not enter into the debate over the efficacy of the machinery designed to promote merit: the important point is that such a debate cannot take place with regard to the Roman bureaucracy of the Principate — there were no formal or impersonal mechanisms for selecting merit, and perhaps more revealing, there was never an ideology of equal opportunity for office-holding.

The question of ideology is important for deciding how influential we should expect patronage to be in Roman society: it is easy to see how, as in China's case, a society might not live up to its professions of equal opportunity, but it is very difficult to see how the inverse might occur, that is, how in the absence of any ideology or institutions of equal opportunity a society might promote men in its institutions primarily on the basis of merit or seniority. The general assumption of both the ancient Chinese and modern sinologists has been that when formal and impersonal mechanisms did not restrain it, patronage became a primary force influencing appointment and promotion in the bureaucracy.[112] If this assumption is applied to the Roman bureaucracy, the conclusion

---

109 Chang Chung-li, *The Chinese Gentry: Studies on their Role in Nineteenth Century Chinese Society*, 187.
110 Cited by P'an Kuang-tan and Fei Hsiao-t'ung in *The Chinese Civil Service*, ed. J. Menzel, 9.
111 Kracke, *Civil Service*, 85.
112 Other state bureaucracies could be used to illustrate this principle. For example, the British administration, like the Roman, was slow to develop rules for appointments and promotions. In the early modern period there were no advertisements, examinations, formal interviews or professional qualifications for government posts. As a result, 'systematic promotion, whether by seniority or merit, was made difficult, indeed all but impossible by the operation of the three "P"s: Patrimony, Patronage, and Purchase' — the main factors also governing initial appointments. These factors did not prevent meritorious candidates from succeeding, but merit without patronage or favor was not enough to guarantee promotion (G. E. Aylmer, *The King's Servants: the Civil Servants of Charles I*, 89). When in the nineteenth century a need was felt for the suppression of patronage in order to achieve more efficient government, selection by open examination was introduced by an Order in Council of 1870 (Roger K. Kelsall, *Higher Civil Servants in Britain from 1870 to the Present Day*, 2f.). For other modern European countries, see J. A. Armstrong, *The European Administrative Elite*. Modern Japan provides an interesting example of how the traditional particularism can be integrated into a modern state and economy. As S. M. Lipset notes, 'members of various Japanese organizations, business, academic, or governmental, are given particularistic protection once they are admitted to membership. There is little competition for promotion or salary increases; men move up largely by seniority... [But] universalism enters into the Japanese educational and business system at two stages, first at admission to university, and second at entrance into the lower rungs of business or government executive ladders.' Thus, a recruitment and promotion system which demands talented and skilled personnel need not exclude personal, protective relationships altogether, but, in Lipset's view, it does require 'either strong values or rules sustaining achievement and universalism'. Rome, like the Latin American countries studied by Lipset, had neither of these, and so men were chosen for high positions on the basis of connections, as in Latin American countries today, which, according to Lipset, 'have not yet found mechanisms to associate talent with elite status'. ('Values, education, and entrepreneurship' in *Elites in Latin America*, ed. S. M. Lipset and A. Solari,

must be that in the absence of any institutional restraints patronage played a fundamental role in the Roman system.

APPENDIX 3B

The proportion of procurators advancing from the centenariate to the ducenariate level

This appendix is designed to show the steps by which it was concluded that about one-half of the procurators holding centenariate posts cannot have advanced to a ducenariate post. The analysis will be done for the two periods 98-192 A.D. and 193-249 A.D. The one assumption required for the analysis is that the length of tenure of office was the same on average at each level. This seems reasonable: if the tenure of ducenariate posts was longer than that of lesser posts, my conclusions are strengthened; only if the ducenariate posts were held for significantly shorter periods are the conclusions vitiated.

The first step is to work out an average of the number of posts available at each level for the two periods. This is done by taking the number of posts at each level by reign and then averaging them after weighting each number according to the length of the reign. So to arrive at the weighted average of ducenariate posts available for the period 98-192, we use the equation:

$$\sum_{\text{Trajan}}^{\text{Commodus}} \frac{(\text{no. of CC posts}) \text{ emperor} \times (\text{length of reign}) \text{ emperor}}{\text{total number of years in the period}}$$

or

$$\frac{(34\,\text{CC posts} \times 19\,\text{years}) + (34 \times 21) + (35 \times 22) + (33 \times 19) + (36 \times 12)}{94} = 34$$

So on average there were 34 ducenariate posts available during the period 98-192. If the same equation is used for centenariate and sexagenariate posts, we derive the averages 38 and 35 respectively.[113]

The next step is to calculate the average number of offices held by each office-holder at a given level. In our period 29 procurators whose careers are shown in Table I held 77 ducenariate posts, or an average of 2.7 posts per man. The averages for centenariate and sexagenariate posts are 1.2 and 1.4 posts per man respectively.

If we then divide the number of posts per man into the number of posts at a given level, we arrive at the average number of posts open to new men being promoted into a given level. Thus in each notional appointment period some 25 sexagenariate posts

---

42ff.) Of course, since imperial Rome did not have the interest in modernization found in Latin America today, there was less motivation to seek the sort of mechanisms mentioned by Lipset.

113   C: $\dfrac{(29 \times 19) + (35 \times 21) + (37 \times 22) + (49 \times 19) + (49 \times 12)}{94} = 38$

LX: $\dfrac{(21 \times 19) + (35 \times 21) + (35 \times 22) + (42 \times 19) + (49 \times 12)}{94} = 35$

opened up to men who had not held a sexagenariate post before. Also some 32 centenariate posts, but only about thirteen ducenariate posts. The difference between the turnover rate of the sexagenariate and centenariate levels is not surprising, since in this period a significant group of *equites* went straight into the centenariate level without holding sexagenariate posts. Quite clearly, however, there was a bottleneck between the centenariate and ducenariate levels. Well under half of the 32 men leaving the centenariate level every notional period could have found their ways into the thirteen ducenariate posts available. These figures surely underestimate the bottleneck, for in addition to centenariate procurators, *primipilares bis* filled procuratorships at the ducenariate level. The conclusion seems reasonable: most procuratorial 'careers' stopped short of the ducenariate level and this usually entailed holding only two or perhaps three procuratorships.

The parallel figures for the period 192-249 A.D. are as follows: 36 ducenariate, 57 centenariate and 75 sexagenariate posts; an average of 1.8 ducenariate posts per holder, 1.8 centenariate posts per holder and 2.0 sexagenariate posts per holder. The situation has changed from the second century: about the same number of offices is held by each man at each level. But since the number of offices at the lower levels has increased, there is still a bottleneck. An average of 20 ducenariate, 32 centenariate and 38 sexagenariate posts are opening up in each notional appointment period. It would look as if the bottleneck were less severe except for the fact that Pflaum's catalogue suggests an increase in the number of *primipilares bis* advancing to ducenariate posts in this period.

The figures in this appendix are not meant to be exact, but the conclusion nevertheless emerges with some clarity. In the earlier period ducenariate procurators held significantly more posts at this level than procurators at the lower levels. There were not more ducenariate posts available and so, unless the tenure of ducenariate posts was much shorter than others, most procurators cannot have gone on from the centenariate to the ducenariate level.

4

The Roman imperial aristocracy

Seneca devoted the longest of his moral essays to the subject of *beneficia* — that is, reciprocal exchange. Concerning the importance of exchange to the fabric of society, the philosopher noted that it was a custom 'which more than any other binds together human society'.[1] Seneca's typology of *beneficia* comprised three categories: the protection of life and liberty for oneself and one's kin; *pecunia* and *honores* (less vital, but nevertheless 'useful' for a full life); and favors which can be described as frivolous luxuries.[2]

Studies of patronage in the Republic have concentrated on the political arena, especially the voting assemblies. Thus, when the selection of magistrates and the passage of legislation were effectively taken out of the hands of the assemblies, it has been thought by some that patronage should have disappeared.[3] But this view does not take account of two facts: political

1 *De Ben.* 1.4.2: 'De beneficiis dicendum est et ordinanda res, quae maxime humanam societatem adligat.'

2 *De Ben.* 1.11.2f. Michel provides a discussion of Seneca's *De Beneficiis* (*Gratuité*, 519ff.) and more generally of the economic and social significance of exchange (552ff.). His conclusion (553f. and 577) that the importance of reciprocal exchange declined differs from the conclusions reached in this chapter and so deserves several comments. (1) The reason given for the decline is that reciprocal exchange requires a social setting of a small, stable group such as the senatorial aristocracy of the Republic (578ff.). Michel's view of Republican exchange seems unrealistic: Cicero's letters prove that senators did not engage in reciprocal exchange solely with other senators, and the senate as a whole did not comprise a stable group from generation to generation (Michel cites Gelzer, *The Roman Nobility,* for evidence of the paucity of *novi homines*, but, as Gelzer himself points out, new men were rare only in the consulate, while 'in the lower magistracies, up to the praetorship, such new men were quite a common phenomenon' (35)). (2) Michel's view of the individualism of the Principate which obviated the need for *amicitiae* seems untenable in view of the evidence presented in this study (584). (3) His evidence for the decline lies partially in the frequency with which private friendships appear in the classical jurists on the one hand, and the Theodosian and Justinian Codes on the other (577) — a comparison whose value is vitiated by the general difference in the subject matter in the two bodies of material (see Honoré, *Tribonian,* 37ff.). (4) Michel's examples of the replacement of friendship by impersonal institutions (553f.) hardly indicate a revolution in social institutions: for instance, the public chairs instituted for teachers were limited in number and did not alter their need for friends and patrons (V. Nutton, 'Notes on Immunities', 55ff.). Michel's examples seem unimportant compared with the functions of *amicitia* described by Michel himself.

3 Pflaum, *Procurateurs,* 195, describes and rejects this view.

competition did shift to another arena but did not disappear, and political support was only one type of *beneficium*, as indicated by Seneca. Indeed, during the late Republic political patronage was less prominent than economic and social *beneficia* in the *commendationes* of Cicero.[4] As A. R. Hands has pointed out, the exchange of these latter favors often performed functions which are the concern of more formal institutions in the modern world.[5] For patronage to have disappeared, the entire nature of Roman society (not just politics) would have had to undergo a radical transformation.

In this chapter I shall endeavor to show that the exchange of economic and social goods and services within the imperial aristocracy continued largely unchanged from the end of the Republic. Further, our study of the imperial court has made it clear that political patronage also continued, though in a somewhat modified form: it has been left to this chapter to describe the resources of political patronage which remained in the hands of the imperial aristocracy. To some extent, the division between economic, social, and political is artificial: the upward mobility of municipal aristocrats and others seeking to make their ways in Rome required various combinations of economic and political aid. Nevertheless the analytical distinction is worth preserving for the sake of clarity and in order to emphasize the pervasiveness of reciprocal exchange in all aspects of life. The remainder of the chapter will be devoted to an analysis of what kinds of people were bound together in patron-client relationships and in what contexts these relationships grew.

The economic aspect of patronage can be described under four headings (not mutually exclusive): loans and debts, gifts, legacies, and property transactions. It is a commonplace that during the late Republic aristocrats, especially senators, frequently faced liquidity problems. Owing to the fact that most of their wealth was invested in land, senators could have serious difficulties raising the cash required for lavish games or electoral bribery. The problem was partially solved by loans (often without interest) between *amici*, which created social and political, as well as financial, obligations.[6] The letters of Cicero show that patronal and *amicitia* bonds were useful for aristocrats in their roles both as borrowers and as creditors. The orator seems to have turned to friends and clients for cash more frequently than to bankers, the most famous instance being the 800,000 sesterces loan from Caesar.[7] What is perhaps less often noted is Cicero's need to exercise influence as a creditor.

---

4 Of 100 Ciceronian *commendationes* two were concerned with electioneering and two with legal cases, while 48 requested financial *beneficia* and 36 ambiguously asked that the bearer be taken into the addressee's *amicitia*.

5 See above, p.14.

6 For the importance of land investment and the problem of liquidity, M.I. Finley, *The Ancient Economy*, 53. I. Shatzman, *Senatorial Wealth and Roman Politics*, 135–42, discusses senatorial loans and their political consequences.

7 Shatzman, *ibid.*, 416ff., provides a list of Cicero's debts and loans.

Taking an aristocratic debtor/friend to court in order to compel repayment was an extreme and unpopular solution which entailed disgrace for the debtor and the end of the friendship. Cicero rarely mentions it as an option in his many letters concerned with debts.[8] Instead, the creditor could turn to the debtor's kinsmen and mutual friends to apply social pressure; alternatively, he could attempt to transfer the debt to another creditor in a better position to exert social pressure.[9]

The heat of the political competition in the late Republic may have magnified the necessity for loans to advance senatorial careers.[10] Though the competition may have cooled in the Principate, the need for financial help from friends remained. Tacitus reports that Curtius Rufus, a new man said by Tiberius to be 'ex se natus', pursued a successful career with the financial help of friends.[11] Many of the expenses of a career remained: conspicuous consumption grew more extravagant in the first century A.D., games still had to be paid for, and even bribery, though it may have declined, did not disappear altogether.[12] Seneca tells of Iulius Graecinus who, when receiving money from friends to meet the expenses of his praetorian games, refused to accept anything from Fabius Persicus and Caninius Rebilus on the grounds that he did not want to be under obligation to men of such *infamia*. Graecinus' action illustrates the importance attached to the social bond created by financial *beneficia*.[13] That such *beneficia* were expected from patrons and friends is suggested by a letter of Fronto. Gavius Clarus, Fronto's senatorial protégé, was compelled by financial need to travel to Syria in order to secure a legacy. Fronto wrote a *commendatio* to Lucius Verus, then on campaign in the East, requesting all possible help for Clarus. If his own fortune were more abundant, Fronto claims, he would obviate the need for the trip by providing Clarus with the required assistance in performing his 'senatoris munia'.[14]

This sort of generosity contributed to an aristocrat's honor: it is noted in the

---

8 M. W. Frederiksen, 'Caesar, Cicero and the problem of debt', *JRS* 56 (1966), 128ff., reviews the harsh nature of Roman laws concerning debt, pointing out that 'for a man of standing it was vital to keep out of the courts as long as possible' (130).

9 Cicero, having troubles recovering his money from Faberius, tried to secure it by persuading Oppius and Balbus on the basis of *amicitia* to act as sponsors for the debt. They apparently refused. Frederiksen (*ibid.*, 131) gives the references with his discussion. Cicero had the tables turned when Terentia countered his delay in repaying the dowry by turning over the loan to Balbus (*Ad Att.* 12.12).

10 Frederiksen, 'The problem of debt', 128.

11 *Ann.* 11.21. Tacitus labels the financial support 'largitiones'. Whether Tacitus would have had precise details about the transactions seems doubtful. I suspect that as Rufus enjoyed increasing success, he would have been in a position to repay the *beneficia* (as Gavius Clarus repaid Pius as soon as he was able (Fronto, *Ad Verum Imp.* 2.7)). See also H.A., *Pius* 8.4.

12 Pliny, *Ep.* 6.19.

13 *De Ben.* 2.21.5f. In the case of Pius' aid to Clarus cited in note 11, the occasion of the expenditure was the Praetorian Games.

14 *Ad Verum Imp.* 2.7.

Historia Augusta in praise of Antoninus Pius that before reaching the throne he used his fortune to help others by lending at the low interest rate of four percent.[15] Pliny lent money to the father of an otherwise unknown Calvina. When the father died, Pliny informed Calvina that he would pay off all other creditors and then write off the debts so that Calvina could take up the inheritance without hesitation — an 'adfinitatis officium'.[16] In this case a loan was eventually turned into a gift. Moreover, the distinction between loan and gift is not always made clear in the sources cited above. In view of the general obligation to repay *beneficia*, we may suspect that the nature of the financial transactions between close friends may not always have been specified and firm: whether the money became a loan or a gift depended upon the friend's eventual ability to repay, as well as his reliability. Thus Martial in several poems satirized the way in which his friends invented excuses to avoid loans which may have turned out to be gifts to himself and others of doubtful ability to repay and without security.[17]

If social relationships provided avenues of approach to lenders, they also continued to be used to apply social pressure on debtors for repayment. For example, Pliny's protégé, Atilius Crescens, loaned an unspecified sum of money to Valerius Varus, who then died leaving his estate to a certain Maximus. Pliny undertook to meet his patronal obligation of protecting Crescens by writing to Priscus, a mutual friend: 'Varus' heir is our friend Maximus, and, as you are closer to him than I am, I ask, or rather demand in the name of our *amicitia*, that you see to it that Atilius recovers not only the principal but also the interest accumulated over the years.'[18] Default on the loan by Maximus would have been understood as an insult to Crescens and also to Pliny as his protector. On a larger scale, loans by Roman aristocrats to provincials continued in the Principate.[19] It seems reasonable to assume that *amici* and protégés in provincial posts were exploited for aid in enforcing repayment, just as Brutus attempted to exploit his friendship with Cicero to secure the extortionate interest from Salamis.[20] All of this evidence suggests that an aristocrat's financial success, or even survival, could depend on the wealth and influence of his friends and patrons.

Closely linked with loans, gifts were another form of status-raising generosity expected of aristocrats. Pliny's letters permit us to document for

---

15 *Pius* 2.8.
16 *Ep.* 2.4.
17 *Epig.* 2.30, 9.46, 12.25; in 4.15 Martial portrays himself evading a friend's request for a loan.
18 *Ep.* 6.8: 'Huius est heres Maximus noster, quem et ipse amo, sed coniunctius tu. Rogo ergo, exigo etiam pro iure amicitiae, cures ut Atilio meo salva sit non sors modo verum etiam usura plurimum annorum'.
19 Dio 62.2.1; see Griffin, *Seneca*, 231f.
20 D. Stockton, *Cicero: A Political Biography*, 239-42. Previously Cicero had himself asked Octavius, governor of Macedonia, to help Atticus with the collection of a debt (*Ad Att.* 2.1.12).

private individuals what public buildings and monuments attest for communities. Romatius Firmus, Pliny's family friend, received a gift of 300,000 sesterces which quadrupled the value of his estate and gave him the equestrian census.[21] Here the connection between patronage and the prospects for social mobility is clear: since Firmus' new status was a gift from Pliny, Pliny warned him to enjoy it with discretion. This is only one of several examples of Pliny helping clients either to achieve higher statuses or to maintain them with gifts. Metilius Crispus obtained a commission as a centurion with Pliny's support and also received 40,000 sesterces to purchase the necessary equipment.[22] On at least two occasions Pliny provided large monetary gifts for dowries to enable daughters of friends to enter into prestigious marriages in style.[23] These substantial gifts should be understood in a social context in which the honor of a man's kin, friends and dependents reflects on his own standing.[24]

Pliny's gifts worth tens and even hundreds of thousands of sesterces cannot have been normal, daily occurrences (though there is no reason to believe that the letters preserve evidence of all his large gifts). Martial's poems yield a glimpse of the ordinary gift-exchange which was part of Roman aristocratic life. Patrons and friends sent out gifts, especially during the Saturnalia and on birthdays. Advocates, poets and others who supplied services without fixed fees looked forward to these occasions for their reward.[25] The variety of gifts seems to have been enormous: Martial himself speaks of receiving, *inter alia*, an estate, a carriage, roof tiles, a fine cloak, silver plate, and a cup which he ridicules.[26] After the death of Domitian, Martial returned to his native Spain, the travelling expenses being paid by Pliny 'in recognition of their friendship and the verses which he composed about [Pliny]'.[27]

Gift-exchange is so pervasive in human cultures that its existence cannot in itself tell us anything very significant about Roman society. What is interesting is that the living standard of a number of people in Rome depended on gifts.[28]

---

21 *Ep.* 1.19. Duncan-Jones reviews Pliny's donations in *The Economy of the Roman Empire*, 27ff.
22 *Ep.* 6.25.2.
23 Pliny gave 100,000 sesterces to Calvina (*Ep.* 2.4.2) and 50,000 sesterces to Quintilianus' daughter (*Ep.* 6.32.2). For Cicero's praise of such gifts, *De Off.* 2.56.
24 For descriptions of such value systems in the modern Mediterranean world, see *Honour and Shame*, ed. J. G.Peristiany.
25 *Epig.* 1.98, 4.46, 4.88, 8.71, 12.72.
26 *Epig.* 11.18, 12.24, 7.36, 8.28, 8.51, 10.57, 12.36, and 8.33 for the ridiculed cup from the praetor Paulus.
27 Pliny, *Ep.* 3.21.2: 'dederam hoc amicitiae, dederam etiam versiculis quos de me composuit.'
28 White, 'Amicitia', 87ff., discusses gift exchange and reaches a different conclusion: 'for the most part, the gifts were not expected to be very large'. Several points should be made: (1) a Fronto passage is used to prove that gifts were in general supposed to be modest (87), but the quotation is taken out of context: Fronto explicitly says that his ideal of modest gifts is not followed in reality (*Epist. Graec.* 5.2); (2) the gifts discussed by White (90f.) are in fact of very

For others gifts (of, for example, ordinary foodstuffs) were of more symbolic than real value, expressions of clients' loyalty. The constant exchange of such gifts with friends and dependents beyond the kinship group served as a reminder and reinforcement of differences of status, as we shall see later.[29]

As we have already noted with respect to the emperor, legacies constituted the final gifts in exchange relationships. In Cicero's day legacies made important contributions to men's fortunes.[30] After the end of the lucrative conquests they must have become relatively more important: most aristocrats could no longer make their fortunes by the capture of booty and they turned instead to the capture of legacies.[31] Notoriously, Seneca accumulated enormous wealth after his return from exile. Suillius Rufus levelled the accusation that this fortune derived from usury in Italy and the provinces, and from inheritances from the childless in Rome — an accusation not at all implausible for an associate of the emperor.[32] Most would not have been as successful as Seneca, but legacies nevertheless made notable contributions to their estates. Pliny was named in a number of wills; one inheritance alone was valued at the senatorial census requirement.[33] It will be remembered that Gavius Clarus travelled to Syria to collect an inheritance which Fronto suggests he needed to keep up his senatorial lifestyle.[34]

A man 'captured' legacies by entering into *amicitia* or patron-client relations with the wealthy, and especially the childless. When Aper lists the advantages of advocacy in the *Dialogus*, he suggests that the effective orator can develop a following of people of all ranks owing to his talent and not to his wealth or lack of children. The implication is that *amici* and *clientes* naturally congregated around the childless hoping for a legacy.[35] The practice was widely condemned. Seneca wrote: 'I call the man *ingratus*, who sits at the bedside of a sick man about to make his will and finds room for any thought of

---

substantial value (gifts in kind need not be token, as indicated by Juvenal's account of Naevolus' assets in which the sort of silver plate received by Martial is included (9.140f.)); (3) of the three ways listed by Martial (somewhat facetiously) in which a man immigrating to Rome might try to earn a living, all involved the sort of exchange discussed in this chapter (*Epig.* 3,38); further, Martial's and Juvenal's barbed comments about the meanness of the gifts from patrons and friends would have had little point if the exchange were expected to be of only token gifts.

29 That the imperial freedman Parthenius was able not only to forward Martial's poems to Domitian but also to give the poet a fine cloak gave proof of a superiority which conflicted with their relative standings in legal *ordines*. (For status dissonance of this kind, P. R. C. Weaver, 'Social mobility in the early Roman Empire: the evidence of the imperial freedmen and slaves', *P&P* 37 (1967), 3-20.)

30 Shatzman, *Senatorial Wealth*, 409ff.

31 M. I. Finley, 'Empire in the Greco-Roman world', *G&R* 25 (1978), 11.

32 Tacitus, *Ann.* 13.42; see Griffin, *Seneca*, 289.

33 Duncan-Jones, *Economy of the Roman Empire*, 25ff.

34 See above, p.121.

35 Tacitus, *Dial.* 6; see also Seneca, *De Ben.* 1.14.3.

an inheritance or a legacy. He should do everything which a good friend mindful of his duty ought to do: but if hope of gain haunts his mind, he is a fisher of legacies who is dropping his hook.'[36] Pliny later echoed these sentiments about generosity in the hope of final profit. Apparently not even the imperial family was immune from it: Marcus Aurelius' great aunt Matidia disappointed all those paying court to her fortune by leaving it to others.[37] Such legacy-hunting provided rich material for the humor of Martial: in one epigram, for instance, Charinus is asked to stop opening his will and rewriting it since the poet can no longer afford to send gifts each time; and in another Oppianus is chided for sending a gift to Salanus after the death of his only son and heir.[38]

Paradoxically, to hunt legacies was base, yet to receive legacies was an honor, an expression of esteem from friends and kin. Thus Seneca, only a few pages after condemning legacy-hunting, suggested that gratitude for services rendered was expressed most selflessly in *testamenta*, since there could be no ulterior motives.[39] Pliny's pride in being named in wills along with Tacitus is unmistakable.[40] As proof of Antoninus Pius' *pietas* towards his family, it is noted that he was honored by legacies from distant, as well as close relatives.[41]

One final financial aspect should not be overlooked: the use of patrons, clients and friends in property transactions. When Cicero sought an estate as a site for a memorial to Tullia, he used Atticus to contact friends who might be persuaded to sell.[42] In his role as protector of Suetonius, Pliny similarly helped to locate an estate suitable for a literary protégé, and then used his influence to ensure that it was sold at a reasonable price. Later, the sister of Pliny's patron, Corellius Rufus, indicated to Pliny that she wanted to purchase an estate near Comum. When Pliny inherited a suitable piece of property, he sold it to her as a favor at 20% below the market price.[43] In addition to *beneficia* such as these, gift-exchange between *amici* seems also to have provided a kind of fire

---

36 Pliny, *Ep.* 9.30; Seneca, *De Ben.* 4.20.3: 'ingratum voco, qui aegro adsidit, quia testamentum facturus est, cui de hereditate aut de legato vacat cogitare. Faciat licet omnia, quae facere bonus amicus et memor officii debet: si animo eius observatur spes lucri, captator est et hamum iacit.'

37 Fronto, *Ad amic.* 1.14.

38 *Epig.* 5.39 and 6.62. In 1.99 and 4.51 Martial writes of characters whose fortunes were radically altered by inheritance. He scorns those paying court to the childless as well as the childless who accept gifts from the self-interested in 4.56, 6.63, 7.66, 8.27, 9.9, 9.48, 11.44, 11.55, and 12.10. How to treat Martial's poetry as historical evidence is, of course, difficult, but the frequent recurrence of the theme, other corroborating sources and the inherent plausibility indicate that Martial is working with a realistic theme in this case.

39 *De Ben.* 4.22.1; see Tacitus, *Ann.* 16.17.5 for evidence that even legacies could have ulterior motives.

40 *Ep.* 7.20.6.

41 H.A., *Pius* 1.9

42 D. R. Shackleton Bailey, *Cicero's Letters to Atticus*, App. 3.

43 *Ep.* 1.24 and 7.11.

insurance for an aristocrat's property: Juvenal cynically suggests that the wealth of gifts a rich man might receive from friends after the burning of his house might lead some to suspect that he set the fire himself.[44]

Altogether, this evidence suggests that loans, debts, gifts and property transactions should be understood in the context of aristocratic exchange relationships and Roman values of honor and prestige. Unfortunately, these examples cannot show just how 'embedded' financial affairs were in the social fabric. Thus, any suggestion about the overall effect of patronage on the economy must be conjectural. But it may be useful to keep in mind the hypothesis of Pitt-Rivers regarding early modern Spain. He has pointed out that the development of 'the spirit of capitalism' (i.e., a mentality interested in capital accumulation and productive investment) is antithetical to and hindered by patronal values which encourage the utilization of wealth primarily as a means of social domination in personal relationships.[45]

The preceding discussion makes obvious the artificiality of separating economic and social exchange. As we have suggested, the patron's economic *beneficia* were often repaid by increased social prestige. These social aspects of patronal exchange deserve fuller consideration.

The most basic premise from which the Romans started was that honor and prestige derived from the power to give what others needed or wanted.[46] Competition for honor and the resulting social subordination were natural parts of life. This is apparent in Pliny's letters to his clients. One commentator speaks of the 'Roman lack of delicacy' displayed in Pliny's letter to Calvina concerning his loans to her father and his gifts to her.[47] While Pliny's language may shock modern egalitarian sensibilities, it is much less clear that it would have been offensive to Calvina, living in a patronal society in which no pretense was made about equality.[48]

44 Juvenal, *Sat.* 3.220; also Martial, *Epig.* 3.52.

45 J. Pitt-Rivers, *The Fate of Shechem, or the Politics of Sex*, 36. Pitt-Rivers' view cannot be applied schematically and our evidence does not permit us to work out the precise effects of patronal values.

46 Pitt-Rivers (*ibid.*, chs. 1-2) distinguishes between honor = precedence and honor = virtue. Seneca and other Stoics propounded the latter view, arguing that a man's honor depended not on external factors such as wealth, but on virtuous character. The evidence cited in this chapter shows that in fact the former equation was dominant in Roman society, or rather that the two were confused (the ability to give to friends and clients was equated with virtue). Such 'confusion of the meanings of honour = precedence and honour = virtue served the function of social integration by crediting the rulers with a claim to esteem and a charter to rule. But it is a function which is fulfilled only as long as the confusion is not recognized as such' (47). One way of conceptualizing the cause of rising tensions in the reigns of Caligula, Nero, Domitian and Commodus is that the emperor's distribution of *beneficia* to unworthy favorites came to seem irresponsible and the confusion was no longer possible.

47 Sherwin-White, *Letters of Pliny*, 149.

48 Boissevain, 'When the saints go marching out', in *Patrons and Clients*, ed. Gellner and Waterbury, 88f., points out that there was no stigma attached to being a client in Malta (for an

The social consequences of patronal exchange are made clear by several corollaries of the above premise. First, in return for a *beneficium* one of the client's duties was to publicize it, along with other honorable acts by the patron.[49] While quaestor in Asia, Egnatius Marcellinus performed an act of financial honesty which the emperor and senate thought noteworthy. Since the equestrian Maturus Arrianus had previously commended his *amicus* Marcellinus to Pliny, Pliny sent news of the glorious deed back to his protégé Arrianus in Northern Italy. Pliny recommended that Arrianus add his congratulations to the rest: 'everyone who is influenced by thoughts of *fama* and *gloria* takes great pleasure in words of praise and appreciation even from lesser men (*minoribus*) [like yourself]'.[50] In one of Fronto's letters we find an even clearer example of reputation-building as an element of exchange. After Avidius Cassius' successes on campaign in the East about 165, his tribune Iunius Maximus returned to Rome with news of the victory. In addition to the public announcement, Maximus fulfilled his *officium* to his *amicus* by making the rounds to private houses with word of the exploits in order to boost Cassius' reputation further. In a *commendatio* Fronto told Cassius of this and concluded: 'he is worthy to enjoy your esteem and to be enhanced by your patronage (*suffragiis*). You will add to your own glory in the measure that you build the *dignitas* of your eulogist.'[51]

A client, by publicizing his patron's *beneficia*, also advertised his own inferiority. If the client was not attempting to compete for honor as an equal, the acknowledgement of subordination need not have presented any problems (Martial seems to have had no qualms about writing verses about his dependence). On the other hand, the response of *amici* in competition might be quite different. Aristocrats sometimes rejected gifts from those whose equality or superiority they refused to concede, as the action of Iulius Graecinus illustrates.[52] If compelled by need to accept, Seneca tells us, some men refused to acknowledge their debt publicly, and so showed themselves to be *ingrati*.[53] Such men may also have attempted to repay their debts immediately and so to absolve themselves of any obligation.[54] Finally, Seneca indicates that some benefactors preferred to forego repayment rather than

ordinary man) until recently, when the old patronal values have radically altered or disappeared.

49 Seneca, *De Ben.* 2.11.2.

50 *Ep.* 4.12: 'Omnes enim, qui gloria famaque ducuntur, mirum in modum adsensio et laus a minoribus etiam profecta delectat'. Another instance of Pliny's 'lack of delicacy', or more proof that the identification of some men as *minores* and others as *superiores* was part of the natural order of things?

51 *Ad Amic.* 1.6: 'Dignus est quem diligas et suffragiis tuis ornes. Tuae propriae gloriae addideris, quantum dignitati praedicatoris tu adstruxeris.'

52 Seneca, *De Ben.* 2.21.5.

53 *De Ben.* 2.23.1.

54 *De Ben.* 6.42f.

accept the return and hence sacrifice the symbol of their superiority.[55] These passages make it clear that, given the basic premise above, the exchange of *beneficia* had a direct bearing on the dynamics of social status in aristocratic circles.

In the Republic the client's presence at the morning salutation was a symbol of respect for his patron and a means of honoring him. Seneca, Martial, Tacitus and Juvenal attest that this most public manifestation of honor and prestige continued in the Principate.[56] Attending a patron at the *salutatio* and throughout the day during his public business was one of several ways listed by Martial in one epigram for a municipal migrating to Rome to earn his subsistence. In his day the going rate for attendance at the salutation was 100 quadrantes.[57] Pliny tells of how two of his *nomenculatores* were paid three denarii each to add their applause in a legal hearing.[58] *Clientes* were also paid to attend their patron's dinners and suffer his abuse as entertainment.[59]

---

55 *De Ben.* 2.17.6.

56 Seneca, *Brev. Vitae* 14.3f.; at least twenty of Martial's epigrams mention *salutationes*, e.g., 2.18. 3.36, 3.38, 3.46; when Seneca retired from political life, he drove away the 'coetus salutantium' (Tacitus, *Ann.* 14.56); Juvenal, *Sat.* 1.127 and 3.124; Columella, *De Re Rust.* 1. praef. 9; *CIL* VI. 21975.

57 *Epig.* 3.7 and 8.42. See R. Marache, 'La revendication sociale chez Martial et Juvenal', *RCCM* 3 (1961), 30-67; J. Le Gall, 'La "nouvelle plèbe" et la sportule quotidienne', in *Mélanges d'archéologie et d'histoire offerts à A. Piganiol*, 1449-53; J. Gérard, *Juvenal*, ch. 6. All three scholars attempt to trace a development in patron-client relationships. In particular, Gérard (following Le Gall) argues that the position of the client gradually worsened and the relationship became more formal and regulated, until in the time of Martial (and not before) *sportulae* in the form of money were distributed daily at the *salutatio*. The case appears to be doubtful for the following reasons. (1) It rests entirely on an argument from silence (i.e., there is no mention of a daily distribution of *sportulae* by Seneca or earlier authors). But this silence is best explained by the fact that authors such as Seneca and Cicero were writing from a different social vantage point and in a different genre from Martial and Juvenal. This explanation must carry some weight in view of the fact that no other authors contemporary with Martial and Juvenal, but in a social position similar to Seneca's, mention the daily distribution of money to clients (even in passages complaining of the drudgery of *salutationes* — e.g., Tacitus, *Dial.* 11 or Quintilian, *Inst.* 12.11.18). (2) There is a passage, missed by Gérard, which seems to hint at the distribution of money at *salutationes* during the era of Seneca: Columella (1. praef. 9) denigrates the *mercenarii salutatores* who hang around the *limina* of the rich. (3) Large crowds of clients attended formally regulated *salutationes* from the late second century B.C. It not clear how Gérard thinks the clients were rewarded for their efforts before the institution of *sportulae*. Whether in the form of money or not, there must surely have been some concrete reward to encourage clients to endure the drudgery.

58 *Ep.* 2.14.6. Several of Martial's epigrams (3.7, 14, 30 and 60; cf. Suetonius, *Dom.* 7.1) indicate that the distribution of *sportulae* to clients was briefly suppressed in the reign of Domitian. Gérard, *Juvenal*, 182, argues that the practice was permitted again only in the reign of Trajan on the grounds that to believe otherwise would mean that Domitian 'se soit donné le démenti de revenir sur sa décision'. Yet Domitian was persuaded to reverse other policies (Millar, *Emperor*, 391f.), and several of Martial's epigrams written during the later years of Domitian's reign (8.42, 50 and 9.100) speak of giving *sportulae* as a contemporary practice.

59 Martial, *Epig.* 4.68; see also Herodian 2.6.7 for another example. For the *beneficium* of housing, *Dig.* 9.3.5.1.

Martial would have us believe that the life of a *cliens* was a rough and tiring one.[60]

Discussions of *salutationes* at aristocratic houses usually concern the lower-class *clientes*.[61] What is less often noted is the attendance of aristocrats paying their respects. Martial writes of a senator out in the early morning 'treading innumerable thresholds' in the hope of securing a consulship, and both he and Juvenal complain of the unfair competition created by senators for the ordinary clients.[62] These passages might be attributed to comic exaggeration, were it not for other evidence. In a letter to Lucilius, Seneca casually mentions that a distinguished *eques* Cornelius Senecio customarily called on him in the early morning.[63] Plutarch, with reference to provincials seeking governorships and procuratorships in Rome, talks of men who 'grow old haunting the doors of other men's houses' — clearly a reference to *salutationes*.[64] The survival of the custom into the third century is proven by an unambiguous passage from Dio: before his fall in 205 the praetorian prefect Plautianus invited friendly senators into his house in the morning 'in advance of the general throng of those who came to pay Plautianus their respects'. This attendance was later used as proof of guilt by association, with painful or even fatal results for some of the senators.[65] Clearer evidence could not be hoped for of the continuation not only of patronage but also of the basic customs associated with it.[66]

60 *Epig.* 10.70, 74 and 82.
61 In addition to the works cited in note 57, modern discussions include L. Friedlaender, *Roman Life and Manners*, vol. 1, 195f.; Fustel de Coulanges, *Les origines du système féodal*, 225-35; A. von Premerstein, *RE* IV. 53f.
62 Martial, *Epig.* 12.26; 10.10; and Juvenal, *Sat.* 1.117.
63 *Ep. ad Luc.* 101.3. In *De Brev. Vitae* 20.1 Seneca says that senators pursuing magistracies have to endure 'mille indignitates': this may be a reference to the humiliations of attending salutations, mentioned earlier in the essay (14.3).
64 *Moralia* 814D: 'οἱ πολλοὶ γηράσκουσι πρὸς ἀλλοτρίαις θύραις'. Pliny, *Ep.* 2.9 may also refer to *salutationes*.
65 Dio 76.5.3f.: 'πρὸ τῶν ἄλλων τῶν ἀσπαζομένων αὐτόν'. Tacitus, *Ann.* 3.55 is ambiguous, if not misleading, about salutations.
66 Gagé, *Les classes sociales dans l'Empire romain*, 128, argues that emperors could not tolerate the continuation of clientèles attached to senatorial houses, but offers no evidence for his view. It is far from clear that such clientèles would have been felt to represent a serious threat to emperors who had the Praetorian Guard at hand to control disturbances. Nor is Yavetz's interpretation of the Augustan legislation about manumission as an attempt to limit the size of aristocratic clientèles convincing, since only testamentary manumission was limited (*Princeps and Plebs*, 96f.). Gérard, *Juvenal*, 190f., asserts that emperors (especially Trajan) showed great interest in regulating clientèles, but the evidence hardly supports the case. Martial, *Epig.* 10.34.5-6 appeal to Trajan to improve the lot of the *cliens* and say nothing of regulations (pace Gérard); Pliny, *Ep.* 10.116-117 show no great interest on the part of Trajan, as is argued, and in any case concern the mass distribution of money at a provincial wedding, not the customs associated with morning salutations in the city of Rome. Domitian's temporary measure is the only secure example of an attempt to regulate patron-client relationships by the emperor and did not produce serious change.

In our discussion in the first chapter we noted that legal services constituted part of an aristocrat's stock of *beneficia*. From the early Republic it was one of the patron's traditional responsibilities to provide legal protection for his clients, and this continued in the Empire to be a basic *officium* expected by the client.[67] From the advocate's point of view, Aper's remarks in the *Dialogus* make it clear that the profits accruing to a successful orator can only be understood in the context of a patronal society: effective oratory allowed one to build a prestigious and financially profitable following by protecting *amici* and *clientes*.[68]

Patronal help with a legal hearing could also take the form of influencing the judge. Tacitus remarked on Tiberius' interference in the courts which limited the influence and so the *libertas* of the *potentes*.[69] In theory, then, emperors could use their powers (e.g., of hearing appeals) to usurp the legal *beneficia* of the aristocracy. But without the means for systematically reviewing the bulk of cases heard by governors and magistrates in Rome, the emperor's real capacity to suppress this sort of patronage must have been limited. Moreover, there is doubt about just how serious was the emperor's interest in suppression: there seems to have been no special policy for the selection of appeal cases towards this or any other end. To the extent that the emperor spent his time listening to cases characterized by their 'routine nature and often insignificant subject-matter', he infringed little on the sum of the legal jurisdiction exercised by Roman aristocrats throughout the empire.[70] As we shall see in our study of provincial patronage, Fronto's letters written in an attempt to influence governors in their judicial capacities differ very little from Cicero's.[71]

Even if he had wished to do so, the emperor, owing to the lack of adequate, centralized, hierarchical administrative machinery, was not in a position to usurp most of the aristocracy's economic and legal patronage resources. Obviously the situation was different with regard to political patronage because of the discontinuity between Republican and imperial political institutions.

Nevertheless, even in the realm of politics and administration the emperor did not usurp all *beneficia*: senatorial and equestrian officials were often left (*de facto* or *de iure*) to appoint subordinate officials. Ordinary consuls were apparently allowed to select their quaestors from the group of those elected.

---

67 See above p. 29; J. Crook, *Law and Life of Rome*, 93.
68 See above, p. 29 and the remark in note 100 about Neuhauser's claims about the declining role of the orator.
69 *Ann.* 1.75. See Garnsey, *Social Status and Legal Privilege*, 208f.
70 Millar, *Emperor*, 240. Suetonius does say that Domitian rescinded *ambitiosas sententias* of the Centumviral Court (*Dom.* 8.1).
71 *Ad Amic.* 1.1, 2.7, 2.8. See de Ste Croix, 'Suffragium', 43f., and for a full discussion of the exercise of *gratia*, J. M. Kelly, *Roman Litigation*, ch. 2, esp. 51-5, 59f.

On the mistaken guess that Minicius Fundanus would be appointed consul the following year Pliny wrote to him, asking that his friend's son Asinius Bassus be appointed consul's quaestor. Pliny described the rank and character of Bassus' family so that Fundanus would know that by the *beneficium* of the appointment he would 'put under obligation' a large and numerous family whose prestige would make it an honor to have a member as his quaestor.[72] Consuls and praetors also had a more junior position at their disposal: they, like governors, appointed *praefecti fabrum* during the first and second centuries. While the duties of the post are uncertain, its nature as a *beneficium* is clear from the fact that some of the appointments were honorary sinecures.[73]

Most of Pliny's *commendationes* concerning appointments were sent to provincial governors (both equestrian and senatorial). Though the emperor's formal approval was required, these officials were permitted to select their own civilian staff, including legates (in the case of proconsuls), assessors, *praefecti fabrum*, and *adiutores*.[74] Fronto gives some indication of the kind of people whom governors selected: after being chosen proconsul of Asia, 'I took active steps to enlist the help of my friends in all that concerned the ordering of the province. Relations and friends of mine, of whose loyalty and integrity I was assured, I called from home to assist me.' Fronto also called upon *familiares* from Alexandria, Cilicia and Mauretania.[75] He had no sons, but other proconsuls with sons seem typically to have taken them out to their provinces as legates.[76] This patronal custom of provincial government remained unchanged from the Republic.

As de Ste Croix points out, the letter of Fronto illustrates 'what a vast amount of patronage a high official such as a provincial governor had it in his power to bestow'.[77] But great as his resources may have been as a proconsul, Fronto did not possess as large a stock of *beneficia* as governors with army commands who were able to fill equestrian military positions. Pliny wrote

72 *Ep.* 4.15; see Sherwin-White, *Letters of Pliny*, 291 for the dating.
73 For a discussion of *praefecti fabrum*, B. Dobson, 'The Praefectus Fabrum in the Early Principate', *Britain and Rome*, ed. M. Jarrett and B. Dobson, 61ff. and esp. 68 for sinecures.
74 The fact that emperors *could* have made these subordinate appointments themselves but chose not to do so suggests that emperors did not pursue a conscious policy of minimizing the patronal resources of senators.
75 *Ad Pium* 8: 'Post illa quaecumque ad instruendam provinciam adtinerent, quo facilius a me tanta negotia per amicorum copias obirentur, sedulo praeparavi. Propinquos et amicos meos, quorum fidem et integritatem cognoveram, domo accivi'. (Loeb translation.) For other evidence for the appointment of friends to staff positions, Lucian's *Apology* and Pliny, *Ep.* 10.51 and 10.94 (on the latter compare Syme, *Tacitus*, 779 with Sherwin-White's cautious position in *Letters of Pliny*, 690); for appointments to legateships, W. Eck, 'Prokonsularen Legationen, 24ff.
76 B. E. Thomasson, *Die Statthalter der römischen Provinzen Nordafrikas von Augustus bis Diocletianus*, 2, 138-42 for a list of the legates of the proconsul of Africa: six were sons of proconsuls.
77 'Suffragium', 40.

bluntly to his friend Priscus: 'your command of a large army gives you a plentiful source of benefits to confer and your tenure has been long enough for you to have provided for your own friends'.[78] Thus Pliny suggested that it was only reasonable for Priscus now to bestow one of his *beneficia* on Pliny's friend Voconius Romanus. The tone of the passage suggests that equestrian *militiae* were assumed to constitute patronal resources to be dispensed first to protégés and then to friends of friends.

The way in which these appointments could be used as rewards for clients is best illustrated by the Gallic inscription known as the Thorigny Marble.[79] The stone was erected in 238 in honor of T. Sennius Sollemnis by the *tres provinciae Galliae* and was inscribed on three faces. The main face contained the dedication to Sollemnis with an account of his benefactions and honors, which included being the *cliens* of two governors of Lugdunensis — Claudius Paulinus, a leading senator, and Aedinius Iulianus, later praetorian prefect. On the other two faces were inscribed letters concerning Sollemnis written by these two men. From the letters we can reconstruct the sequence of events which led to Sollemnis' appointment as tribune under Claudius Paulinus during his governorship of lower Britain. The first is a *commendatio* sent by Iulianus, now praetorian prefect, to the current equestrian governor of Lugdunensis, Badius Comnianus. Iulianus recommends Sollemnis as a useful friend for any governor with the following explanation: during Iulianus' administration accusations against the previous governor Paulinus were discussed in the provincial assembly with a view to a possible prosecution; Sollemnis announced that as a delegate he was not authorized by his city to initiate charges against Paulinus — on the contrary, his fellow citizens had only praise for the former governor; as a result, the charges were dropped; 'this man I began to love and to approve of more and more'. As might be expected, Sollemnis' reward from Paulinus was more concrete. In the other inscribed letter Paulinus, now governor of Britain, notified Sollemnis of his appointment as *tribunus semestris*, which would take effect when the position became vacant. Paulinus sent ahead the salary of 25,000 sesterces, together with numerous luxurious gifts. (The association of gifts and offices is very suggestive.)

The influence of patronage on the distribution of these *militiae* seems often to be overlooked in discussions and comparisons of equestrian careers where comments about patronage in early careers are largely reserved for *praefecti fabrum*. In his catalogue of procuratorial careers, for example, Pflaum often remarks on the special senatorial patronage signalled by the latter office.[80]

---

78 *Ep.* 2.13.2: 'Regis exercitum amplissimum: hinc tibi beneficiorum larga materia, longum praeterea tempus, quo amicos tuos exornare potuisti.' (Loeb translation.)

79 *CIL* XIII. 3162; see Pflaum, *Le Marbre de Thorigny*.

80 Pflaum, *Procurateurs*, 196f., provides a list of procurators who had served as *praefecti*

Jarrett, in his study of African *equites*, wrote: 'prospects for the man appointed as *praefectus fabrum* appear to have been extremely good, due no doubt to the senatorial patronage implicit in the appointment'.[81] The implication seems to have been drawn that *praefecti fabrum* were somehow specially favored with regard to patronage. Yet the figures adduced for Africans in the emperor's service show that *praefecti fabrum* were hardly more successful in proceeding to higher offices than the whole group of equestrian officers.[82] Moreover, if the careers of the *praefecti* in Pflaum's catalogue are compared with other procuratorial careers, it becomes clear that the *praefecti* constitute a representative cross-section, no more and no less successful than other procurators.[83] In short, like the office of *praefectus fabrum*, equestrian *militiae* and other offices should be understood as signs of favor in as much as they were obtained through patronage.

At first sight these first-order resources left to senators and equestrians by the emperor might seem relatively unimportant owing to the subordinate nature of the positions. But their significance should not be underestimated. The single most common request in the corpus of *commendationes* extant from the principate is for equestrian *militiae*.[84] More than half of those pursuing equestrian procuratorial careers in the first and second centuries began as equestrian officers, and so as a result of distributing *militiae*, senatorial governors (and their senatorial friends who sent the *commendationes*) established patronage bonds with potentially influential *equites* very early in their careers.[85] Even those equestrians who held only one *militia* and then returned to their provincial cities could be useful clients, as the case of Sollemnis shows. Moreover, the *commendationes* suggest that the

fabrum. For typical comments about the office see *Carrières*, 295 ('*praefectus fabrum*, charge toujours avantageuse, qui assure de la protection du senateur influent'), 344, 510, 555, 707. In *Procurateurs*, Pflaum argues that the post was abolished by Septimius Severus. The circularity of his argument should be noted: his evidence lies in the fact that no *praefectus fabrum* appears after the reign of Commodus; on the other hand, in his catalogue he gives the reign of Severus as a *terminus ante quem* for the prefectures of M. Veserius Iucundianus (no. 209) and M. Porcius Aper (no. 187) because Severus abolished the post.

81 M. Jarrett, 'The African contribution to the Imperial Civil Service', *Historia* 12 (1963), 222.

82 *Ibid*. Seven of sixteen *praefecti* became equestrian officers and four of the seven (57%) succeeded to procuratorships, while nine of eighteen (50%) of all African equestrian officers of the same period succeeded to procuratorships — an insignificant difference with such a small sample.

83 For *praefecti fabrum* pursuing procuratorial careers in the second century the average number of sexagenariate offices held before advancement was 1.0 and the number held before promotion to ducenariate posts was 1.8. Compare these figures with the similar averages for all procurators: 0.75 and 1.9, respectively.

84 *Ep*. 3.2, 3.8 (indirect evidence of a recommendation), 4.4, 7.22, and Fronto, *Ad Amic*. 1.5. In *Ep*. 3.8 and 7.22 Pliny apparently secured the tribunate without naming his candidate to the governor — an indication of how little consideration was given to merit.

85 Pflaum, *Procurateurs*, 259. In the third century slightly fewer than half of the procurators of known background served in *militiae*.

appointment of a client constituted a *beneficium* for his recommender who
was also put under obligation.[86] Thus, it is one more type of favor whose
exchange cemented *amicitia* bonds between leading aristocrats. In his
recommendation of Faustinianus for an equestrian post under Claudius
Iulianus, Fronto wrote: 'if I had had any children also of the male sex and these
were of age for the discharge of military duties at this particular time, when you
are administering a province with an army, my children should serve under
you. This that each of us would desire will almost be fulfilled. For I love
Faustinianus, the son of my friend Statianus, not less, and I desire him to be
loved no less, than if he were my own son.'[87] It seems, then, that the exchange
of such favors for clients was thought to play a role in aristocratic friendships.

These subordinate appointments (the first-order resources) were only part
of a leading aristocrat's political *beneficia*. Often a patron's efficacy depended
more on his second-order resources, i.e., his connections with those who
directly controlled the appointments. It has already been suggested that,
though the emperor took control of many political resources, he permitted his
senatorial and other friends to act as his brokers for the distribution of these
beneficia.[88] Needless to say, the most important single criterion governing a
patron's power was his influence on imperial grants. The *commendationes*
cited above indicate that another element in a patron's second-order resources
was his links with other leading members of the aristocracy. While a senator
could at most hope to be of direct assistance to his clients in one province at a
time for several years of his life, through powerful *amici* who could be called
upon for favors he could influence decisions throughout the empire. Fronto
perhaps never enjoyed any first-order political resources as a governor, yet he
was able to secure appointments and to influence judgements from North
Africa to lower Germany, and so was cultivated assiduously by a clientèle.[89]

With their economic, legal and political resources Roman aristocrats bound to
themselves large clientèles of men from all *ordines*. The composition of the
lower-class clients who lined up outside the doors of the great houses is
impossible to determine. Fortunately, however, since the *commendationes*
contained as a standard element a description of the patron's relationship with
his protégé, we are able to describe the composition of this part of the
clientèle.[90] From Pliny's and Fronto's letters emerge several main social

86 Pliny, *Ep.* 3.2.6 and 4.4.2.
87 *Ad Amic.* 1.5: 'si mihi liberi etiam virilis sexus nati fuissent, eorumque aetas hoc potissimum
    tempore ad munia militaria fungenda adolesceret, quo tempore tu provinciam cum exercitu
    administrares, uti sub te mei liberi stipendia mererent. Non longe aberit quin hoc, quod
    uterque cuperemus, evenerit. Nam Faustinianum Statiani mei filium, non minus diligo neque
    minus eum diligi cupio, quam si ex me genitus esset'. (Loeb translation.)
88 See above, pp. 74 f.
89 Fronto, *Ad Amic.* 2.8.
90 Pflaum, *Thorigny Marbre*, 22.

groups from which patrons frequently drew their protégés: kin, fellow *municipes*, literary colleagues and students, and *contubernales* in military service.

Exchange between kin is normally excluded from patronage studies by anthropologists on the grounds that it is governed by a set of mores different from those of patronage relationships.[91] This rationale is justified in the case of Rome for close relatives: a father bestowed *beneficia* on his son *qua* father, not *qua* patron. On the other hand, as the kin became more distant and their obligations as kin less strong, close relationships between distant relatives may have been conceived of in terms of the roles of patron and protégé.[92] To discover at what degree of kinship this change may have occurred would require a full study of kinship roles and exchange which lies outside the scope of this study. However, because of our interest in the distribution of *beneficia* and social mobility, the importance of kinship ties deserves a few rudimentary remarks.

A number of successful, prominent aristocrats of the Principate are known to have benefited from the help of relatives, especially affines. A common avenue of entry into the Roman aristocracy for municipals was by marriage links with aristocratic families. Seneca and his brothers enjoyed the support of their aunt's husband, the Egyptian prefect C. Galerius, and the initial impetus for the younger Pliny's career came from his maternal uncle.[93] Parallels to these two examples can be discovered in the epigraphic evidence.[94] With entry into the aristocracy secured, families might hope for further marriage ties which would provide 'decus ac robur' — the words of Tacitus for Agricola's marriage which could also have described his own.[95] In Stein's *Der römische Ritterstand* appear other examples of marriage bonds successfully negotiated by equestrians with senatorial families.[96] We would like to have quantitative evidence to assign a relative importance to this type of bond in the patronage network, but it is, of course, lacking. These examples, however, should warn against the overemphasis on relationships arising from common literary and cultural interests found in some recent work.

Syme in his discussion of the entry of new families into the aristocracy lays stress on the patronage ties formed between men of common municipality or region.[97] A survey of Pliny's clientèle indicates that the emphasis is properly

---

91 Gellner, 'Patrons and clients', in *Patrons and Clients*, ed. Gellner and Waterbury, 2.
92 See Evelyne Patlagean, *Pauvreté économique et pauvreté sociale à Byzance, 4ᵉ-7ᵉ siècles*, 119.
93 Seneca, *Cons. Helv.* 19.2 (see Griffin, *Seneca*, 43ff.); Syme, *Tacitus*, 60.
94 See below, pp. 200 ff.
95 *Agric.* 6 and 9.7.
96 E.g., C. Betitius Pietas (221f.), C. Flavonius Anicianus Sanctus (314), M. Ulpius Carminius Claudianus (315), C. Fufidius Atticus (319).
97 *Tacitus*, 591, 595, 606.

placed.[98] His letter to Romatius Firmus announcing a gift of 300,000 sesterces opened: 'you and I both come from the same town, went to the same school, and have been friends since we were children. Your father was a close friend of my mother and uncle, and a friend to me too, as far as our difference in age allowed; so there are sound and serious reasons why I ought to try to improve your position.'[99] That Pliny took his patronal responsibility towards friends of common municipality or region seriously is seen clearly in a list of other such protégés: Maturus Arrianus, a Transpadane commended for an Egyptian staff position; Varisidius Nepos, a relative of a Comum friend and commended for a *militia*; Atilius Crescens from nearby Milan; Metilius Crispus, a decurion of Comum commissioned as a centurion at Pliny's request; Cornelius Minicianus, described as the 'ornamentum regionis meae' and also recommended for an equestrian *militia*.[100] Thus, the largest single group of Pliny's protégés were able to place themselves under his patronage as a result of the geographical proximity of their origins. Pliny himself had earlier reaped the benefits of similar associations, enjoying the patronage of two leading Transpadane senators, Verginius Rufus and Corellius Rufus (a family friend of Pliny's mother).[101]

Several of his local friends were also linked with Pliny by common literary and educational interests, and in Fronto's *commendationes* literary students and friends are predominant.[102] Education and literary culture supplied several different contexts for the development of patron-protégé relationships. During childhood schoolmates formed close friendships which could endure for life. Explaining his obligation to help promote the career of a Spaniard, Voconius Romanus, Pliny wrote in a *commendatio* to Priscus: 'he was my close and intimate friend when we were students together, my *contubernalis* inside the city and out of it; with him I shared everything, work and play'.[103] In the case of Pliny's friendship with Romatius Firmus, their time at school together permitted the development of an existing bond between local families, while Voconius' relationships depended entirely on his attending the same school at the same time as Pliny.

98 Syme, 'People in Pliny', *JRS* 58 (1968), 135-51.
99 *Ep.* 1.19: 'Municeps tu meus et condiscipulus et ab ineunte aetate contubernalis, pater tuus et matri et avunculo meo, mihi etiam quantum aetatis diversitas passa est, familiaris: magnae et graves causae, cur suscipere augere dignitatem tuam debeam.' (Loeb translation.)
100 *Ep.* 3.2, 4.4, 6.8, 6.25, 7.22.
101 Syme, *Tacitus*, 77f. For the friendship of Pliny's mother and Corellia, see *Ep.* 7.11.3.
102 Pliny's local protégés with literary interests include Maturus Arrianus (*Ep.* 3.2), Atilius Crescens (6.8), Varisidius Nepos (4.4); for a survey of Fronto's clients and friends, see H.-G. Pflaum, 'Les correspondants de l'orateur M. Cornelius Fronto de Cirta', in *Hommages à J. Bayet*, 544-60.
103 *Ep.* 2.13.5: 'Hunc ego, cum simul studeremus, arte familiariterque dilexi; ille meus in urbe ille in secessu contubernalis, cum hoc seria cum hoc iocos miscui.' (Loeb translation.) Champlin, *Fronto and Antonine Rome*, 45f., stresses the importance of *contubernium*.

In addition to *amicitiae* between students, schools encouraged teacher-pupil friendships, as illustrated by Fronto's relationships with his student protégés. They lived with Fronto, studying oratory, and after their education Fronto continued to take an interest, helping to promote their careers and interests. One particular aspect of this aid was the introduction of his students into the law courts of the forum: for instance, Sardius Lupus, 'having been instructed in the noble arts', was introduced into the forum from Fronto's house and *contubernium*.[104] It was not always the teacher who took responsibility for the introduction, and sometimes the apprenticeship involved in the introduction provided a context in which patron-protégé relationships grew as the protégé accompanied his patron in public.[105] Pliny wrote to a legal client requesting permission for Cremutius Ruso to appear with him at the hearing: 'this is my usual way of treating young men of distinction, for I take special pleasure in introducing promising young people to the courts and setting them on the path to fame'.[106] In another letter Pliny pointed to a decline in the tradition requiring aspiring advocates to be introduced into court by a senior advocate of consular status, but clearly this patronal custom had not entirely died out by Fronto's day.[107]

In addition to oratory and the courts, literary culture and circles provided common interests out of which grew friendships. We have already noted in the first chapter that men like Pliny and Titinius Capito assumed patronal responsibility for the young litterateurs in their circles.[108] The sum of the evidence, especially from Fronto, has led to strong statements in recent studies about the importance that literary education and talent held for social mobility.[109] While their significance should not be underestimated, several qualifying remarks should be added. It may be admitted that a certain minimum of Latin education was necessary for entry into the aristocracy, but that does not by itself warrant singling out literary cultivation as a chief determinant of success. In the letters of recommendation, Fronto's and Pliny's protégés (about whom we have most information) are frequently praised for their literary interests or their eloquence. It must be remembered, however, that both patrons were notable for their literary pursuits, and so their protégés should not be thought representative. As the leading teacher of oratory of his day, Fronto possessed a following made up largely of former students with

104 *Ad Amic.* 1.10.
105 *Dial.* 34.
106 *Ep.* 6.23.2: 'Solitum hoc mihi et iam in pluribus claris adulescentibus factitatum; nam mire concupisco bonos iuvenes ostendere foro, adsignare famae.' (Loeb translation.)
107 *Ep.* 2.14.2-3.
108 p. 28.
109 For instance, Pflaum, 'Les correspondants', 560, singles out wealth and education as the important factors in social mobility. For Millar's view of the importance of literary culture and some doubts, see below, pp. 190 f.

special interests in rhetoric.[110] Of course, as Pliny himself indicates, not all aristocrats were as intensely interested in literature as he, and Tacitus' report of Suillius' attack on Seneca may suggest the resentment in certain circles towards the arrogant bookishness of some senators.[111] We would expect the literary interests of the protégés in such circles to be of much less consequence. Moreover, even within the circles of Pliny's and Fronto's protégés success may not have depended on talent as much as on the personal relationship established. In a typical *commendatio* Pliny praised Iulius Naso for befriending Pliny, for using him as a model of behavior, for accompanying his patron in the law courts and at literary readings, and for reading Pliny's literary efforts.[112] Naso's own literary talent received no mention, and literary culture apparently played a role in the patronage relationship to the extent that it allowed Naso one among several opportunities to display his loyalty and common interests. In the end, the importance of literary culture should not be denied, but it would be a mistake to lose sight of the fact that our evidence for aristocratic society has been observed almost exclusively through the eyes of litterateurs.

Through *commendationes* young aristocrats secured military and civilian staff positions under governors with whom they sometimes had no previous special relationship. The recommendations frequently stressed qualities which would make the young men appear to be good prospects for companionship in the provinces, and during their service it was expected that a friendship would develop from the *contubernium* with the result that the young man would enjoy the patronage of his superior in his later career.[113] Avidius Cassius' responsibility for promoting the career of his tribune Iunius Maximus has been discussed. Similarly Iunius Avitus' service with Iulius Ursus Servianus in Germany gave rise to a friendship with the result that Avitus accompanied him to his next command in Pannonia.[114]

The above account of situations in which patronage flourished is, of course, not comprehensive: any contact between Romans could develop into a reciprocal exchange relationship. Plautianus, for example, is said to have taken

110 'Les correspondants', 544.
111 Pliny, *Ep.* 1.13 and 8.12.1. The context of Suillius' remark that Seneca was 'studiis inertibus suetus' was an attack on Seneca's lifeless oratory (Tacitus, *Ann.* 13.42). Syme notes the domination of literature of the age by provincials — an indication that their cultural energies were not fully shared by the older aristocracy (*Tacitus*, 609).
112 *Ep.* 6.6.5f. No mention of eloquence is made by Pliny with regard to several of his protégés (Romatius Firmus, Iunius Avitus, Erucius Clarus).
113 Pliny, *Ep.* 8.23.5 emphasizes that Iunius Avitus won the heart of his commander through the quality of his companionship, rather than as a soldier. The importance of companionship may explain why the literary interests of a protégé are often noted in recommendations for staff positions (*Ep.* 3.2, 4.4, 7.22).
114 *Ep.* 8.23.5; see Eck, 'Prokonsularen Legationen', 32. For the Republican roots of this patronal practice, M. Gelzer, *The Roman Nobility*, 101ff.

notice of the future emperor Macrinus' πίστις while the latter was pleading a friend's case before him in court; as a result, Macrinus was taken on as Plautianus' personal procurator.[115] Nevertheless, the four basic contexts discussed recur in a way which attests to their importance both for the Roman aristocracy and (as we shall see) for the provincial aristocracies as well.[116]

Having described the web of personal relationships in Roman aristocratic society, we can give some consideration to its political and social consequences. Obviously, it would be impossible in the space available to discuss each political event in which patronage can be documented or conjectured. Rather, the aim is to point out some of the general implications for approaches to understanding the history of the Principate.

In Chapter 2 it was suggested that the notion of the emperor exploiting antipathies between ordines to secure his own power faces serious objections inasmuch as the emperor used senators as brokers for the distribution of equestrian offices.[117] However we evaluate the emperor's intentions, the possibility remains that class (or ordo) interests and consciousness existed and were important. The evidence adduced in this chapter, however, suggests that they did not constitute a strong force directing the course of imperial history.

The bonds between the senatorial and equestrian orders were so numerous that it cannot be doubted that the two orders were fully integrated socially and culturally. In addition to the numerous kinship ties, documented by Stein, there was a constant exchange of beneficia between senators and equites.[118] As we have noted, large numbers of equites depended on senatorial patronage for their first appointments, the equestrian militiae. It is revealing that even as important an equestrian as C. Calvisius Statianus (about to be appointed ab epistulis Latinis and then Egyptian prefect) turned to Fronto to secure a militia for his son Faustinianus.[119] In Pliny's letters we can find a reversal of the situation, with a leading senator putting himself under obligation to the Egyptian prefect, Vibius Maximus, by requesting a staff position in Egypt for a protégé.[120]

These are but two of the many amicitia and patronage relationships which can be documented between leading senators and equites. Praetorian prefects from Sejanus to Plautianus are known to have had senatorial followings, and one of Fronto's letters of gratitude was addressed to the prefect Cornelius

---

115 Dio 78.11.2.
116 See below, pp. 176 ff.
117 See above, p. 77.
118 *Ritterstand*, 293-357. Alföldy, *Römische Sozialgeschichte*, 109ff. stresses links between the senatorial and equestrian orders.
119 Fronto, *Ad Amic.* 1.5.
120 *Ep.* 3.2; Pliny dedicated the first book of his letters to another prominent equestrian Septicius Clarus.

Repentinus.[121] One of the best examples of the unity of the aristocratic network concerns Fronto's friend Niger Censorius. Owing to the abuse expressed in Censorius' will toward Gavius Maximus, Censorius posthumously fell out of favor with Pius. In defense of his friendship with Censorius, Fronto felt compelled to write an apology to the emperor. 'When I first came to be his friend, his strenuous achievements, civil and military, had already won him the love of others. Not to mention his other friends, he was on the most intimate terms with Marcius Turbo and Erucius Clarus, who were both eminent men in the front rank, the one of the Equites, the other of the Senators.'[122] Underlying this passage is Fronto's assumption of two paths to high honors, but a single network of *amici* and a single set of values concerning honor and friendship. In view of this unity, it seems to me that any historical explanation relying on attitudinal differences or hostilities between the senatorial and equestrian orders will require concrete evidence of divisions along *ordo* lines for justification.

In explanations about the development of the *familia Caesaris* (similar to those about the equestrian bureaucracy), it is frequently claimed that the emperors employed their freedmen as administrators because their loyalty could be trusted.[123] This may be true on the whole, but imperial freedmen were not completely isolated from the web of aristocratic social relationships and hence independent. Fronto in a letter to Marcus Aurelius described his attachment to the imperial freedman Aridelus and recommended him for a procuratorship.[124] Whether this sort of patronage had a strong influence on careers in the *familia Caesaris* is difficult to say and requires further study. Certainly patronage relationships between aristocratic officials and *liberti Augusti* cannot be thought unusual. In a dedication to the procurator C. Postumius Saturninus Flavianus, Victor, a *libertus Augustorum*, described himself as a *cliens*.[125] The inscription does not indicate whether Victor was serving in a subordinate post, but other imperial freedmen who dedicated stones to aristocratic officials clearly were.[126] If, as Dio indicates, emperors were motivated to appoint freedmen (and equestrian) assistants in order to have watchdogs, the efficacy of the policy must have been partially

---

121 Sejanus: Tacitus, *Ann.* 4.74; Burrus: Syme, *Tacitus*, 591; Aemilius Laetus: H.A., *Sev.* 4.4; Plautianus: see above, p. 129.

122 *Ad Pium* 3.3: 'Ego quidem quom ad amicitiam eius accessi, ⟨iam ei amorem aliorum⟩ strenua opera domi bellique promeruerant. Ut ceteros eius amicos omittam, Turboni Marcio et Erucio Claro erat familiarissimus, qui duo egregii viri alter equestris alter senatorii ordinis primarii fuerunt.' (Loeb translation.)

123 E.g., Petit, *Pax Romana*, 67.

124 *Ad M. Caes.* 5.37.

125 *CIL* VIII. 11175.

126 *CIL* III.431 (= *ILS* 1449): 'Hermes Augusti libertus adiutor eius honoris causa' to the procurator Valerius Eudaemon; also see *ILS* 8849, *IGR* III.1103 and *AE* (1956), 123.

undermined by such patronal ties.[127]

In general, then, it seems to me that we should be wary of structural interpretations of the Principate which are based on interactions between what might be called horizontal groups (that is, groups of people of similar class or status backgrounds, or with common interests and consciousnesses). In ancient society the vertical personal bonds between individuals of different orders were usually predominant, inhibiting the development of any class consciousness or horizontal group action. This has been increasingly emphasized in Republican studies with regard to the alleged conflict between senatorial and equestrian orders, and in recent work in political science it has been argued that this 'group theory of politics' is in principle of limited value for the understanding of patronal societies.[128] But these views do not yet seem to have made an impact on traditional ideas about the Principate.[129]

Finally, we may turn to the political and social significance of patronage within the senatorial order. During the Republic a senator's political effectiveness was related to the strength of his clientèle and the power of his *amici*. With the emergence of a single *princeps* this changed, and proximity to the emperor became the most important single determinant. While lower-class clientèles lost most of their relevance to political power after 14 A.D., a man's senatorial following continued to have political value. Some senatorial magistracies continued into the second century to be filled by free elections in the senate, and a senator's *amici* and protégés could be decisive for his own promotion or that of his protégés. Iulius Naso's career suffered a setback when he lost his father and his father's connections. But in Pliny, Naso found a patron who would call on his friends for help with canvassing for Naso's election.[130]

Perhaps more important than elections, political trials in the senate could be decisively influenced by the extent and power of a man's *amici*. In many trials, of course, the emperor's attitude was the critical factor, but when the emperor

127 Dio 52.25.5. The same point should be made about equestrian procurators appointed as watchdogs over senatorial officials: in an inscription from Ephesus P. Celer, a procurator, calls himself a *comes* of the quaestor of Asia, C. Helvidius Priscus (*AE* (1924), 79a).

128 P. A. Brunt, 'The equites in the late Republic', in *The Crisis of the Roman Republic*, ed. R. Seager, 83. For modern views see C. H. Landé, 'Networks and groups in Southeast Asia: Some observations on the group theory of politics', *Am. Pol. Sci. Rev.* 67 (1973), 103-27; S. Sayari, 'Political patronage in Turkey', and M. Johnson, 'Political bosses and their gangs: Zu'ama and qabadayat in the Sunni Muslim quarters of Beirut', in *Patrons and Clients*, ed. Gellner and Waterbury, 103ff., 207ff.

129 P. Petit, *Pax Romana*, 169f. gives a common view of the development of the equestrian administration based on a view of some universal characteristics ascribed to *equites*: 'we may... feel confident that the knights were adherents of the regime and the principal buttresses of the state, and that their role in administration, as public functionaries, in municipal affairs, in law, in public works, gave their order a certain class-consciousness and a lawyerlike mentality.'

130 *Ep.* 6.6.

abstained from intervention, a man's *amici* could protect him from prosecution or secure his acquittal.[131] When Pliny threatened to prosecute Publicius Certus, he was warned against it partially on the grounds of the danger from Certus' powerful *amicitiae*.[132] We have suggested that childlessness produced clientèles of legacy-hunters. To such a clientèle Tacitus ascribes the acquittal of Pompeius Silvanus, accused by Africans of maladministration. (Tacitus adds ironically that Silvanus outlived the fortune-hunters who voted for his acquittal.)[133] Conversely, the support of *amici* could help to convict enemies.[134]

The senate under the emperors continued the tradition of factional infighting which it inherited from the Republic. More generally, senators and *equites* can be said to have perpetuated Roman aristocratic culture — something which calls for explanation in view of the rapid turnover of senatorial families and the entry of provincials from diverse parts of the empire.[135] Much of the cause should be attributed to the education of the provincial aristocracies in Graeco-Roman culture. But with regard to conservative senatorial mores in particular, some of the responsibility should be ascribed to the patron-protégé relationships. During the Republic the traditions were learned as sons of the great senatorial houses accompanied their fathers in their public affairs. The great senatorial families died out in the Empire, and the function of enculturation was fulfilled in the patron-protégé relationships, as Pliny's letters show. As a young man Pliny attended his patrons and was introduced in the forum, just as his protégés served a sort of apprenticeship with him a generation later.[136] When Pliny sought office his patrons supported him and then accompanied him during his tenure of office, giving advice and guidance.[137] With respect to matters arising in the senate, Pliny always sought the advice of his patrons (with one exception).[138] In return for his support, Pliny performed many filial *officia* for Corellius Rufus and Verginius Rufus in their old age and after their deaths.[139] The description given by Pliny of his relationship with his own senatorial protégés is very similar.[140]

---

131 Dio 58.10.8 claims that the consul Memmius Regulus did not immediately put the death penalty or imprisonment of Sejanus to a full vote of the senate after the reading of Tiberius' letter because he feared opposition from Sejanus' numerous kin and friends.

132 Pliny, *Ep.* 9.13.11.

133 *Ann.* 13.52.

134 Seneca, for example, used his influence in his indirect attack on P. Suillius which ended with Suillius' conviction in the senate and exile (Tacitus, *Ann.* 13.42ff.).

135 M. Hammond, 'Composition of the Senate, A.D. 68-235', *JRS* 47 (1957), 74-81.

136 Pliny, *Ep.* 6.6.6; see above, p. 27. For this general phenomenon in the Republic, see Thomas N. Mitchell, *Cicero: the Ascending Years*, ch. 1, esp. 42ff.

137 *Ep.* 4.17.6 and 2.1.8f.

138 *Ep.* 9.13.6.

139 *Ep.* 4.17.9f. and 2.1.9.

140 Pliny emphasizes how Iunius Avitus and Iulius Naso seek his advice and use him as a model (*Ep.* 8.23.2 and 6.6.5f.).

Its quality of fictive kinship is underlined by the fact that Pliny performed in his home the ritual normally carried out by the father in the Republic, the assumption of the *latus clavus*. In Pliny's letters we can see the senatorial aristocracy reproducing itself in its own image through three generations without the appearance of a natural son. Municipal aristocrats were coopted and then tutored, promoted, and advised by their patrons, just as Republican senators had done with their sons. Thus, I think we must believe that the institution of patronage made a considerable contribution to the conservatism and continuity of traditions in senatorial society.

In this chapter we have found reason to reaffirm the conclusion which Fustel de Coulanges reached nearly one hundred years ago with regard to bonds of dependence: 'la substitution de l'Empire à la République n'a pas été cette révolution complète et radicale que plusieurs historiens modernes se sont figurés. Le pouvoir a été seulement déplacé; les lois ont été peu modifiées, et les moeurs ne l'ont pas été.'[141] We have been able to find no reason or evidence to suggest that the importance of patronage and *amicitia* declined substantially in the day-to-day economic, social and political affairs of Roman aristocrats. And so it is not surprising to find that patronal *officia* remained a standard element in discussions and complaints about the duties and drudgery of aristocratic life in the city.[142]

---

141 *Origines*, 225.
142 Pliny encouraged Bruttius Praesens to return to Rome and his 'dignitas, honor, amicitiae tam superiores quam minores' (*Ep.* 7.3.2). But Pliny himself complained of having to waste his time performing *officia* while in Rome (*Ep.* 1.9.2f.). Seneca frequently cites patronal duties as one of the ways people fritter away their lives in Rome (*Brev. Vitae, passim*, e.g., 2.4f., 3.2, 7.2).

5

Patronage and provincials:
the case of North Africa

The further we move our attention away from the emperor and Rome, the less adequate the information of our literary sources, especially the historical narratives, becomes. Nevertheless, it is vital to our understanding of the empire to have some idea of how the provincials related to Rome and Roman officials in the provinces. In this final chapter I wish to consider how patronage functioned in this relationship. The discussion will concern provincial patronage as a whole insofar as it has been necessary to draw on literary sources from all regions for a few scattered bits of information. The conclusions drawn from the literary passages can often be corroborated by the epigraphic evidence. With regard to the inscriptions, a somewhat different approach has been adopted: rather than utilizing scattered stones from the whole empire in a haphazard fashion, I have decided to study the whole corpus of material from one region in order to discover whether patterns emerge. North Africa appeared to be a good choice for several reasons. A large corpus of inscriptions has been collected from the area, and useful preliminary studies are available.[1] More importantly, during the second century North Africans came to be more successful than men from any other region outside Italy in securing positions in the imperial aristocracy.[2] Despite their success, the relation between Rome and the North African aristocracies has not received as much attention and emphasis as the influence of prominent figures from the Greek East, especially the famous figures of the Second Sophistic. The reason, no doubt, is that the Sophists captured the lion's share of the attention in our literary sources: a careful study of the inscriptions from the Latin-speaking

---

1 A. Pelletier, 'Les sénateurs d'Afrique proconsulaire d'Auguste à Gallien', *Latomus* 23 (1964), 511-31; R. Duncan-Jones, 'Equestrian rank'; H.-G. Pflaum, 'Les juges des cinq décuries originaires d'Afrique romaine', *Ant. Afr.* 2 (1968), 153-95; M. Jarrett, 'An album of the equestrians from North Africa in the emperor's service', *Epigraphische Studien* 9 (1972), 146-232; B.E. Thomasson, *Statthalter*.
2 Pflaum, *Procurateurs*, 260ff.; Jarrett, 'African contribution'; Hammond, 'Composition of the the Senate', 77. During the second century Eastern senators outnumbered African *clarissimi* by two to one, but, given the much smaller population of Africa, Africans were more successful *per capita*.

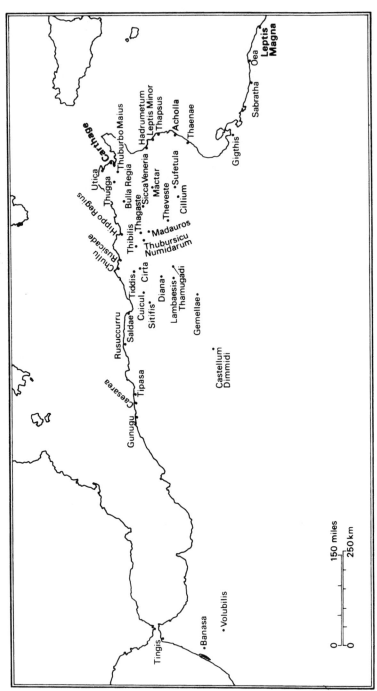

Map of North Africa

West offers some hope of achieving a more balanced view of the interaction of provincials with Rome. Unfortunately, even with a massive body of inscriptions at hand to supplement our knowledge, this picture will be admittedly conjectural at times because of the elliptical nature of the inscriptions. But the interpretations offered are not without foundation: their plausibility derives from the ideology described in the first chapter.

As an analytical tool for organizing this chapter, two different but overlapping types of patronage will be distinguished. The first section will describe and analyze patrons with what we have called first-order resources, that is, patrons with direct control over the distribution of certain favors. Since a provincial seeking a favor did not always enjoy a relationship with the appropriate patron of this kind, he often had to find friends or other patrons through whom he could approach the men in control. This latter group comprises what can be described as mediators, and will be the subject of the second section. In an appendix at the end of the chapter can be found a table and discussion of the North African patronage inscriptions.

POLITICAL AND ADMINISTRATIVE BACKGROUND OF NORTH AFRICA
Before proceeding to an examination of patronage in North Africa, it may be useful to provide a very brief account of the historical context. Roman annexation in Africa followed the defeat of Carthage in 146 B.C. Having razed Carthage, the conquerors granted the status of *civitas immunis et libera* to seven cities which had supported them, and confiscated the lands of the other, hostile cities, including the *territorium* of Carthage as far as the *fossa regia*. The land beyond this boundary was given to the Numidian king Masinissa.[3]

The new province was governed by a proconsul. During the final century of the Republic, the Roman impact on Africa was relatively limited, with the local administration of the native cities remaining Punic in character. In 122 B.C. Gaius Gracchus led out a group of Romans to establish the Colonia Iunonia Carthago; the colony was suppressed in the subsequent reaction against Gracchus, but the settlers were confirmed in their land by a law of 111 B.C. Two decades later viritane grants were made by Saturninus' law to Marian veterans of the war against Jugurtha (many of whom were native Africans).[4] By 49 B.C., then, there was a small number of Roman citizens in North Africa (compared with the native population), but no Roman communities.

After his victory in North Africa in 46 B.C., Julius Caesar began to introduce substantial political changes. The privilege of autonomy was

3 G. Charles-Picard, *La civilisation de l'Afrique romaine*, 22f.
4 J. Gascou, *La politique municipale de l'empire romaine en Afrique proconsulaire de Trajan à Septime-Sévère*, Coll. Ec. Fr. de Rome; P.A. Brunt, *Italian Manpower, 225 B.C.- A.D.14*, App. 12.

revoked for the cities opposing him. Western Tunisia was annexed and added to the province of Africa, while P. Sittius of Nuceria, a Caesarian condottiere, was left as ruler of a semi-autonomous kingdom in the region of Cirta. In 44 B.C. Caesar ordered the foundation of a colony at Carthage; the order was carried out after Caesar's death, and the new colony was later reinforced by Augustus. Other *coloniae* were founded by the dictator, in particular on the coast of Cape Bon, but their identity and number are uncertain owing to the difficulties of distinguishing Caesar's foundations from those of his successor.[5]

Some time shortly before 35 B.C. *Africa vetus* and *Africa nova*, including Cirta, were combined to form the province of *Africa proconsularis*.[6] Under Augustus, this province was left in the hands of a proconsular governor with a legion (a military force of some 13,000 including auxiliaries).[7] Further west, Juba II was installed as a client king of Mauretania in 25 B.C. In addition to reinforcing the colony at Carthage, Augustus founded a number of colonies in the grain-growing areas of the African province and on the coast of Mauretania, and made Utica a Roman *municipium*.[8]

During the reigns of the later Julio-Claudians there appears to have been a lull in the process of founding new colonies.[9] There were, however, other important political and administrative developments. The area to the south of the Roman occupation was inhabited by native tribesmen, who were useful to the Romans as recruits for auxiliary units, but who also represented a source of unrest. Over time the Romans evolved a *modus vivendi* with these peoples, in part through military compulsion, most notably during the reign of Tiberius, when the proconsuls with the aid of the Mauretanian king finally suppressed the Tacfarinas revolt. The violent confrontations between tribesmen and Romans, so frequent during the early years of the Principate, gradually declined, leaving Roman Africa in relative peace during the second century.[10]

Gaius and Claudius introduced certain changes which gave North Africa the basic administrative structure which was to remain stable for the next century and a half. In 37 Caligula, not wishing to entrust the African proconsul with an army, sent out a *legatus pro praetore* to command *legio III Augusta*.[11] The legate was *de facto* governor of Numidia, until Septimius Severus separated it from Proconsularis as a *de iure* province.[12] While in Lugdunensis in 40,

---

5 Gascou, *La politique municipale*, 19f.; Charles-Picard, *L'Afrique romaine*, 2; Brunt, *Italian Manpower*, 593-97.
6 D. Fishwick and B.D. Shaw, 'The formation of Africa Proconsularis', *Hermes* 105 (1977) 369-80.
7 Charles-Picard, *L'Afrique romaine*, 6f.
8 Gascou, *La politique municipale*, 24.
9 *Ibid.*, 11.
10 B.D. Shaw, 'Pastoralists, Peasants, and Politics in Roman North Africa'.
11 Charles-Picard, *L'Afrique romaine*, 9; M. Benabou, 'Proconsul et légat en Afrique. Le témoignage de Tacite', *Ant. Afr.* 6 (1972), 129ff.
12 The date of the separation is uncertain; the *terminus post quem* appears to be 198/9 A.D. (M.

Caligula summoned Ptolemy, king of Mauretania, had him executed, and annexed his kingdom.[13] Several years later Claudius then divided Mauretania into two provinces, Caesariensis and Tingitana, each governed by a senior equestrian procurator with auxiliary units.[14] In addition to the governors of the provinces, several other important equestrian officials deserve brief mention: from the reign of Augustus a provincial procurator was appointed for Africa, but disappears from the record after the reign of Trajan;[15] a *procurator IIII publicorum Africae* can be found managing the collection of indirect taxes (documented from the reign of Hadrian);[16] and, finally, a variety of procurators were appointed to supervise the emperor's vast imperial estates in the province.[17]

The political stability enjoyed by North Africa from the Flavian period, together with the increased cultivation of the olive tree in more arid regions, permitted the spread of sedentarization south and west of the old province, reaching as far as Cillium under Trajan, Gemellae under Hadrian and Castellum Dimmidi under Septimius Severus.[18] At the same time there was a large-scale creation of *coloniae* and *municipia;* Roman municipal institutions came to dominate the old Punic system; and gradually the Latin language became predominant in the urban areas. In short, African municipal life grew to resemble that of Romanized cities in other provinces: we find in Africa the familiar competition between individuals as well as cities for honors.[19] Thus, in a study of North African inscriptions, we shall address ourselves to questions also relevant to urbanized areas of other provinces in the empire. How and under what circumstances did municipal aristocrats deal with imperial officials sent to the provinces? To what extent were personal relationships important? What role did patronage play in provincials' dealings with Rome? What effect did the increasing number of African patrons in the imperial aristocracy have on the interaction between imperial government and the provinces?

OFFICIALS AS PATRONS OF FIRST-ORDER RESOURCES

In a recent essay 'Patronage and power', A. Weingrod has pointed out that authors of patronage studies today usually adopt one of two approaches.[20] The first is the functionalist approach of the anthropologist, who is interested in the

---

Speidel, 'The singulares of Africa and the establishment of Numidia as a province', *Historia* 22 (1973), 125ff.).

13 D. Fishwick and B.D. Shaw, 'Ptolemy of Mauretania and the conspiracy of Gaetulicus', *Historia* 25 (1976), 491ff.

14 Gascou, *La politique municipale*, 27.

15 H.-G. Pflaum, *Abrégé des procurateurs équestres*, 21.

16 Pflaum, *Procurateurs*, 61 and S.J. De Laet, *Portorium*, ch. 10.

17 Pflaum, *Procurateurs*, 44, 56f., 68.

18 Gascou, *La politique municipale*, 40.

19 *Ibid.*, 41-66.

20 *Patrons and Clients*, ed. Gellner and Waterbury, 41.

broad effects of patronage for the whole society (e.g., cohesion, integration, or schism) and tends to pass over an analysis of the specific locations of power and decision-making. The other approach is that of the political scientist, whose interests are the reverse: a concentration on power politics at the expense of an analysis of the social implications. An ideal study would integrate these two approaches. Unfortunately, the epigraphic evidence is not dense enough to permit us to move beyond the level of speculation with regard to the anthropologist's questions. As a result, we are left to proceed with the political scientist's approach in this section. By drawing on what is known about provincial society and administration, the positions of power in the provinces can be located. Then the relevant literary evidence and North African inscriptions will be adduced to confirm that the patronage bonds are to be found where we would expect them, that is, radiating out from these *loci*.

The most important centers of power in the provinces were the governors, and so it should come as no surprise that they represent the most prominent group in the table of patronage inscriptions. In this section several questions will be considered: (1) what sorts of *beneficia* governors distributed; (2) how patronage bonds with governors were formed; and (3) what form reciprocity from the client could take. Proconsuls, imperial *legati* and praesidial procurators can be treated together here, since all shared many of the same responsibilities and patronal resources. To the extent that some imperial legates and procuratorial governors had additional military, and, in the latter case, fiscal responsibilities, they possessed correspondingly greater resources for patronage, as will be noted. Work on this section has been greatly facilitated by recent studies of the activities and duties of provincial governors: it has been shown how ambiguous were the rules guiding the governor's actions and how much discretion he enjoyed — conditions in which patronage was likely to prosper.[21]

In a speech cited in the first chapter, Apuleius said that in contrast to the philosopher who loves the governor for the public example he sets, 'most people esteem the *fructus* of his *bonitas*'.[22] What form might this *fructus* take? What were these favors appropriate to friends? Even with all the literary evidence and the numerous inscriptions concerning North African governors, there is little hope of providing complete answers, but several important spheres of patronal activity can be delineated.

Most of a governor's time in civilian administration was likely to be taken up with legal cases,[23] and it is in this sphere that we have most evidence for the role

---

21 G. Burton, *Powers and Functions of Proconsuls in the Roman Empire, 70-260 A.D.*; 'Proconsuls, assizes and the administration of justice under the Empire', *JRS* 65 (1975), 92-106. For a brief description of official duties, Charles-Picard, *L'Afrique romaine*, 12.
22 *Flor.* 9.
23 Burton, *Powers and Functions of Proconsuls*, ch. 1.

of social relationships. The governor's favor was important for both the advocates and the parties to the case. Though outside the chronological limits of this study, Libanius' autobiographical oration gives a more vivid account of patronage related to the provincial administration of law than any literature surviving from the Principate. I see no reason to think that in this particular respect anything changed substantially from the second to the fourth century and that the evidence of Libanius should not be considered. Bits of literary evidence and some inscriptions from Africa provide a few hints that Libanius' description is applicable.

Libanius describes his life as a series of peaks and valleys, his good fortune depending largely upon whether he was in the good graces of the current governor. When he was known to be in favor, people with court cases and other problems flocked to Libanius: 'those people who had suffered injury at the hands of men of greater influence, those who, indicted in anger, now needed the governor for their deliverance, and those desirous of a speedy trial — and many other favors too a governor can grant without harm to the law — all these, either in person or through their wives, begged me to approach him on their behalf'.[24] This remark refers to the praetorian prefect Strategius, but it is clear that Libanius' friendships with other governors benefited himself and his friends in similar ways.[25]

The people for whom visible friendship with governors and favoritism in the courts would be most valuable were advocates. This supposition appears to be confirmed by the fact that they erected a significant proportion of the patronage dedications to North African governors. One, T. Flavius Silvanus, was quite explicit in his gratitude to the governor of Numidia: 'M. [Au]reli[o] Comi[n]io Ca[s]siano, leg. Augg. pr. pr. c.v. patrono, T. F. S[il]vanus eq. R. [ad]vocat., Q. Pin[ar]ius Urban[us] IIvir et L. [Gar]gilius Fel[ix] fl. pp. qui iu[dicia] eius for[i iustitiamque] tot[ies admirati sunt]' (no. 14 in appendix). (Though Mommsen's complete restoration here is not certain, the references to the advocate and the legal decision are clear enough.) Another advocate, L. Valerius Optatianus, erected dedications 'to two consecutive *legati pro praetore* of Numidia, T. Iulius Tertullus Antiochus (attested for 242) and M. Aurelius Cominius Cassianus (c. 244-9).[26] Perhaps these stones advertised what became known about Libanius by word of mouth — that the man had a personal relationship with the governor and so might bring favorable results in

---

24 *Or.* 1.107: οἵ τε γὰρ δὴ ὑπὸ δυνατωτέρων ἀδικούμενοι οἵ τε κατ᾽ ὀργὴν ἐγγεγραμμένοι, τῆς ἀρχῆς δὲ εἰς ἀπαλλαγὴν δεόμενοι οἵ τε ἐπιθυμοῦντες ὡς τάχιστα ψήφου τυχεῖν — πολλὰς δ᾽ ἂν καὶ ἄλλας ἀρχὴ δοίη χάριτας οὐ λυποῦσα τὸν νόμον — οὗτοι, οἱ μὲν αὐτοί, τῶν δὲ γυναῖκες, ἤτουν καὶ ὑπὲρ σφῶν ἐλθεῖν ἐκεῖσε. (Translation by A.F. Norman in his edition and commentary on *Libanius' Autobiography*.)
25 *Or.* 1.232.
26 E. Birley, 'The governors of Numidia, A.D. 193-268', *JRS* 40 (1950), 65. See nos. 12 and 31 in the table

legal cases. Altogether, there are five inscriptions in the table dedicated to governors by *advocati*, a clear reflection of the *beneficia* which they could hope to secure.[27]

In more specific terms, what were the legal favors which might be granted 'without harm to the law' (a familiar phrase echoed in a letter of Marcus Aurelius cited below and in a letter of Fronto)?[28] The favor specified by Libanius and found again in Apuleius' *Apologia* was the scheduling of the trial. This could represent a considerable *beneficium*, because, as stressed in a recent study, there was no set schedule for cases and it was important to many people to receive a court hearing quickly and in a town close to their homes. 'In general it was precisely the absence of any formal structure for the preliminaries to the hearings themselves that ensured the effective operation of the informal social influences of status (*honos*) and bribery (*improbitas*)' which Ulpian mentions in the *Digest*.[29] Apuleius thought that the speed with which his case was heard was of great importance, preventing the forgery of documents by his accusers. Indeed, Apuleius thanked the proconsul Claudius Maximus for this *beneficium* in his speech.[30]

Another traditional and legitimate favor, defended and utilized by Fronto, was the acceptance of letters of recommendation as character references for the parties involved. The *commendandi mos*, according to Fronto's explanation, 'grew up even on behalf of those who were involved in public or private lawsuits to the actual judges or their assessors — and nothing reprehensible was seen in the practice. This was not done, as I see it, in order to tamper with the fairmindedness of the judge or to cause him to depart from giving a true judgement. But as there was a time-honored custom in the courts of bringing on witnesses to character, after the case had been heard, to declare what they honestly thought of the defendant, so these letters of recommendation were treated as fulfilling the function of testimonials.'[31] The claim here that the *commendatio* was just a character testimonial is not quite true: it was a testimonial whose efficacy derived from the author's friendship with the judge. The accuser or defendant became credible because he

---

27 Nos. 3, 12, 14, 30, 31.
28 See footnote 97 and p. 164 below; Fronto, *Ad Amic.* 1.1.1; and also see de Ste Croix, 'Suffragium', 42f. for similar evidence from Cicero and a discussion of the Fronto letter.
29 Burton, *Powers and Functions of Proconsuls*, ch. 4, and 'Proconsuls, assizes', 102. The reference to the *Digest* is found in 1.16.9.4.
30 *Apol.* 84.
31 *Ad Amic.* 1.1.1: 'progressus est, ut etiam eos qui publico vel privato iudicio disceptarent, non tamen improba res videretur iudicibus ipsis aut iis, qui consilio adessent, commendare, non, opinor, ad iustitiam iudicis labefactandam vel de vera sententia deducendam. Sed iste in ipsis iudiciis mos inveteratus erat causa perorata laudatores adhibere, qui quid de reo existimarent, pro sua opinione cum fide expromerent; item istae commendantium litterae laudationis munere fungi visae sunt.' For the translation and a discussion, see de Ste Croix, 'Suffragium', 43f.

happened to be a friend of a friend, and so the favor really requested may sometimes have been nothing less than a favorable verdict. We would very much like to know what impact Apuleius' letter from his friend Lollianus Avitus, the previous proconsul of Africa, had in his trial before Claudius Maximus, who was said also to have been a friend of Avitus. After reading the letter (not a *commendatio*), Apuleius asked his accuser: 'will you attack with accusations of magic and the black art the man whom Avitus describes as a good man, and whose disposition he so warmly praises in his letter?'[32]

The modern ideal of strictly impartial court hearings differs from the Roman acceptance of limited favoritism or favoritism 'without harm to the law'. The more vague the law and its procedures, the more patronage could be exercised without clear violation. In addition to this legitimate patronage, illegitimate patronage in court cases requires some consideration. Most of the available evidence centers on intrigues, convictions and acquittals at Rome owing to *gratia*. There is every reason to think that this went on at the less well-documented provincial level as well. In an oration delivered in Prusa, Dio Chrysostom defended himself against the charge that in his local political struggles he had used his connection with the proconsul of Bithynia to have his enemies tortured and exiled.[33] Whatever the truth of this particular accusation, this regrettable consequence of municipal infighting can be documented for North Africa. Pliny prosecuted a case against Marius Priscus, former proconsul of Africa, in the senate. Priscus pleaded guilty to the charge of having accepted bribes from two provincials for harassing their enemies, including *equites Romani*, with flogging, exile and execution.[34] In Pliny's account it is not clear whether the provincials' relationship with Priscus had been established before the bribery and so would qualify as patronage under our definition. In any case, the point remains that in the Principate, as in Libanius' time, one of the governor's potential *beneficia* was harassment of his clients' enemies. At the other extreme, friendship with the governor or his powerful friends at Rome could provide protection from prosecution, as demonstrated by a dispute related by Lucian. He waged a continuing battle with a certain Alexander who claimed to have magical and oracular powers. A senator named Rutilianus allegedly came under Alexander's influence. At one point in the struggle Alexander was supposed to have tried to kill Lucian. This naturally provoked Lucian to undertake a prosecution, 'but the governor of Bithynia and Pontus at the time, Avitus, held me back, all but begging and entreating me to stop. For on account of his goodwill toward Rutilianus he

---

32 *Apol.* 96. Pliny *Ep.* 9.5 shows that governors, like emperors, felt the conflicting claims of equality and 'gratia potentium' in court. See above, p.56.
33 *Or.* 43.11; C.P. Jones, *The Roman World of Dio Chrysostom.*
34 *Ep.* 2.11.8.

could not punish Alexander, even if he found him clearly guilty of wrong-doing.'[35] This story illustrates how powerful patrons at the center of the empire-wide patronage network in Rome could provide protection from legal accusations for their provincial friends. Although Lucian may have exaggerated the bluntness of Avitus' response, Aulus Gellius in a thoughtful and detached mood concluded that protection of a friend by a judge should sometimes take priority over strict justice, should the two conflict in a court case before him.[36] All of these details seem to me to add up to a potentially considerable role for patronage in a governor's activities as judge.

The other main civilian administrative duty of the governor was oversight of the provincial communities. Here again the opportunities for exercise of patronage were great because there were no detailed rules regulating the relationship between cities and the governor.[37] As a result, Plutarch in his advice to a young man intending to pursue local political offices recommended that the young man cement friendships with important Romans: 'Not only is it necessary for a statesman to keep himself and his home city blameless toward the rulers, but also always to have some friend in the circles of the most powerful as a firm support for the city. For the Romans themselves are best disposed toward the civic exertions of friends. And it is good that those who enjoy benefits from friendship with the powerful use it for the prosperity of the people.'[38] So it was important for the local notable to possess a means of tapping the patronage of the Roman rulers. This need not mean that he must be a friend of the current governor, but rather that he have access into the proper network of friends at Rome. As we shall see, once he gained access he could be passed along a chain of contacts until he could introduce himself to the governor as a friend of a friend. Fronto claims that once his friendship with Arrius Antoninus, *iuridicus per Italiam regionis Traspadanae*, became widely known, 'as a result of this public knowledge I was approached by many people who desired [Antoninus'] *gratia*'.[39] The letters show that these people were municipal aristocrats passed on to Fronto by mutual friends with requests concerning local administration. Fronto had become a funnel at Rome through

---

35 Alexander the False Prophet 57: ἀλλ' ὁ τότε ἡγούμενος Βιθυνίας καὶ τοῦ Πόντου Αὔτειος ἐπέσχε, μονονουχὶ ἱκετεύων καὶ ἀντιβολῶν παύσασθαι· διὰ γὰρ τὴν πρὸς Ῥουτιλιάνον εὔνοιαν μὴ ἂν δύνασθαι, καὶ εἰ φανερῶς λάβοι ἀδικοῦντα, κολάσαι αὐτόν.

36 N.A. 1.3: the discussion includes more than a judge hearing charges against a friend in court, but his initial anecdote concerns such a case and so the general discussion by implication pertains to such a situation.

37 *Powers and Functions of Proconsuls*, ch. 3.

38 *Moralia* 814C: οὐ μόνον δὲ δεῖ παρέχειν αὑτόν τε καὶ τὴν πατρίδα πρὸς τοὺς ἡμεμόνας ἀναίτιον, ἀλλὰ καὶ φίλον ἔχειν ἀεί τινα τῶν ἄνω δυνατωτάτων, ὥσπερ ἕρμα τῆς πολιτείας βέβαιον· αὐτοὶ γάρ εἰσι Ῥωμαῖοι πρὸς τὰς πολιτικὰς σπουδὰς προθυμότατοι τοῖς φίλοις· καὶ καρπὸν ἐκ φιλίας ἡγεμονικῆς λαμβάνοντας... εἰς εὐδαιμονίαν δημοσίαν ἐξενέγκασθαι καλόν.

39 *Ad Amic.* 2.8.

which such requests were routed.

These friendships, however, could be a danger as well as a boon to the community. Though he does not specify particular issues or quarrels, Plutarch notes that it was all too tempting for a local aristocrat entangled in a municipal dispute to resort to his powerful Roman friends to settle the matter, rather than settling it internally in a way to preserve community autonomy and dignity as far as possible.[40] Whatever the dangers, some African municipal leaders seem to have followed Plutarch's advice: inscriptions permit us to name several municipal magistrates who possessed the patronage of governors.[41] Of course, the inscriptions do not reveal how the local magistrates used their links: whether they used them for the benefit of the community or for personal advancement is uncertain, though the latter was the more common course of action according to Plutarch.[42]

What specific forms might a governor's influence in municipal affairs take? There were three main spheres of gubernatorial interference — municipal elections and honors, finance, and building — and in each of these we can document patronage.[43] In the *Digest* is recorded Ulpian's suggestion that 'the provincial governor should see to it that obligations and offices in cities are distributed equitably (*aequaliter*) by turns according to age and *dignitas* in accordance with the prestige of the obligations and offices which have long been established, in order that, without danger and the frequent oppression of some, the cities not be deprived of their men and strength'.[44] *Aequaliter* of course involves a value judgement and great influence might be exerted in the process of coming to a 'fair' decision. There is no need to repeat here Professor Bowersock's account of how Aelius Aristides summoned all the influence at his disposal, including that of the emperor himself, in order to persuade reluctant proconsuls of Asia to confirm his immunity from office-holding and the *munera* involved.[45] Influence was not exercised only for purposes of escaping public honors. In a letter to be discussed below Fronto tried to exert influence on Arrius Antoninus to reinstate Volumnius Serenus on the municipal council of Concordia in Italy. There is no evidence to indicate whether Fronto's effort was rewarded. Such a use of patronal connections must have been common, since Dio of Prusa could boast of having refrained

---

40 *Moralia* 814Ff. Dio Chrysostom prided himself on not having gone to the Roman authorities and urged others to do the same (*Or.* 45.8ff.).

41 Nos. 3, 28, 52.

42 *Moralia* 814D.

43 Burton, *Powers and Functions of Proconsuls*, ch. 3; Jones, *Dio Chrysostom*, ch. 11.

44 *Dig.* 50.4.3.15: 'praeses provinciae provideat munera et honores in civitatibus aequaliter per vices secundum aetates et dignitates, ut gradus munerum honorumque qui antiquitus statuti sunt, iniungi, ne sine discrimine et frequenter isdem oppressis simul viris et viribus res publicae destituantur.'

45 *Greek Sophists*, 36-40

from using his influence with proconsuls and the emperor to his advantage in Prusa's quarrels over the election of municipal decurions.[46]

At a lower level, teaching positions in provincial cities also seem to have been allocated through patronage channels.[47] Fronto sent a *commendatio* on behalf of Antoninus Aquila to Aufidius Victorinus, his son-in-law and *legatus Germaniae superioris*, requesting him to exert his influence in order to secure a public teaching position in one of the German *civitates*.[48] These examples of the effect of patronage by Roman aristocrats come from scattered areas of the empire: since they concern basic elements of life common to all areas with developed municipal institutions, there is good reason to believe that they are representative of what happened throughout much of the empire.

By discussing the governor's oversight of the distribution of *honores* we have already in effect discussed one aspect of his intervention in the financial affairs of the cities: involvement in distribution and enforcement of *munera* afforded opportunities for patronage.[49] Another aspect was his oversight of public building projects. Because the same municipal leaders proposed, planned, financed and carried out the projects, and then were responsible to themselves and other municipal aristocrats, obvious possibilities existed for financial mismanagement and fraud. In order to restrain misconduct and prevent financial chaos governors might intervene from the time a project was proposed.[50] Various African inscriptions attest to such involvement: L. Claudius Honoratus, for instance, in accordance with a promise made by his father before his death to the *populus Cuiculitanorum* built a hall in Cuicul with a statue and marble columns 'ex decreto Fontei Frontiniani legati Augusti pro praetore'.[51] Now such intervention seems to have been haphazard and subject to the governor's discretion,[52] and so a governor's favor might be useful. Fronto once again supplies an example of influence being brought to bear: his letter on behalf of a certain Baburiana to Arrius Antoninus is badly damaged, but it can be discerned that in order to oblige his friends Fronto was

---

46 *Or.* 45.8; Jones, *Dio Chrysostom*, 99.

47 In *Ep.* 4.13.10 Pliny asked Tacitus to send one of his students to begin a school at Comum.

48 *Ad Amic.* 1.7.

49 A local aristocrat might promise more than the compulsory *summa legitima*; once made, the promise could be enforced by the governor. But enforcement was probably not uniform and 'there are indications that powerul individuals and groups within cities were prepared to call in friendly governors in order to win short-term victories over their rivals' (P. Garnsey, 'Taxatio and pollicitatio in Roman Africa', *JRS* 61 (1971), 129).

50 Dio Chrysostom, *Or.* 40, 45, 47 and Pliny, *Ep.* 10. 17a, 17b, 81 illustrate the quarrelling, fraud and mismanagement that might arise; see Jones, *Dio Chrysostom*, 111ff.

51 For the inscription and a discussion of other gubernatorial interventions to enforce the fulfillment of *pollicitationes* by municipal aristocrats, see Garnsey, 'Taxatio', 116–29.

52 The governor was supposed to travel around the province inspecting public buildings (*Dig.* 1.16.7.1). If, as in the case of Pliny, something in these spot checks aroused his suspicion, he could make further enquiries (*Ep.* 10.17a.3).

asking Antoninus for some favor 'de opere extruendo'.[53] Of course, a few scattered examples cannot prove the general impact of governors' patronal connections on municipal finance and public building, but several indirect indicators are available. In Dio's speeches concerning the local quarrels at Prusa, the possibility of the intervention of the governor on behalf of local favorites is always taken into account (if only to be denied or warned against).[54] Moreover, it should be noted that Fronto uses the word *plurimi* to describe the number of people approaching him alone to contact a single *iuridicus* in Italy concerning local affairs.[55]

Epigraphic evidence for the last gubernatorial resource, appointments and promotions, is more explicit. The resources varied according to the type of governorship. For example, from the reign of Gaius the proconsul of Africa no longer commanded a legion and so no longer was able to distribute army posts, but he, like other governors, continued to make appointments to his staff for civilian administration. The staff of a governor comprised three groups: the aristocratic companions whom the governor took out to the province with him, the military *officium*, and the humble staff (e.g. lictors).[56] The group of aristocratic friends and protégés which accompanied governors to their provinces has been discussed in a previous chapter. As for the clerical and sub-clerical staff who accompanied the governor (for example, the *scribae* and lictors) little can be said. In theory, at least, these men were probably selected by lot in Rome, so that the posts were not in the gift of the governor. A. H. M. Jones, however, notes the case of Verres' *scriba* in the Republic who accompanied Verres on too many tours of duty to have been selected by a random process.[57] The lack of evidence for the Principate does not allow us to draw any conclusion.

Appointment to the governor's military *officium* represented a substantial promotion from the ranks. Egyptian papyri show governors making these appointments, and further indicate that in addition to *commendationes*, bribery was thought necessary to secure such posts.[58] The patronal relationship between these *beneficarii* and the governor is attested by relatively numerous dedications.[59] For instance, T. Flavius Serenus, *praeses* of both Mauretanias, received an honorary inscription from Iulius Sabinus and his brother Pontianus, 'adiutor et strator eius' (no. 24). The words 'patrono incomparabili' in the inscription specify the nature of the relationship more clearly than in

53 *Ad Amic.* 2.8.
54 Jones, *Dio Chrysostom*, ch. 11.
55 *Ad Amic.* 2.8.
56 Burton, *Powers and Functions of Proconsuls*, ch. 1 and A.H.M. Jones, 'The Roman Civil Service' in *Studies in Roman Government and Law*, 153-75.
57 'Roman Civil Service', 155.
58 G. R. Watson, *The Roman Soldier*, 37f.
59 See, for example, *CIL* VIII 2746, 2750, 2751, 2733; *AE* (1917-18), 71, 72, 77, 78.

most other dedications. We also find patronal dedications from *domicuratores* (nos. 27 and 43), one of whom explicitly attributes his promotion to his patron, the governor of Numidia.

Command of an army provided more appointments for imperial legates and procurators in charge of auxiliary units — as Pliny implies, the larger the army, the greater the number of *beneficia* at the commander's disposal.[60] The appointment of aristrocratic protégés to equestrian *militiae* has been described elsewhere. Here we shall briefly survey appointments at a lower level, without attempting to offer a comprehensive discussion of the topic. The governor was responsible *de iure* for appointments below the grade of centurion and often *de facto* for appointments to the centurionate for which the emperor was formally responsible. E. Birley has outlined the evidence for patronage in the appointment of both civilians and soldiers from the ranks to centurionates.[61] In some instances the evidence for patronage is clear: Ti. Iulius Pollienus Auspex, legate of Numidia c. 217-20, received a dedication from the centurion C. Publilius Septtiminius (sic) *candidatus eius* (no. 29). For others the evidence is indirect: Birley has noticed cases in which the promotion and movement of centurions are parallel to the movements of senatorial legates and hence are suggestive of patronage relationships. At a lower level we find several dedications to African governors by *decuriones alae* (commanders of the *turmae* of the *auxilia*). A commander of III Augusta, M. Aurelius Cominius Cassianus, was thanked by a *decurio alae*, 'ex corniculario provectus ab eo' (no. 13).[62] These examples cannot indicate the frequency of patronal influence in these appointments, but it is clear that the placement of loyal clients in positions of responsibility (especially centurionates) could be of considerable importance. Tacitus reports that upon arriving in Syria Cn. Piso replaced the serving centurions with his *clientes*, and later Vitellius appointed centurions loyal to his cause in the British legions.[63]

Governors also recommended provincials for high equestrian and senatorial offices filled by the emperor. The description of this mediation is left to the latter part of the chapter. A letter of Fronto suggests that mediation is not the only type of patronal resource left out of the basic list given in this section. Fronto wrote to Caelius Optatus, possibly the Numidian legate, on behalf of Sardius Saturninus.[64] He requested help for Saturninus with his *negotium*. The

---

60 *Ep.* 2.13; see above, p.132.
61 'Promotions and transfers in the Roman army', *Carnuntum Jahrbuch* 7 (1963-64), 22ff. Dedications from centurions to the Numidian legate include *CIL* VIII. 2730, 2737, 2742, 2753, and *AE* (1917-18), 50, 51, and (1954), 138. Note also *ILAlg.* II.i.634 which may represent the same sort of case of patronage.
62 See *CIL* III.6154 (= *ILS* 1174) for a non-African example.
63 *Ann.* 2.55 and *Hist.* 3.44.
64 *Ad Amic.* 1.9; for further discussion, see p.163 below. Whether this Caelius Optatus should be identified with the Numidian legate has been doubted by Champlin, 'The chronology of

nature of the help is not specified. It seems unlikely that it falls into the categories discussed above. Perhaps Saturninus required assistance in the collection of a debt or rent, *beneficia* known from Cicero's letters in which similar language is found.[65] Such suggestions, however, must remain speculative in the absence of any specific evidence, and we must be content with the suggestion that governors provided other services in their patronal roles for which no evidence survives.

It seems reasonable to conclude that in all gubernatorial administrative activities provincials could profit from patron-client bonds with governors. How, then, were these bonds established? What avenues were open to the governor's favor? The variety of ways in which a governor might be contacted and a patronage relationship established must have been almost limitless. From the time the governor entered his province he listened to orations in the provincial capital and in each of the cities through which he passed on his assize circuit (Sabratha and Utica are documented for Africa Proconsularis).[66] The speeches offered orators opportunities to shower praise on the governor and so win his favor. In an oration before the proconsul Severianus in Carthage, Apuleius expressed his regret that he could not read out his complete works. It was his desire 'to offer all of my works and to enjoy your praiseworthy testimony to all the offspring of my muse! Not on account of lack of praise, which has long been preserved fresh and brilliant up to you through all your predecessors, but because I wish to be praiseworthy to no one more than the man whom I myself esteem for virtue above all others.'[67] Reference to Severianus' *antecessores* suggests that Apuleius regularly gave such orations, and we have part of another oration to another proconsul, Scipio Orfitus, in which Apuleius also speaks of seeking the proconsul's *amicitia*.[68] As Apuleius points out (and Libanius vividly confirms), praise of the orator was a sign of *amor* on the governor's part. Apuleius claims to be different from the rest of mankind on account of the total lack of self-interest in his friendship with the

Fronto', 151. The letter can be used here with some reservations for the following reasons. (1) Champlin's arguments do not appear entirely compelling: the *nomen* Sardius is so rare as to be indecisive and Fronto's use of 'frater' and 'filius' to his addressees need not reflect strict considerations of age (the use of *filius* with regard to Arrius Antoninus could be explained on the basis of a patron-protégé relationship, and in any case the senatorial *cursus* was not so highly structured that Optatus could not have been somewhat older than Antoninus in 167). (2) The numerous parallel requests from Cicero for help with a client's *negotia* strongly suggest that this can be used as an example of a letter sent to a governor — even if not a governor of Africa (see *Ad fam.* 13.11, 14, 26, 27, 30, 56, 57, 63).

65 See references in previous note.
66 Burton, *Powers and Functions of Proconsuls*, ch. 2 and *Dig.* 1.16.7 for orations; Burton, 'Proconsuls, assizes', 96 for assize centers.
67 *Flor.* 9: 'offerre ac praedicabili testimonio tuo ad omnem nostram Camenam frui! non hercule penuria laudis, quae mihi dudum integra et florens per omnes antecessores tuos ad te reservata est, sed quoniam nulli me probatiorem volo, quam quem ipse ante omnis merito probo.'
68 *Flor.* 17

governor.[69] He is no doubt right that other orators were willing to exploit their *amicitiae* with governors; his own selflessness may be open to doubt after reading his *Apologia.* However that may be, the point is that the literary culture of the empire provided common interests and common grounds for *amicitiae* between orators and educated governors. Just as Greek sophists were thought worthy of imperial friendship and rewards for moving rhetorical displays before the emperor,[70] so a provincial orator might thrust himself into the good graces of the governor and thus benefit.

It was suggested above that most of the governor's time in civilian administration was devoted to hearing legal cases. This provided *advocati* with a number of opportunities for contact, as the patronal dedications from them attest.[71] Moreover, for some governors the greater part of the year was spent travelling around the assize circuit. The cities which the governors visited had the opportunity of cementing *hospitium* bonds.[72] During these rounds the governors apparently stayed in the houses of local notables, who were able to impress the Roman officials with lavish entertainment and form private ties of *hospitium.*[73] The connection between *hospitium* and individual patronage is well known for the Republican period, and the custom of *hospitium,* together with the route of the assize circuit, must have continued to be important in the distribution of patronal favors during the Empire.[74] On the one hand, those cities off the assize circuit might rarely receive gubernatorial visits with the result that opportunities for contact with the governor and hence for his patronage were rare. On the other hand, families with a *hospitium* relationship with a senatorial or high equestrian provincial official must have been prime candidates for *beneficia* while the governor was still in his province, and also for opportunities arising after his return to Rome. These conjectures find support in evidence from the later Empire, when patronage came to be considered an abuse and a threat to imperial administration: part of the campaign to suppress certain aspects of patronage included laws prohibiting governors from staying in or even visiting the houses of private individuals.[75]

Occasions on which a town's leading citizens contacted governors on

---

69 *Flor.* 9; see Libanius, *Or.* 1 *passim* (esp. 180f., 232) for the importance of giving or not giving orations before governors.

70 Philostratus, *V.S.* 533, 589f., 626.

71 See above, note 27 with text.

72 *CIL* VIII.68 and *AE* (1913), 40.

73 Burton, *Powers and Functions of Proconsuls,* ch. 1: Apuleius remarks very briefly about the time 'quo provinciam circumibas [sc. Severianus]' (*Flor.* 9).

74 For the link between *hospitium* and patronage of municipal aristocrats in the Republic, T.P. Wiseman, *New Men in the Roman Senate, 139 B.C.-A.D. 14,* 33ff.

75 Libanius, *Or.* 1.211; *C.T.* 1.16.12.1 (369 A.D.) for comment on which see J. Matthews, *Western Aristocracies and the Imperial Court A.D. 364-425,* 29. For the dating of the beginning of the anti-patronage legislation and the idea that it had not been a threat to government and so not prosecuted earlier, de Ste Croix, 'Suffragium', 44.

municipal business probably also provided opportunities for the cementing of personal bonds. Philostratus indicates that this occurred in meetings between emperors and ambassadors from Greek cities who received personal favors for their effort.[76] It is clear from Pliny's letters, Dio's orations and inscriptions such as that documenting Frontinianus' involvement in the Cuicul building project, that governors were in frequent contact with municipal aristocrats in matters of local administration. Moreover, governors constituted the single largest group of municipal patrons and one would expect that in this capacity too governors would have been open to the initiation of personal friendships by the towns' notables.[77] Such may have been the circumstances for the development of patronage relationships between two Numidian governors and municipal aristocrats from Lambaesis. Both Q. Anicius Faustus (197-201) and M. Aurelius Cominius Cassianus (246-7) were patrons of Lambaesis and inscriptions suggest that they were involved there in local affairs, especially building activities.[78] It was perhaps through these activities that the municipal leaders who dedicated inscriptions to them as patrons came into contact and established bonds with them (nos. 3 and 14). Of course, the reverse sequence is also possible: personal friendships with local leaders may have involved governors in municipal affairs and led them to accept positions as municipal patrons.[79] Whatever the sequence, the existence of a link between private and public patronage is likely owing to the personal nature of the governor's administration.

Direct contacts with the governor provided provincials with opportunities for developing patronage relationships. In addition to these, and perhaps more important, were indirect methods of contact. Several of our patronage inscriptions are dedicated to wives or sons of governors.[80] Typical is *AE* (1946), 64, from Thamugadi: 'M. Aemilio Macro Dinarcho M. Aemili Macri leg. Aug. pr. pr. cos. desig. filio patrono P. Iulius C. f. Papiria Iunianus.' Unfortunately, such a brief inscription cannot provide a clear idea of what was happening. It is impossible to know from the stone whether the relative of the governor was a patron in his own right or whether his patronage consisted

---

76 Hadrian of Tyre before Marcus Aurelius: *V.S.* 589; Heliodorus before Caracalla: *V.S.* 626.

77 Lists of municipal patrons for North African cities can be found in B.H. Warmington, 'The municipal patrons of Roman North Africa', *PBSR* n.s. 9 (1954), 39-55 and L. Harmand, *Le patronat.*

78 Thomasson, *Statthalter,* 2, 197ff. and 216ff. for the epigraphic evidence for the terms of office of Faustus and Cassianus, respectively.

79 For discussions of municipal patronage, see Warmington, 'Municipal patrons', 39-55 and L. Harmand, *Le patronat.* (The reader should be warned that Harmand's list of municipal patrons is not only incomplete, but also unreliable: for example, C. Iulius Lepidus Tertullus is listed as a patron of Diana Veteranorum on the basis of *AE* (1934), 26 which is a dedication by M. Aemilius Felix Iunior to his *optimus patronus* — clearly *patronus* here refers to Tertullus' relationship with Iunior.)

80 Nos. 2, 18 and 27.

mainly of influencing the governor. At the imperial court at Rome women seem to have been important mainly in the second way (or so our sources lead us to believe).[81] There is every reason to expect governors' wives to have been a source of patronage in the same way.[82] Tacitus relates a debate in the senate during the reign of Tiberius over a proposal to ban governors from taking their wives out to the provinces with them. Speaking in favor of the ban, Caecina Severus argued that the basest provincials attached themselves to the wives who then interfered in the governors' *negotia*.[83] Besides influence on the governor, sons of proconsuls often possessed their own patronage resources in their capacity as legates with delegated responsibility for dealing with legal and administrative matters. Apuleius praised Severianus' son Honorinus in the same way as the father: there was 'paternal fairness in the son, the prudence of an old man in the youth and consular authority in the legate' — and also, we might add, patronal resources comparable in some respects with the governor's.[84] Wives may also have had some independent resources, such as money.[85] In addition, in Aemilius Florus' dedication to Vergilia Florentina, wife of Iulius Fortunatianus, Florus' position in the household as *domicurator* (a post in the governor's *officium*) suggests that he may have been able to benefit directly from Vergilia.[86]

Finally, the method of contact for which we have most evidence is the *commendatio*. Jeremy Boissevain has described a modern parallel phenomenon in southern Italy and Sicily: the professional calling card. In these areas an individual wanting any sort of action from a government official must try to find a chain of relatives, friends and patrons through which he can approach the official. He goes to a friend and is passed on to a friend of a friend and so on until he reaches the official in question; at each stage he picks up the mediator's calling card to carry on to the next stage in order to identify himself as someone worthy of consideration. The calling cards are indispensable to his progress because 'the non-kin with whom [the official] deals in his official capacity, unless they are introduced by a third party who is a kinsman, friend, patron or client, receive short shrift. He is not only impartial, he is so detached as to be remote.'[87]

81 See above, pp.64f.
82 *CIL* VIII.2739 is very suggestive of female avenues of access to the governor: 'Munisiae P. fil. Celerinae coniugi D. Fontei Frontiniani leg. Augustor. pr. pr. cos. desig. Magnia Procula mater Caecili Concessi corniculari' (Lambaesis). The fact that Procula specifies that her son was serving under Frontinianus perhaps suggests that she used her contact with Celerina for his benefit. Another inscription in the table indicates that *corniculari* benefited from gubernatorial patronage (no. 13).
83 Tacitus, *Ann.* 3.33; also Martial, *Epig.* 2.56 and Juvenal, *Sat.* 8.128f.
84 *Flor.* 9.
85 For an example (not a governor's wife), *ILAfr.* 454.
86 *AE* (1917-18), 52; cf. Domaszewski, *Die Rangordnung des römischen Heeres*, rev. B. Dobson, 68.
87 'Patronage in Sicily', 21.

In many respects the function of the *commendatio* resembles that of the calling card. Consider, for example, the three fragmentary recommendations of Fronto addressed to men probably governing in North Africa at the time (two to proconsuls and one to a *legatus pro praetore*). All three are letters of introduction in the same tradition as Cicero's *commendationes*, varying in length but with the same essential components.[88] First come a few lines describing Fronto's relationship with the man and then a request for the governor to take the man into his *amicitia* and give him help in every possible way. Though more verbose than modern Sicilian calling cards, these *commendationes* are similar in purpose. In none of these letters (nor in many of Cicero's)[89] is the favor spelled out. In the letter to Lollianus Avitus, Fronto says that Licinius Montanus 'in accordance with his modesty has asked nothing except what is right and honorable both for you to give and for him to ask... Since I love him as I do very few other men, please enjoy the company of one dear to me, receive him when he comes, embrace him with kind concern and give him the best counsel appropriate to friends.'[90] It is possible that something more concrete was in the gaps in the manuscript, but nothing in the tone of the letter seems to suggest it. The other two *commendationes* are equally vague. Fronto wrote to Aegrilius Plarianus nothing more specific on behalf of Iulius Aquilinus than 'it is right that a man learned as well as cultured as Aquilinus is should not only be protected but also promoted and honored by a man as serious and wise as yourself'.[91] In the third letter Fronto asked Caelius Optatus simply: 'if any [of Sardius Saturninus'] *negotium* brings him to you, you should judge him a man worthy of every honor, a man dear to me, and should protect him with all your power'.[92] The message in each case is the same: not a specific favor, but a request to add the protégé or client to the governor's group of kin, friends and friends of friends, who because of their personal links deserve special consideration and favor.[93]

The letter of Optatus deserves a brief remark for another reason. Fronto's *familiaritas* with Sardius Saturninus arose *per filios suos* who were students of

---

88 For a similar form, see for example Cicero, *Ad Fam.* 13.45-47.

89 Cicero's two *commendationes* (*Ad Fam.* 13.6a, b) to a proconsul of Africa, Valerius Orca, on behalf of provincial friends of P. Cuspius are ambiguous about the nature of the favor. Of course, in some letters Cicero explains what is required, but often he does not (e.g., *Ad Fam.* 13.46, 47, 49, 51, 52).

90 *Ad Amic.* 1.3: 'Nihil postulavit pro sua verecundia nisi quod probum honestumque sit et tibi datu et sibi postulatu... Quom eum inter paucissimos ultro amem, fac mihi caro fruaris, eum praesentem accipias et propitia cura ambias et auxilium summum ei amicis consiliis feras.'

91 *Ad Amic.* 1.4: 'Decet a te gravissimo et sapientissimo viro tam doctum tamque elegantem virum non modo protegi sed etiam provehi et illustrari.'

92 *Ad Amic.* 1.9: 'si quid negotii eum ad te adduxerit, carissimum mihi virum omni honore dignum iudices et ope tua protegas'. For the problem of identifying the addressee, see note 64 above.

93 Of course, some *commendationes* do carry specific requests, most notably for staff offices, but none of these are addressed to governors of North Africa.

Fronto. It is quite possible that Fronto never met Saturninus: in another recommendation Fronto admits that he was not personally acquainted with the beneficiary of the letter.[94] The point is that here we see the chains of friends of friends which Boissevain found in modern Sicily. As Boissevain points out, the links in the chain can be vertical (up to a higher status group) or horizontal. So Saturninus made the vertical ascent through his sons — the shortest, most intimate path possible — to Fronto in the highest aristocratic circle in Rome, and then Fronto supplied the horizontal link back to Africa and the governor.

Fronto supplies three examples of the network being circuited through Rome. This need not happen: Apuleius indicates that he wrote a letter of recommendation to Lollianus Avitus in Carthage on behalf of his stepson Sicinius Pontianus. The precise nature of the request is not clear: all that is said is that Pontianus was going to Carthage and 'tirocinio orationis suae fuerat a me commendatus' ('and had been introduced by me for his oratorical début').[95] Apuleius' subsequent account is interesting because, if it bears any resemblance to the events, it underlines that *commendationes* were not simply polite formalities which a man could just as easily dispense with. After the initial recommendation was sent to Avitus, Apuleius fell out with Pontianus over the question of inheritance. This apparently generated much bitterness, and Apuleius wrote another letter to Avitus about the quarrel — the essential message being, no doubt, that Pontianus is not 'one of us' after all. When Pontianus later came on his knees to Apuleius, tearfully begging forgiveness, his foremost request seems to have been getting another favorable letter from Apuleius to reverse his standing with Avitus again. What exactly Pontianus hoped to gain from the good graces of the proconsul we do not know, but it is clear that his favor was of paramount concern.

I have concentrated here on *commendationes* related to North Africa. These, together with the other surviving *commendationes* and evidence of other methods of contacting the governor, suggest that from the time a governor took up office he faced a barrage of requests to take orators, friends of friends, local notables, etc. into his *amicitia*. The requests came from every quarter, from the emperor down to humbler local friends,[96] and no doubt every avenue of approach was exploited to win a share in what Marcus Aurelius himself described as 'the things appropriate to friends which faith and scruples of conscience allow a proconsul to distribute without harm to others'.[97]

Since patron-client relationships in the Roman world were reciprocal, we must ask finally how a provincial who approached a governor would display his

94 *Ad Amic.* 1.7.
95 *Apol.* 94; H. Pavis-d'Escurac gives brief consideration to this passage in 'Pour une étude de l'apologie d'Apulée', *Ant. Afr.* 8 (1974), 95.
96 For *commendationes* from emperors to governors, Pliny, *Ep.* 10.58.6 and Fronto, *Ad M. Caes.* 5.36.
97 Fronto, *Ad M. Caes.* 5.36.

gratia. Of course, much of the evidence for patronage has survived precisely because one of the expressions of *gratia* was a dedication inscribed on stone. The gratitude took other forms as well. Beyond the ordinary expressions of gratitude between private individuals discussed elsewhere (e.g., legacies), two are specific to governor-provincial relations and so deserve comment here. The first group consists of gifts given to governors. These could range from small *xenia* to large-scale bribes: the latter were clearly illegal and the former expressly legal by the Severan period.[98] Marius Priscus did not seem to be in doubt that his acceptance of a total of one million sesterces for the exile and execution of *equites Romani* and others was illegal. On the other hand, Ulpian devoted a paragraph to the problem of *xenia* which shows that the strict rules of the early Principate were formally modified at some point. He cites Septimius Severus who said: 'in so far as *xenia* are concerned, hear what we think: there is an old proverb: οὔτε πάντα οὔτε πάντοτε οὔτε παρὰ πάντων [not everything, not every time, not from everyone]. For to accept gifts from no one is exceedingly discourteous, but to do so indiscriminately is very base and to accept everything is most greedy.'[99] The limitations on *xenia* thus were nebulous and Ulpian could not provide any clearer definition than Severus.[100] Though governors were left in some doubt as to where this line between illegal and legal was to be drawn, they were apparently expected to profit from their sojourn in the province. The *salarium* paid out to them was supposed to be for travelling and living expenses.[101] And yet senators who asked to be excused from service traditionally requested the *salarium* despite the lack of expenses.[102] The implication may be that, whatever its purpose, governors expected legally to clear at least their *salarium* as profit by (at the minimum) living off provincial *xenia* and other income and hospitality.

Because the law concerning bribery and *xenia* as well as other administrative rules was vague, prosecution by provincials often was a matter of discretion. Consequently, patronage ties with leading provincials might be very useful for a governor after his tour of duty. Dio of Prusa urged the Bithynians not to engage in internal quarrelling precisely on the grounds that it would allow a governor to establish favorable relationships with factions, and then to wrong the province with impunity, knowing that he would enjoy the support of his local favorites in any prosecution for maladministration.[103] It

---

98 Pliny's letters (*Ep.* 4.9) concerning the trial of Iulius Bassus indicates that acceptance of any gifts by governors was illegal at the time.
99 *Dig.* 1.16.6.3.: 'quantum ad xenia pertinet, audi quid sentimus: vetus proverbium est: οὔτε πάντα οὔτε πάντοτε οὔτε παρὰ πάντων, nam valde inhumanum est a nemine accipere, sed passim vilissimum est et omnia avarissimum.'
100 Sherwin-White, *Letters of Pliny*, 277 notes that the date of the change of rules is uncertain.
101 Dio 52.23.1 and 52.25.3.
102 Tacitus, *Agric.* 42.2.
103 *Or.* 38.36f and 39.4; also Philostratus, *Apoll.* 6.38; Jones, *Dio Chrysostom*, ch. 10.

appears from other evidence that Dio's warning to the Bithynians was justified. Evidence for the same phenomenon in the West can be found in the Thorigny Marble from Gaul.[104] The sequence of events described in Iulianus' letter illustrates the kind of impact a leading provincial could have on efforts to prosecute a governor and therefore the importance of a governor developing a clientèle among such men. The traditional idea that Rome supported municipal aristocracies across the empire and in return benefited from their allegiance had its parallel here at the personal level.[105] Just as at the imperial level the emperor distributed his stock of *beneficia* to buy the loyalty of the Roman aristocracy, so the governor built up a loyal and useful clientèle among the provincial aristocracy, both by favoring clients in local disputes and by supplying the patronage needed to enter the imperial aristocracy.

The above discussion relates to praesidial procurators in their capacity as governors. We must now turn to their financial responsibilities and to non-praesidial procurators. The expectation that their financial powers provided them with resources for patronage is borne out to some extent by the epigraphic evidence. Brunt has described the ebb and flow of procuratorial jurisdiction from the reign of Claudius.[106] For the most part procurators were limited to hearing cases related to the fiscus. Some of these cases might require the procurator's 'interpretative judgement' and involve local quarrels.[107] Procurators were accused of sometimes favoring their patron and employer.[108] We might suspect, then, that they could also be 'lenient' (or 'fair', depending on the viewpoint) when other, closer personal ties outweighed their concern for the emperor's interests. Dio of Prusa claimed that he had never accused an enemy of having infringed on imperial estates: presumably this sort of accusation would be heard by an imperial procurator who could use his judicial power just as governors did, to injure or favor locals in accordance with his patronal connections.[109] Needless to say, people were not keen to leave dedications to patrons explicitly indicating that by their favor cases were won at imperial expense. As a result, we should not be surprised that no epigraphic evidence survives from North Africa to confirm these suggestions.

An invaluable piece of evidence does survive to document patronage by procurators of imperial estates. The vast tracts of imperial land in Africa, administered by equestrian procurators, were leased to *conductores* who in turn subleased plots to *coloni*. A *lex Hadriana* set out the obligations of the

---

104 See above, p.132.
105 For *beneficia* distributed by the Roman government to its African supporters and potential supporters, P. Garnsey, 'Rome's African Empire under the Principate', in *Imperialism in the Ancient World*, ed. C.R. Whittaker and P. Garnsey, 223.
106 P.A. Brunt, 'Procuratorial jurisdiction', *Latomus* 25 (1966), 461-89.
107 *Ibid.*, 475.
108 *Ibid.*, 480f.
109 *Or.* 46.7-8.

coloni on the *saltus Burunitanus* to the *conductores*, such as six days per year of corvée labor. The procurator had soldiers at his disposal to enforce the obligations as he saw fit. In this situation a patronage relationship between the procurator and his *conductores* presented opportunities for mutual profit at the expense of the *coloni*. In the reign of Commodus the *coloni* took their complaints about collusion to the emperor through a representative, Lurius Lucullus.[110] The *coloni* alleged that Allius Maximus, a *conductor*, enjoyed the favor of a series of procurators partly on account of his *largitiones* to them. As a result, the procurators not only refrained from investigating alleged violations of the *lex Hadriana*, but even sent soldiers to enforce the illegal demands for extra labor by violence. Now if this were a simple case of bribery, then it would not meet our definition of patronage. But the *coloni* imply that the relationship consisted of more than isolated exchanges of money: in their view the *conductores* won support from the officials not only by the *largitiones*, but also because the *conductores* were personally known 'to each of the procurators on account of the contract' (ll.20f.).

How much the tenants exaggerated the pervasiveness of this patronage is difficult to ascertain. In addition to another inscription complaining about similar abuses, a dedication survives testifying to an open and friendly relationship between *conductores* and patrimonial procurators: 'T. Flavio T.f. Quir. Macro IIvir, flamini perp. Ammaederensium, praef. gentis Musulamiorum, curatori frumen. comparandi in annona urbis facto a divo Nerva Traiano Aug., proc. Aug. ad praedia saltus Hipponiensis et Thevestini, proc. provinciae Siciliae, collegium Larum Caesaris nostri et liberti et familia item conductores, qui in regione Hipponiensi consistent.'[111] Why the first three groups of dedicators, the administrative personnel under Macer, decided to set up the stone we do not know, but a good guess can be made for the *conductores*. The fact that the *conductores* felt free publicly to thank a procurator of imperial estates indicates perhaps that the complaints of the *coloni* were not exaggerated.

Up to this point our discussion of the *loci* of power and patronage has concentrated on the highest senatorial and equestrian officials, for whom we have most information. To the extent that their subordinates shared in or were delegated the power to make decisions, they also shared patronal resources. This was briefly suggested above in relation to legates with legal and administrative duties delegated by proconsuls, and seems to be confirmed by

---

110 *CIL* VIII.10570 + 14464 = Abbott and Johnson no. 111 = *ILS* 6870; Rostovtzeff, *Studien zur Geschichte des römischen Kolonates*, 370ff.
111 *AE* (1922), 19 = *ILAlg.* I.3992; for comment, see the original publication by Albertini, *BCTH* (1921), CCVIf. For the other record of complaint by African *coloni*, *CIL* VIII. 14428. The motivation behind one other dedication by a local notable to an African procurator (no. 46) is difficult to discern; perhaps this man could also have been a *conductor*?

the fact that they undoubtedly possessed the resources to act as municipal patrons.[112] At a lower level, clerks and notaries on the governor's staff could occupy quite influential positions owing to their control of access to the governor and to files of documents. Philo indicates that Egyptian prefects were frequently at the mercy of their clerks, who were thus able to help friends, clients and anyone else with enough money for bribery.[113] Egypt, with its complex administrative system, was something of a special case in this respect, but there is evidence that elsewhere clerical and sub-clerical staffs also had opportunities to exercise influence on behalf of those enjoying their favor. The experience of Aristides, for example, shows that in Asia the goodwill of the governor's staff might be necessary to ensure that petitions and letters came to the governor's attention.[114]

To summarize, wherever we have located official power in provincial government, we also have been able to document patronage. Unfortunately, the fragmentary positive evidence does not enable us to decide whether it was an aberration or the norm. But it seems probable that patronage was as pervasive as it has been in other societies with similar patronal ideologies: not only were patron-client relationships with officials not suppressed in the Principate, they were openly advertised in every major city by inscriptions erected in public by proud clients. Furthermore, if the common view is accepted that interference in local affairs by the emperor's officials increased as time passed,[115] then it seems quite likely that the opportunities and motivations for developing ties with governors and procurators also grew, as both the ruling power and provincial aristocrats attempted to manipulate one another for their own benefit. The consequences of this will be discussed at the end of this chapter.

PROVINCIALS AND THEIR MEDIATORS

In his speech before Scipio Orfitus, proconsul of Africa, Apuleius poured scorn on those provincials who gathered subserviently around the governor, men who 'gloried in the pretended expressions of your friendship'. Apuleius, by contrast, had moved in Orfitus' circle of friends at Rome. His connections and reputation were such that he could confidently tell the governor 'that my *amicitia* ought to be eagerly taken up by you no less than yours ought to be desired by me'.[116] This passage provides an example of a provincial's

---

112 *IRT* 330, 342; *AE* (1935), 32; *ILAfr.*506. See Dio 72.11 for examples of bribery of legates by provincials.
113 Brunt, 'Administrators of Roman Egypt', 135 and 140f.
114 Burton, 'Proconsuls, assizes', 101.
115 For the argument for increasing interference in the East and the resulting increase of references to governors as benefactors, V. Nutton, 'The beneficial ideology', in *Imperialism*, ed. Whittaker and Garnsey. Nutton uses the study by L. Robert, 'Epigrammes relatives à des gouverneurs', *Hellenica* 4 (1948), 35.
116 *Flor.* 17: 'ut non minus vobis amicitia mea capessenda sit quam mihi vestra concupiscenda'.

connections with private circles of Roman aristocrats, and the importance of these contacts is illustrated by the boldness with which Apuleius addressed the governor, treating him more as an equal than as a superior. In the previous section these Roman connections were introduced as one means of establishing patronage relationships with provincial administrators. Now I want to consider what other *beneficia* a provincial might seek through the patronal mediators which linked him with Rome. Then, after consideration of the contents of the exchange, will follow an examination of how provincials, especially Africans, established the personal bonds with their mediators.

The list of benefits which a provincial could hope to obtain in Rome through effective influence included citizenship, equestrian honors, the *latus clavus*, various offices and administrative decisions. In his recent book Millar set out a full treatment of citizenship grants, collecting the 'sporadic individual instances' from the first and second centuries.[117] Those who mediated the provincials' requests included provincial officials and private individuals. Pliny is found submitting requests for citizenship to Trajan in both capacities. For instance, as governor of Bithynia he forwarded a centurion's *libellus* requesting citizenship for his daughter.[118] We possess epigraphic evidence from Africa for this phenomenon of forwarding *libelli* in the form of the Tabula Banasitana.[119] In Banasa were found copies, inscribed on bronze, of the imperial replies to requests from tribal leaders for citizenship for their wives and children. In each case the emperors' letters make it clear that the procurators of Mauretania Tingitana did more than simply forward the *libelli*: the governors also played the part of *suffragatores* providing letters testifying to the *merita* and *fides* of the two leaders of the Zegrenses ('suffragante... per epistulam'). It seems likely that in backward areas of the provinces such as this, imperial officials would have been the only men available capable of supplying the necessary mediating link with the emperor.

By contrast, in the better developed areas which boasted native-born senators and *equites*, private mediators must have been relatively more important. The tone of Pliny's requests to Trajan written before his governorship of Bithynia indicates that such letters were routine.[120] As Millar points out, 'the very randomness of the examples [of individual grants] is some indication of how general a form of *beneficium* this was.'[121] It is possible to speculate from nomenclature about the patrons who secured citizenship, as a recent biographer does for the ancestors of Septimius Severus.[122] But the

---

117 *Emperor*, 482ff.
118 *Ep.* 10.106.
119 W. Seston and M. Euzennat, 'Un dossier de la chancellerie romaine: la *Tabula Banasitana*', *CRAI* (1971), 468-90; cf. Millar, *Emperor*, 261f.
120 *Ep.* 10.5, 6, 7, 10, 11.
121 *Emperor*, 482.
122 Birley, *Septimus Severus*, 304, where he suggests that the *nomen* came from Septimius

uncertainties involved are such that we cannot progress much beyond Millar's generalization.

It is worth mentioning briefly in this context the kind of patronage that falls between municipal and personal. Duncan-Jones has discussed the use of influence to secure civic statuses. Grants of full citizenship to whole communities do not fall within our topic. But when Latium maius or Latium minus was granted to a city, the patron benefited a small group of leading citizens and no doubt enjoyed their personal gratitude in return. *CIL* VIII.22737 was set up to a local man from Gigthis for securing Latium maius for the city on his second attempt in Rome. Duncan-Jones concluded his article with the remark that 'given better backing, M. Servilius Draco Albucianus of Gigthis might have achieved Latium maius for his town without travelling to Rome twice on that account'.[123] It might be added that Albucianus may well have taken the precaution of securing more effective influence after his initial failure.

The uncertainties raised by the grant of the *equus publicus* and membership in the *quinque decuriae* were discussed in the context of imperial *beneficia*.[124] Of interest here is what the African inscriptions indicate about their distribution to provincial notables. Duncan-Jones in his article about African *equites* maintains that 'it is very rarely possible to make any suggestion about the identity of the officials to whose help particular knights may have owed their promotion'.[125] There are, however, a few more plausible examples of patronage than listed in this survey. The relatively large number of men *exornati equo publico* in Cirta, it was suggested, was the result of patronage by their fellow *municipes* in the Roman senate.[126] Men from smaller towns, such as Cuicul and Castellum Tidditanorum, held magistracies in the Cirtan confederation and quite possibly benefited from the friendships made there to gain the public horse.[127]

Patronage can be conjectured with more assurance in those cases in which an inscription links a man holding some equestrian honor to an imperial aristocrat: both C. Didius Maximus and Q. Asturnius Lappianus, *equites*, had senatorial brothers-in-law; the equestrian Q. Cornelius Rusticus was a teacher of a *clarissimus vir;* and C. Volumnius Marcellus Caecilianus expressed his *pietas* to the memory of the son of P. Porcius Optatus Flamma, a senator of

---

Flaccus, the legate of III Augusta in c. 79.

123 'Patronage and city privileges — the case of Giufi', *Epigraphische Studien* 9 (1972), 16.
124 See above, pp.51ff.
125 'Equestrian rank', 154.
126 *Ibid.*, 154.
127 *Ibid.*, 161f. Duncan-Jones' speculation on p. 154 about Lollius Urbicus' patronage of Q. Sittius Faustus faces the criticism that Faustus was 'in quinque decurias adlectus' some ten years after Urbicus probably died (*PIR²*L 327). On Urbicus' career, see A.R. Birley, 'The Governors of Roman Britain', *Epigraphische Studien* 4 (1967), 71 n. 24.

praetorian rank.[128] These examples will be discussed further in the next section.

For the vast majority of men with equestrian rank we do not know enough to make plausible guesses concerning the personal networks through which the awards were secured. As a result of his research, Duncan-Jones suggested that a correlation in the evidence exists to indicate that the requisite census and effective patronage were not the only factors in the distribution:

Although most of the inscriptions are uninformative or inconclusive about access to equestrian rank, usually some clearly show a sequence in which municipal activities, including the tenure of magistracies or priesthoods, were followed by promotion to equestrian or juror rank. It is reasonable to see a causal relationship between the two parts of this sequence, since the promotion of obscure provincials was probably closely related to paper qualifications, and can have depended little upon direct assessment of personal ability.[129]

This view, based on a large body of evidence, is quite important because, if correct, it introduces some universalistic criteria into Millar's image of a very particularistic process of petition-and-response for imperial grants. The conclusion is based on several observations about the *cursus* inscriptions of equestrians who held a series of local magistracies. Those inscriptions in which equestrian rank is placed ahead of the municipal offices are set aside quite properly on the grounds that the grant of equestrian status may have been placed at the beginning of the *cursus* to emphasize its importance rather than to indicate its temporal priority. Of the remaining careers of two or more offices, it is noted that in the great majority of cases equestrian rank is placed after the local offices, and in only four instances can the grant be shown to have come at the beginning or in the middle of a municipal career.[130] Thus, the conclusion is that a completed municipal career was a criterion for the distribution of the *equus publicus*. Several objections to this argument may be raised. It is quite possible that it was customary to keep municipal offices and equestrian grants separate in the inscription, with the result that we should not expect to find equestrian status listed between local posts, even if they were

---

128 See below, pp.202, 203, 184 for the first three men. For Caecilianus and Flamma see *ILAlg.* II.i.648.

129 'Equestrian rank', 153. I wish to thank Dr Duncan-Jones for discussing this issue in detail with me, though I am unable to accept some of his conclusions.

130 *Ibid.*, 155, where a list is supplied of 14 men who held magistracies and priesthoods before the grant of equestrian rank, 8 who held priesthoods, and 5 who held magistracies — a total of 27 out of 33.

131 It is not surprising that only one definite case of equestrian rank granted before a municipal career can be found, given the very exacting conditions required to show it — i.e., an equestrian whose career was inscribed during the brief period when he was *designatus* for his first magistracy (a *cursus* inscribed at any other point in the career would be ambiguous, since the placement of the equestrian rank at the head of the career could be for reasons of prominence rather than chronological priority).

received in that sequence.[131] Moreover, no account is taken of the significant number of local aristocrats with equestrian rank whose *cursus* inscriptions include only one of the lesser municipal magistracies — an indication that the *equus publicus* was granted before or in the middle of their local careers.[132] It may be true that a majority of African *equites* held municipal office, but this would indicate nothing about a causal link: if most wealthy locals held municipal office, then office-holders should constitute the more numerous group of local equestrians, given a random distribution of the rank among wealthy, freeborn citizens.[133] It is possible that local magistrates had a somewhat better chance of securing equestrian rank — not because the emperor intended it to be 'a recognition of local eminence which had not so far received any institutional expression' (for which there is no evidence), but because, as we shall see, participation in civic life afforded opportunities to initiate potentially profitable relationships.[134]

The grant of the *latus clavus* completes the basic list of promotions into higher legal *ordines* available from the emperor through patronage (with the exceptions of grants of the *ius anulorum* and the *ius ingenuitatis* for which I know of no provincial evidence). The grant of the *latus clavus* and entry into the senate through patronal support have been considered with special regard to Pliny's protégés.[135] There is every reason to think that the same process was at work, especially in the second century, drawing Africans and other provincials into the senate in great numbers.[136] For example, during his African proconsulship Vespasian is said to have obtained the *latus clavus* for a young man from his province for the sum of 200,000 sesterces, and Septimius Severus received the broad stripe with the help of his consular uncle of the same name.[137] The paternal tone of Fronto's letter to the Cirtan Arrius Antoninus is suggestive of a similar relationship.[138]

After promotion into a new order provincials sought procuratorial and senatorial offices with the help of patrons. These careers have been analyzed in

131 Nos. 97, 99, 113, 120, 133 in Duncan-Jones' list possessed equestrian rank though they had only reached the aedileship when their careers were inscribed. It seems plausible to suggest that those equestrians who list themselves only as *decuriones* also had not reached the duumvirate or some comparable office before receiving the *equus publicus* (nos. 104, 105, 116, 117, 123, 126, 142, 143, 159, 167). If these examples are accepted, then instead of 27 out of 33 cases of equestrian rank after completing a municipal career, we have only 27 out of 48 — hardly a marked correlation.

133 Duncan-Jones, 'Equestrian rank', 153, attaches significance to the fact that the majority of African *equites* were men who took part in municipal activities, without consideration of what proportion of the wealthy aristocracy these men represented.

134 'Equestrian rank', 153.

135 See above, pp.142f.

136 Pelletier in 'Les senateurs', 511-31, gives a list of more than one hundred senators certainly from Proconsularis. The list does not include Numidia nor is it entirely reliable (Garnsey, 'Rome's African Empire', n. 118).

137 Suetonius, *Vesp.* 4 and H.A., *Sev.* 1.5.

138 See below, p.181.

an earlier chapter; it remains here only to summarize briefly the corroboration to be found in the African epigraphic evidence. In two cases the term *candidatus* leaves little doubt about the patron's role in securing offices. The first case concerns the office of *fisci advocatus*, established by Hadrian and serving as a civilian antecedent to a procuratorial career.[139] Philostratus indicates that the office was used by emperors as a reward for men winning their favor.[140] An African inscription suggests that it is one more type of *beneficium* in which the emperors allowed others a share. L. Titinius Clodianus served as *procurator provinciae Numidiae partes praesidis agens* some time between 238 and 253.[141] Later, when Clodianus was in Rome as *procurator ludi magni*, C. Vibius Maximus, *eques Romanus, flamen perpetuus, fisci advocatus* and *candidatus eius*, dedicated an inscription to him (*patrono rarissimo*) in Lambaesis, Maximus' native city.[142] Though not certain, it seems very likely that this relationship was a result of Clodianus' governorship.[143] The second inscription (*CIL* VIII.25382) illustrates a patronage relationship between two men from Utica: 'L. Calpurnio Fido Aemiliano c.v., quaest. Cret. Cyr., trib. pleb., P. Sicinius Pescennius Hilarianus candid. eius amico incomparabili.' There is no way of deducing for which office Hilarianus might have been a candidate and so it is not certain that it was an equestrian or senatorial post. Because of the absence of the phrase *candidatus eius* in most inscriptions, the exercise of patronage to secure equestrian office can only be guessed at in other cases: several procurators from leading Lepcitane families erected dedications in Lepcis Magna to their fellow townsman, the emperor Septimius Severus, and Valgius Mauricus dedicated an inscription to his *condiscipulus*, the ducenarian procurator, Pomponius L [...]murianus to whom he may have owed his post as *fisci advocatus*.[144]

Up to this point we have concentrated on the *beneficia* distributed *ad hominem* by the emperor. This distribution has been characterized as a petition-and-response process. Here personal networks and personal petitions were, so far as we know, the only means of acquisition for provincials, not merely an alternative to some formal, impersonal administrative structure. We should not lose sight of the fact, however, that as a 'predatory state' Rome and especially the emperor had two vital and

---

139 *RE I*, col. 438-39 (Kubitschek).
140 *V.S.* 626 concerning Heliodorus' favor with Caracalla and appointment as *fisci advocatus*.
141 E. Birley, 'Governors of Numidia', 66f. and Pflaum, *Carrières*, 859f.
142 No. 51.
143 It should not be assumed automatically that Maximus necessarily established the relationship while Clodianus was still governor (though it seems likely). It may have been that Clodianus' stay in Numidia established the chain of links so that Maximus could contact him later through friends of friends (as in Fronto's letters).
144 See below, p.184.

continuing interests in the provinces: order and taxation. To secure these two interests an administrative system existed and patrons, in turn, can be found exerting influence within the system on behalf of provincials.[145]

Given the severe limitations on our knowledge, it is impossible to present compelling evidence for the pervasiveness of this patronal influence, but we can offer two African examples to show that it existed. The first concerns tax collection. Fronto sent a recommendation to Marcus on behalf of his friend Saenius Pompeianus, the *conductor IIII publicorum Africae* (probably a private citizen who contracted with the imperial government to collect taxes).[146] Pompeianus' accounts were to be scrutinized by Pius, and Fronto asked Marcus that he be shown *benignitas*. Marcus wrote back that he had befriended Pompeianus and that he desired that everything turn out in accordance with Pompeianus' wishes 'ex indulgentia Domini mei patris'.[147] These letters raise more questions than they answer. Clearly Fronto was trying to exert influence on behalf of the tax collector; his letter seems to be a veiled request for Marcus to intervene with his father. Marcus' response is wholly ambiguous: it is not clear whether he intends to become involved or to leave the matter to his father's kindly disposition. We would perhaps most like to know whether there existed some regular mechanism for reviewing suspect accounts, which involved the emperor as a matter of course and so regularly required patrons close to the emperor. The letter gives no hint about how well defined the rules and procedures concerning such reviews were — that is, how much was left as a matter of course to the emperor's discretion and beneficence without violating rules or custom. If Marcus' ambiguity is a sign of reluctance to intervene, could this be a hint of the existence of some rules which he was unwilling to bend? All that can be concluded with assurance is that tax collectors in Africa could hope to benefit from their friendships with men in the inner imperial circles such as Fronto.

The second example concerns both taxation and public order. Permission for the holding of periodic markets in the provinces had to be obtained in Rome from the senate or the emperor.[148] The imperial government's interest stemmed from the revenues to be collected and the opportunities for breaches of public order afforded by market-days. A letter of Pliny concerning Italy shows that a conflict of interests could arise over the establishment of new

---

145 This analytical distinction, suggested by Blok in 'Variations in patronage', seems to me an important one for understanding how far a society is actually structured by patronage institutions (as opposed to being merely 'lubricated' by patronage).

146 *Ad M. Caes.* 5.34. For the problem of the nature of the *conductores*, see De Laet, *Portorium*, 401f. and Rostovtzeff, *Social and Economic History of the Roman Empire*, rev. ed. P. Fraser, 389.

147 *Ad M. Caes.* 5.35.

148 Ramsay MacMullen, 'Market-days in the Roman Empire', *Phoenix* 24 (1970), 333ff.

nundinae on senatorial estates, for example.[149] As a result, the case for permission might be contested and so it was useful to have friends in Rome to influence the decision. Lucilius Africanus, a senator who owned land in the *territorium Musulamiorum* of the *regio Beguensis* in Africa, possessed such friends, as the *senatus consultum* granting permission for the *nundinae* tells us. In 138, after the consuls spoke 'de desiderio amicorum Lucili Africani c.v.', the senate decided to permit Africanus to hold *nundinae* on his estates provided that the markets take place 'sine iniuria et incommodo cuiusquam' ('without harm or inconvenience to anyone').[150] Strictly speaking this case may not fall under our definition of patronage, since the *amici* could have been friends on equal terms with Africanus rather than patrons. Nevertheless, it points up the sorts of decisions taken in Rome which required provincials to have friendly connections to present and defend their cases.

Altogether, a wide variety of *beneficia* were available to the provincial who had patrons or friends with influence in Rome. Most of the favors derived ultimately from the emperor, and their distribution, as Millar has shown, must be understood in the context of petition-and-response. We may now turn finally to the question of who served as mediators linking provincials to Rome.

We have already briefly noted the mediating role of public officials. On the whole the contacts with governors and the other officials probably constituted short-term relationships, the active exchange lasting for the duration of the official's tenure. This was not always the case. As Cicero's letters show for the time of the Republic, friendships cemented while an official was in his province might endure and entail the writing of *commendationes* later.[151] The third-century dedication to L. Titinius Clodianus was noted above as an example of an ex-governor helping a former subject: it appears that Clodianus supported C. Vibius Maximus as *candidatus eius* for a position in the imperial administration only after Clodianus had returned to Rome to take up a position as *procurator ludi magni*.[152] This instance, however, is the exception rather than the rule.[153] Virtually all other African inscriptions to provincial officials were dedicated during their tenure of office, that is, during the period when they had resources of *beneficia* directly related to provincial life. The fact that very few of the inscriptions thank ex-governors for *beneficia* or *merita* after their tenure suggests that, though ex-officials often remained *patroni* in name, active exchange normally broke off when the official left his province. This is what might be expected: it would have been impossible for a senator or

149 *Ep.* 5.4 where Pliny relates Vicetia's attempt to prevent the senator Sollers from holding *nundinae* on his estate.
150 *CIL* VIII.270.
151 *Ad Fam.* 13.32, 34, 36, for example.
152 No. 51.
153 The case of Sollemnis from the Thorigny Marble presents another exception, but here the importance of Sollemnis' *beneficium* to Paulinus provides an explanation.

equestrian who had served in several provinces to continue an active exchange with all or most of the contacts that he had made.

The relationships which come under consideration in this section form a contrast to the short-term relationships of officials. They lasted (or were intended to last) a lifetime or even several generations. From the African inscriptions emerge the same four types of relationships discussed with regard to the imperial aristocracy in Rome: kinship, *communicipes*, *contubernales* (or *commilitones*) and *condiscipuli*.[154] Of these the first two types can be described as ascriptive, that is, they were normally part of a provincial's lot at birth. The second two, by contrast, were part of what he could achieve by joining the army or pursuing an education. This dichotomy is of some importance for interpreting the social mobility of provincials and their movement to Rome.

In this discussion of kin and *communicipes* we are interested in the Janus-figures who rose from the municipal to the imperial aristocracy, mediators who looked toward Rome and back toward their families and friends in their *patria*. The figure is a familiar one from the Republic. Cicero, for example, in two letters to M. Iunius Brutus requested help for a group of *equites* from his home town Arpinum who were in Gaul to take care of business concerning their municipal estates there.[155] In other words, Cicero was supplying the necessary mediation between the municipal aristocracy and the Roman rulers to allow the former to claim some benefits from the rulers. This phenomenon became more important in the Principate as provincials from across the empire were integrated into the imperial aristocracy.

Most of our evidence provides only a static picture of the kinship ties between the Roman and provincial aristocracies. One of the rare cases from the Latin-speaking West where we can trace the development of such ties through several generations is the family of the Septimii from Lepcis Magna, for whom an imperial biography and several inscriptions give information. Unfortunately, even the evidence for the Septimii is problematic, and it is not possible to construct a certain stemma for the family.[156] All that can be said

154 For the question of inclusion of kinship, see above, p.135.
155 *Ad Fam.* 13.11, 12.
156 The arguments for and against the identification of the emperor's grandfather with Statius' friend put forward by A.R. Birley and T.D. Barnes, respectively, seem to me inconclusive. Both in the final analysis rest on the assumption that one collateral line or the other owned land near Veii and, if we can decide which one, we shall have the key to which line Statius' friend, who is said to have owned land near Veii, belonged (*Silv.* 4.5.54f.). But this assumption can be challenged. On the one hand, it is quite possible that such a farm was passed from one line to the other by testament, and on the other, it is possible that both lines owned land near Veii. When the future emperor decided to pursue a senatorial career, he would have had to acquire Italian land if he did not already own some, and he may have acquired an estate near that of his kin. Birley acknowledges that the Veientine estate mentioned in the Historia Augusta (*Sev.* 4.5) is the only piece of positive evidence for his view. It seems to me too fragile to bear the weight of any argument. For Barnes' view, see 'The Family and Career of Septimius Severus', *Historia* 16 (1967), 88. For Birley's rebuttal, 'The

with assurance is that the emperor's grandfather was a municipal magistrate at Lepcis and a *iudex selectus*.[157] Of the same family, probably of the same generation as the grandfather, and possibly identical with the grandfather, is Statius' friend, Septimius Severus.[158] Statius' friend made his way from Lepcis to Rome and into a circle of literary friends which included at least one consular. Nothing is known of the emperor's father except his name, P. Septimius Geta. The two alternative stemmata are shown below.[159]

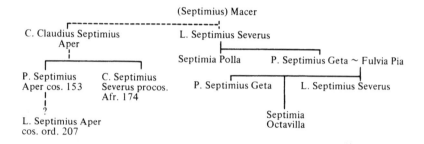

OR

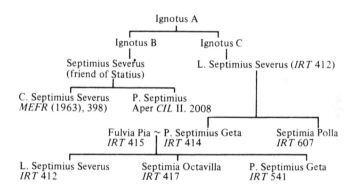

The fact that we cannot place Statius' friend in the stemma with certainty is not important to the argument here. Wherever he is placed, it is clear that members of the Septimii family went to Rome over several generations while

coups d'état of the year 193', *BJ* 169 (1969), 253 and 'Some notes on HA Severus 1-4', *Bonner Historia-Augusta-Colloquium 1968/69* (1970), 63f. For the requirement for senators to own Italian land see Pliny, *Ep.* 6.19 and H.A., *Marc.* 11.8.
157 *IRT* 412 and 413.
158 *Silv.* 4. praef. and 4.5.
159 Barnes, 'Septimius Severus', 107; A.R. Birley, *Septimius Severus*, 307.

others remained in Lepcis. Contacts were maintained between the two lines and, as certain members achieved positions and made contacts of importance, they used their influence to help advance relatives from Lepcis.

For the relationship between the future emperor and his *patruus* we have the testimony of the *Historia Augusta:* 'after going to Rome to pursue his studies, Septimius sought and received the *latus clavus* from Divus Marcus, enjoying the support of his uncle Septimius Severus, already twice consul.'[160] A dedicatory inscription from an arch in Lepcis provides testimony that this same uncle later took Lucius along with him as a legate during his term as proconsul of Africa — a customary form of patronal support for relatives.[161]

Patronage relationships among the Septimii of earlier generations are more uncertain. Statius dedicated Book IV of his *Silvae* to Vitorius Marcellus, an equestrian who married the daughter of the consular Cn. Hosidius Geta and then was promoted to consular rank himself.[162] In Book IV is a *lyricum carmen ad Septimium Severum*, whom Statius describes as a friend and *condiscipulus* of Marcellus. It seems quite likely that the value of these connections to the Septimii became evident in the next generation when both P. Septimius Aper and C. Septimius Severus rose to consulships in the 150s. Whether Statius' friend supplied the connections in his capacity as father or uncle of the consuls remains uncertain. What is important is that here we see an extended family from the African municipal aristocracy capitalizing on the increasingly influential contacts of kin at Rome.

This phenomenon was in all probability a common one, but it can rarely be documented in detail over several generations. The epigraphic record does, however, permit glimpses of bits of the web of kinship relations tying provincials to the Roman aristocracy. Dedications from North Africa (examined in detail in the appendix) show provincial families receiving imperial honors and appointments after their sons and daughters married prominent members of the imperial aristocracy. It seems only reasonable to suppose that in most cases the prominent relative was the channel through which imperial favor was secured. In other dedications provincial families are found expressing gratitude to their successful maternal uncles in the imperial service. The existence of individual instances of these kinship relations involving patronal support will not surprise anyone familiar with the evidence, but the number of the connections must be kept in mind and their consequences analyzed, as I shall attempt to do at the end of the chapter.

A wealthy provincial in an urbanized region was born not only into a kinship

---

160 *Severus* 1.5: 'Postea studiorum causa Romam venit, latum clavum a divo Marco petiit et accepit, favente sibi Septimio Severo adfini suo, bis iam consulari.'
161 *MEFR* 1963, 398; see above, p.131.
162 *Silv.* 4. praef.; on Vitorius see *RE* Suppl. IX, col. 1744 (Hanslik) and T. Mommsen, *Ges. Schr.* VII (Berlin, 1965), 221f.

network, but also into a relatively small aristocratic circle in his city. As a normal part of his activities he would maintain family friendships and develop new ones. These friends might have useful contacts in the imperial aristocracy or might themselves be promoted by grant of an equestrian or senatorial office, in either case providing links in a chain which allowed provincials to influence decisions at Rome. The most that could be hoped for was that one's home town would give birth to an emperor. This of course became the case for Lepcis Magna with Severus' accession in 193. T. D. Barnes (following R. M. Haywood) has shown convincingly, I think, that Septimius Severus did not pursue a policy of favoritism toward all Africa.[163] But his roots and those of his praetorian prefect Plautianus in Lepcis gave Lepcitanes special connections which can be seen to have produced benefits for the local aristocracy. Though the total number of equestrians in the emperor's service from Africa did not increase in the Severan period,[164] Lepcis, which had not previously produced a procurator whose name has survived in our evidence, suddenly produced three in the reign of Septimius. All three, Q. Marcius Dioga, M. Iunius Punicus and D. Clodius Galba, probably came from aristocratic families of Lepcis and so are likely to have long been on friendly terms with the Septimii and Fulvii, themselves leading Lepcitane families.[165] Galba and Punicus are known from dedications which they set up to the emperor, perhaps as expressions of gratitude. In another inscription it is Plautianus who is in effect thanked: 'C. Fulvio Plautiano praef. praet. M. Cornelius Bassus Servianus e.m.v. fieri iussit Cornelia Servianilla c.f. filia et heres posuit.'[166] Behind this dedication may well lie another procuratorship (*egregii memoria viri*) going to a Lepcitane, this time through the agency of Plautianus. The stone is a reminder of the fact that we should not view the success of the Lepcitanes simply as a direct result of some active, favorable policy of Septimius toward Lepcis; rather Lepcitanes enjoyed the benefits of being very close to the source of favors in the network of personal ties. Some Lepcitanes enjoyed direct familial friendships with the Septimii; others were somewhat more removed, having to approach the emperor through Plautianus.[167]

---

163 'Septimius Severus', 87f. and R.M. Haywood, 'The African policy of Septimius Severus', *TAPhA* 71 (1940), 175ff.

164 Jarrett, 'African contribution', 220.

165 Barnes, 'Septimius Severus', 105; *IRT* 392, 403, 422, 434 for Punicus; *IRT* 395, 407, 424 for Galba; *AE* (1926), 160 for Dioga. See M. Torelli, 'Per una storia della classe dirigente di Leptis Magna', *RAL* 28 (1973), 378f., 388, 392 for a discussion of the Lepcitane families of these men.

166 *IRT* 524.

167 Jarrett's comment ('Album', 198) that Dioga was 'probably an adventurer who made his way to Rome in order to profit from the presence of a dynasty from Lepcis on the imperial throne...' is an odd way to describe a man who belonged to a family which had been part of the Lepcitane aristocracy for a century and so had certainly been known to, and probably friends with, the Septimii for generations.

The case of Lepcis Magna introduces the issue of differential access of provincial towns to imperial favors. While an emperor would be the best fellow *municeps* as patron, influential senators or *equites* could also be effective. Duncan-Jones has pointed out a general pattern in the distribution of equestrian rank in Africa: the large cities, Cirta and Carthage, began producing senators and *equites* earlier and in greater numbers than smaller towns.[168] Unfortunately, the epigraphic record for Carthage is badly preserved, but the evidence for Cirta in comparison with other Numidian cities seems to corroborate this suggestion. The explanation offered for the pattern is in part that Carthage and Cirta 'were assize towns and as such they would automatically receive visits from the proconsul or his legates, which small secondary towns could not expect'.[169] Later in the third century 'differentiations between the availability of equestrian rank at major and minor towns seem to have been less marked.'[170]

This explanation of the distribution is useful: in the first and early second centuries governors were probably the most prominent of the few available patronal links to Rome. But as the second century progressed and more and more towns placed leading citizens in the aristocratic circles at Rome, gubernatorial patronage became relatively less important. Prominent African senators and *equites* provided the necessary patronage for their kin and *municipes* from home so that the success of municipal aristocrats became 'almost a self-generating process'.[171] Though we cannot show patronage in action for all or even most Africans who received offices and honors (the evidence is too scarce), it is possible to argue that patronage by Africans of *municipes* and kin provides the best explanation of the patterns documented by Duncan-Jones and that the specific examples from the literature and inscriptions illustrate the explanation.

On this 'patronage' explanation the differential success rate for large and small cities is simply an epiphenomenon of differential access to patronage, as the exceptions to the pattern show. As citizens of Carthage and Cirta began to find their way into the imperial aristocracy in the first century, the patronage opportunities increased mainly for their fellow citizens. As more and more Africans entered, the network gradually penetrated to the smaller towns. If this model is correct, then we would expect small towns whose citizens had close links with the centers of patronage to be exceptions to the large-small pattern. This is precisely the case:[172] Thugga, for example, started producing *equites* and senators relatively early owing to its close contacts with Carthage,

168 'Equestrian rank', 161f.
169 *Ibid.*, 161.
170 *Ibid.*, 162
171 *Ibid.*, 154.
172 *Ibid.*, 161.

which are demonstrated by the fact that four men from Thugga — A. Gabinius Datus, *adlectus in quinque decurias* and granted the public horse, and the three Marcii brothers, adlected *in quinque decurias* — held magistracies at Carthage before rising to equestrian rank in the early and mid-second century.[173] In Numidia two towns with close connections with Cirta, Rusicade and Cuicul, produced *equites* in the first half of the second century.[174] 'Close connections' here means at a concrete level *amicitia* bonds between aristocrats of the cities derived from participation in another city's civic life.

In the literature and inscriptions only traces of the broad networks survive. Fronto, for example, had no interest in passing on much information about his continuing ties with Cirta, but they did exist. There are several Cirtans whom Fronto probably had a hand in helping to consulates.[175] The Iulius Celsinus whom Aulus Gellius accompanied to the house of Fronto for an erudite discussion is probably the Cirtan landowner and consul designate, P. Iulius Proculus Celsinus.[176] 'Marcianus noster' appeared with Fronto before Marcus in the prosecution by Herodes Atticus — probably the Cirtan P. Iulius Geminius Marcianus who held a suffect consulship in 167.[177] The patron-protégé relationship between Fronto and C. Arrius Antoninus (suff. cos. 170) is directly attested: Fronto himself says that Antoninus esteemed him 'non secus quam parentem'.[178] Altogether, Fronto's protégés illustrate clearly why citizens of Cirta had better chances of securing *beneficia* at Rome than other Numidians: through Fronto their requests had a short, direct route to the emperor.

This Cirtan phenomenon was no doubt repeated, usually later and in a smaller way, in other African towns. Again and again we find dedications by locals to senators and *equites* from their *patria*, sometimes with the phrase *amico et municipi*.[179] By the Hadrianic period Saldae in Mauretania

---

173 For references, *ibid.*, 161.

174 Rusicade was one of the four *coloniae* in the Cirtan confederation and produced C. Caecilius Gallus, *exornatus equo publico*, before 115 (*ILAlg.* II.i.36, 71); men from Cuicul, such as Crescentianus (discussed below, pp.201f.), held magistracies at Cirta. Cuicul enjoyed some success during Pius' reign with Cosinii Maximus and Primus *adlecti in quinque decurias*, L. Claudius Honoratus receiving a tribunate and Crescentianus receiving a public horse. Jarrett ('African contribution', 220) notes the success of these men and the connection between Cuicul and Cirta. The overall distribution of senators and *equites* from Numidia also supports this suggestion. Cirta produced senators and *equites* at a roughly constant rate through the second and third centuries. The other Numidian towns produced only a few in the early second century, a few more in the later second century, and more than half of the total in the first half of the third century. The pattern of men from Rusicade and Cuicul, by contrast, resembles that of Cirta — i.e., evenly distributed over the whole 150 years.

175 Champlin, *Fronto and Antonine Rome*, 13ff.

176 *N.A.* 19.10.1; *ILAlg.* II.i.638.

177 Fronto, *Ad M. Caes.* 3.4; *PIR²* I.340.

178 Fronto, *Ad Amic.* 2.8; *PIR²* A.1088.

179 *CIL* VIII.26475 and nos. 1, 5, 7, 17, 19, 22, 23, 35, 37, 40, in the table. Nos. 1 and 5 for *amicus* and *municeps*.

Caesariensis, for example, could boast two citizens in procuratorial service. One of them, Annius Postumus, held at least four procuratorships and received a dedication from Horatius Marcianus, a fellow *municeps*, to an 'amico indulgentissimo ob beneficia quae in se contulit' ('a most indulgent friend on account of the *beneficia* which he bestowed on me').[180] Whatever the precise nature of the *beneficia*, Marcianus clearly profited from the continuing relationship between Saldae and its successful *municipes*.

It would be tedious to describe in detail all the dedications by Africans to their fellow *municipes* in the imperial aristocracy, since few of them give any more than names and careers. But the very fact that they were set up at considerable expense and in significant numbers is evidence for the continuity and strength of private exchange relationships through which were channelled imperial *beneficia*. The emphasis here is on private bonds as opposed to any sort of imperial policy with universalistic criteria: the result is that an understanding of the patterns of distribution must ultimately rest on understanding the nature of the private network which has been described above.

By far the largest group of non-official patrons in our table of African inscriptions comprises kin and *communicipes*. A few African inscriptions, however, remind us that a provincial's life chances were not completely defined at birth. The institutions and culture of the empire provided contexts in which a provincial could meet a variety of people and cement new and potentially important friendships. The two most important were the army and literary education.

We have already discussed some of the evidence for patronage within the army. What is of interest here is how the army supplied a setting conducive to the formation of friendships which then continued after the tours of duty were completed. That provincials thought of *amicitiae* as one of the natural byproducts of military service is suggested by a metaphor of Apuleius. Concerning his relationship with the consular Aemilianus Strabo, he said 'between us the bonds of *amicitia* began honorably a *commilitio studiorum* under the same teachers'.[181] Pliny's recommendation to Trajan on behalf of Nymphidius Lupus is a good illustration of how this might work.[182] Pliny had served with Lupus' father, a *primipilaris*, in Syria some thirty years before his governorship.[183] When Pliny went out to Bithynia, he called the ex-centurion to be his assessor. The continuing friendship profited the son when Pliny wrote to Trajan requesting an equestrian *militia*.

180 No. 7.
181 *Flor.* 16: 'inter nos iura amicitiae a commilitio studiorum eisdem magistris honeste inchoata'. For a similar view, Plutarch, *Moralia* 816B.
182 *Ep.* 10.87
183 Sherwin-White, *Letters of Pliny*, 683ff.

African inscriptions once again provide corroboration of the importance of military friendships. M. Sempronius Liberalis from Acholla pursued a very successful equestrian career in the mid-second century, reaching the Egyptian prefecture in 154.[184] Other than this, nothing is known of Liberalis' career except his service as *praefectus alae* about 130. A military diploma from Banasa which names Liberalis also names M. Gavius Maximus as his commander, the procurator of Mauretania Tingitana.[185] Pliny's letter indicates that commanders became patrons of their subordinates, writing recommendations for them later. And so it is surely not an accident that Liberalis was enjoying great success in his career precisely when Maximus was a very influential figure at Rome as Pius' praetorian prefect from 139 and then sole prefect from 143. The opportunity which military service afforded for establishing a link with Maximus may well have been of decisive importance for Liberalis' success, since to the best of our knowledge his *patria* Acholla had not yet produced any potential patrons of its own.[186]

Education performed a similar function of promoting social mobility in the empire. A son of a provincial aristocrat might begin his education in his home town, and then later move to more important provincial centers of learning. In the fourth century, for example, Augustine started his schooling in his *patria* Thagaste and later went to Madauros and then finally to the most prestigious African center of learning, Carthage.[187] In pursuit of further education provincials could then move on to the centers for the empire, Rome and Athens. At each stage along the way, opportunities were offered for cementing friendships between master and pupil, and between fellow students. As shown in Chapter 4, the recipients of Pliny's patronage were frequently *condiscipuli* or literary protégés.[188] Certainly more than one African can be seen to have benefited in a similar way from his school and literary friends.

The first teachers in a student's career, the *grammatici*, were likely to be of lower social status than the student and so were in a position to profit from the patronage of the student's family or the student himself later in life. Apuleius, explaining how he used his inheritance, says that he bestowed gifts on his

184 Pflaum, *Carrières*, 251.
185 *CIL* XVI.173.
186 Pflaum, *Carrières*, 247ff. The next figure of importance from Acholla after Liberalis (in our record) was M. Asinius Rufinus Valerius Verus Sabinianus, consul in the mid-180s (*AE* (1954), 58). The fact that Liberalis was at the height of his career about the time when Sabinianus was beginning his suggests the possibility of patronage. For another example of military service and patronage in North Africa, see *CIL* VIII.9371 (= *ILS* 1355) and Pflaum, *Carrières*, 603.
187 B.H. Warmington, *The North African Provinces from Diocletian to the Vandal Conquests*, 104-6; also T.D. Barnes, *Tertullian*, 194ff. M.K. Hopkins, 'Social mobility in the later Roman Empire: the evidence of Ausonius', *CQ* n.s. 11 (1961), 239-49, provides a useful analysis of the role of education for social mobility in the later Empire.
188 See above, p 136.

magistri.[189] Similar circumstances may be the background for an African inscription dated to the beginning of Caracalla's reign: 'Q. Cornelio M.f. Quir. Rustico, eq. pub. exorn., Q. Geminius Q.f. Quir. Marcianus c.v., quaestor candidatus a domino nostro invictissimo Imp. designatus, magistro fidelissimo ac karissimo posuit.'[190] Here we have a young senator from Thibilis at the outset of his career dedicating an inscription to his teacher back at home, possibly (we may speculate) on the occasion of securing the *equus publicus* for him.

A dedication from Sufetula illustrates the lasting friendships formed by *condiscipuli.*[191] The poorly preserved inscription is dedicated to Pomponius L [...]murianus, a ducenarian *procurator dioceseos Hadrumetinae*, by L. Valgius Mauricus, *vir egregius* and probably *fisci advocatus* (though Dessau seems less certain of the restoration than Pflaum).[192] Mauricus set up the stone 'ob eximiam condiscipulatus adfectionem'. Both men seem to have come from Sufetula, and so it is impossible to know whether they were fellow students there early in their educational careers or perhaps later at a larger city such as Carthage. In any case, since the office of *fisci advocatus* was often filled through patronage, it seems a reasonable guess that Pomponianus displayed his *adfectio* by securing the office for his fellow-student.

Our best evidence for the importance to men from the western provinces of educational and literary centers concerns Athens and Rome. Several examples have already been mentioned. Apuleius met his future stepson and protégé Pontianus as a *condiscipulus* in Athens where he may also have begun his *amicitia* with the senator Aemilianus Strabo who is said to have studied under the same *magistri* as Apuleius.[193] At Rome Fronto was one of several provincial teachers who enjoyed the rewards of having served as a teacher of Latin rhetoric for the future emperors Marcus Aurelius and Verus; the African Eutychius Proculus, a *grammaticus Latinus* from Sicca Veneria, was promoted as far as the proconsulate by Marcus, who shouldered the financial burden of the career.[194] Other Africans followed Fronto to Rome both to study under him and also to enjoy his patronage. We have already discussed the *commendatio* on behalf of Sardius Saturninus whose sons studied with Fronto and lived in the same house.[195] This latter custom must have provided a context for especially close personal relationships. The potential importance of literary

189 *Apol.* 23.
190 *CIL* VIII.5528-9.
191 No. 44.
192 Pflaum, *Carrières*, 826 and Dessau, *ILS* 9016.
193 *Apol.* 72; *Flor.* 16.
194 *Marc.* 2.3, 5. See A.R. Birley, 'Some teachers of M. Aurelius', *Bonner Historia-Augusta Colloquium 1966/67* (1968), 39ff., for an argument that this man should be identified with M. Tuticius Proculus of *CIL* VIII.1625 from Sicca Veneria.
195 *Ad Amic.* 1.9.

circles is perhaps best exemplified by the success of the Septimii during the second century. As pointed out above, Septimius Severus (friend of Statius) moved from Lepcis and became a member of a literary circle in Rome, one of the most prominent members of which was the senator M. Vitorius Marcellus from Teate, specifically named by Statius as a *condiscipulus* and friend of Septimius.[196] This is an excellent illustration of how literary education provided opportunities for a provincial to cement friendships with powerful aristocrats from other parts of the Roman world and so to overcome whatever drawbacks his provincial origins may have entailed (at least in the early Principate).

At the beginning of this discussion of the four types of patronage relationships, I noted their long-term nature. It is worth concluding the discussion with a brief consideration of how provincials kept up personal relationships with the imperial aristocracy and then of the evidence for the inheritance of patron-client bonds. The patronal relationship could be renewed both when provincials travelled to Rome and when the imperial aristocrats returned to their native communities. With respect to the first case, *hospitium*, an important element in relationships between provincials and Romans in the Republic, continued to be a part of the exchange in the Empire.[197] Fronto wrote a letter to Lollianus Avitus, proconsul of Africa, on behalf of Licinius Montanus, a native of Cirta. The letter is damaged and it is not clear what Montanus wanted from the governor. At the beginning of the letter, in order to impress upon Avitus how close he was to Montanus, Fronto wrote that he shared his house and table with Montanus when he came to Rome. Further, Montanus was second in his affection to none of those 'quiscum mihi hospitii iura sunt' ('with whom I share the rights of hospitality').[198] This last clause suggests that a Roman aristocrat, especially a recent migrant who still had numerous ties with his *patria,* was expected to host provincial visitors as a routine duty, and so renew and strengthen his bonds with them.

On occasion imperial aristocrats returned to their *patriae,* either temporarily or permanently in retirement.[199] When this happened, they had opportunities to become involved again with fellow *municipes* in local politics. Their prestige made them valuable patrons for the influence which they could exert locally as well as in Rome. The inspiration for some of the dedications cited above may have come from patronal help in local affairs. Direct evidence for prestige of Roman senators back in their provinces is found in Apuleius'

196 See note 46 above.
197 For the Republic see E. Badian, *Foreign Clientelae*, 11f.
198 *Ad Amic.* 1.3.
199 Garnsey, 'Rome's African Empire'.

Florida.[200] The consular Aemilianus Strabo, a long-time friend of Apuleius, proposed in the Carthaginian *curia* and ostentatiously gave his vote to a measure honoring Apuleius with a prominently placed statue. Strabo said that he was going to erect another statue to Apuleius at his own expense. And so, according to Apuleius, the Carthaginian senate postponed the vote until the next meeting so that 'out of veneration and reverence for their *consularis* they would seem not to imitate his deed but to follow it'. When it came to the vote, 'all followed his *auctoritas*'. It seems quite likely that Strabo's intervention in local affairs here yielded opportunities for his acquaintances not only to renew their friendships with him but also to lay some claim to his *gratia* by supporting the motion.

The best proof of the durability of these patron-client ties is evidence for their inheritance. Of course, by their very nature kinship relations were inherited and so the concomitant patronage relationships were as well. It is less obvious that the other types of patrons and clients need be passed on from generation to generation. The epigraphic evidence confirms that they were, and a good illustration of this is *CIL* VIII.610 from Mididi: 'C. Mevio Silio Crescenti Fortunatiano c p. patrono, C. Iuli Fortunatiani e.v. patroni filio, Sextus Volussius Maximus cum liberis posuit.' This inscription seems to show both clients and patrons being passed on from father to son. Other North African inscriptions also show clients passing from father to child. The dedication of one from Thamugadi is more explicit and interesting than usual: 'Valubi: Flaviae Severineti Petronianae M. Virri Fl. Iugurthae eq. R., fl. pp. filiae Pompeii Fuscus et Felix fidem paternae amicitiae ista memoriae perpetuitate testantes l.d.d.d.'[201]

Finally, there is one other patronage inscription which probably reflects inheritance of patrons and clients and deserves comment in any case because of its uniqueness in Africa. 'Memoriae patronis et dominis meis, Q. Bullati Sabini patris [...] vi et QQ. Bullati (orum) Sabini et Donati filiis eius et Bullatiis Sabino et Honoratae nepotibus eius, [Q.] Bullatius Sabinus tribunus cohortis I Syrorum.'[202] Jarrett has plausibly explained the tone of the inscription (especially 'meis dominis') and the fact that the client is a homonym of the patron by the suggestion that the tribune was the son of the eldest Sabinus' freedman.[203] This would of course mean that the tribune inherited his father's patron. Further, this case represents a higher degree of social mobility than

---

200 *Flor.* 16; Strabo's participation in the Carthaginian *curia* gives reason to believe that Carthage was his *patria*, though certainty is impossible since men from surrounding African *municipia* also participated in Carthaginian local affairs.

201 No. 53; no. 45 is the other.

202 *AE* (1892), 13.

203 Given the patronage that the tribune enjoyed, it is difficult to see any justification for Jarrett's speculation that 'the tribune was a veteran granted a commission on retirement' ('Album', 163).

nearly all others discussed in this chapter, which have involved wealthy municipal aristocrats.[204]

To summarize, I have tried to provide as complete a description as possible of the role of patronage in linking the provinces, especially Africa, with Roman administration and the aristocracy. The lacunae have been large, and quantitative evidence for frequency of patronal contacts completely absent. But it has been possible to demonstrate from the literature that in a qualitative sense patronage permeated the links. All types of regular judicial and administrative decisions taken in Rome and by officials in the provinces seem to have been subject to patronal influence. For other grants (statuses, offices, etc.) personal contacts, either directly with the emperor or through patrons, were the only means of acquisition. We have found these personal contacts to have been what anthropologists call 'multiplex' or 'multi-stranded' — that is, the relationship was not narrow or for a single purpose, rather the patronal element was an integral part of other forms of relationships (e.g., kinship).[205] The literature and especially the epigraphic evidence have enabled us to illustrate these kinds of relationships along which patronal influence flowed. In doing so, we have glimpsed a fragment of the web of personal contacts between the municipal and imperial aristocracies which bound the provinces to Rome. As Millar summarized with a touch of understatement, 'the whole nature of the assumptions within which the government of the empire worked gave an advantage to individuals from those provincial aristocracies whom a network of ties bound to the emperor and his circle'.[206]

HISTORICAL IMPLICATIONS FOR THE PROVINCES

The descriptive material just presented is very fragmentary. It is notoriously difficult to use such evidence to demonstrate historical trends or see the empire as an integrated, functioning whole. But we can turn to comparative evidence for help in formulating some general implications of the system described. In particular, I wish to concentrate on two historical trends, one which clearly was present, the other which has been postulated but seems overstated in light of the patronage evidence.

The first trend is the increase throughout the Principate in the number of provincials in the imperial aristocracy having links with their *patria*. The increase in Africans occurred especially in the later first and second centuries. The trend is obvious, but its causes and consequences in the context of the personal network ought to be pointed out. First, there is the question of how

---

204 One other exception is M. Pompeius Quintianus (see Appendix 5, p.204.).
205 J. Boissevain in his preface to *Network Analysis: Studies in Human Interaction*, ed. Boissevain and Mitchell, xi.
206 *Emperor*, 476.

provincials were initially introduced into the Roman aristocracy, and especially what role was played by the emperor. In discussions of this question, Tacitus' account of the senatorial debate about the Aedui is frequently adduced and treated as paradigmatic. For instance, it has been suggested that 'if the success of Africans in public life was to become almost a self-generating process from the late second century onwards, it cannot have been so from the outset. The entry of Africans into the Senate may have owed its origin to definite central initiatives, akin to Claudius' admission of the Aedui.'[207] The phrase 'central initiatives' here may imply too much. In the case of the Aedui Tacitus says that the initiative came from the Gauls who asked for the '*ius adipiscendorum in urbe honorum*'.[208] The nature of the *ius* is unclear (that is, whether it had any formal legal status or was simply a synonym for *latus clavus*, as elsewhere in Tacitus), but it is certain that as a result of Claudius' speech the *ius* (and not actual entry) was extended to the Aedui.[209] It is conceivable, though unlikely, that at some point a similar right was formally extended to other provinces, but this would not in any way explain how individual provincials took advantage of the opportunity with increasing success. Certainly it should not be thought that the only two possibilities for entry were 'a self-generating process' of provincials patronizing other provincials, or 'central initiatives'. As we have seen there were other sources of patronage: governors and other officials had from the time of the Republic become patrons of leading provincials and instrumental in the extension of citizenship and other rights to them; in addition, Romans in their private capacities (e.g., the senators who owned provincial estates) may also have had contacts with provincial aristocrats and patronized them. In short, we can explain the gradual entry of provincials with a model of patrons approaching an essentially passive emperor on their behalf. This has the advantage of avoiding references to 'central initiatives', which are out of character in Millar's view, and which even in the case of the Aedui are misleading.[210]

Millar also emphasizes the role of the emperor in the trend: 'the fact that senatorial rank, virtually confined to Italians at the beginning of the period, was steadily extended to men from all the more civilized provinces in both the Latin west and the Greek east, and thence to their descendants, was entirely a function of imperial patronage'.[211] Of course, this statement is correct to the

207 Duncan-Jones, 'Equestrian rank', 154.
208 Tacitus, *Ann.* 11.23; see now A. Chastagnol, 'Les modes d'accès au Sénat romain au début de l'Empire: remarques à propos de la table claudienne de Lyon', *BSAF* (1971), 282-310, who reviews the evidence, arguments, and bibliography, but adduces no new compelling reasons for believing that there existed an inferior type of Roman citizenship without the *ius honorum* at this time.
209 Tacitus, *Ann.* 11.25; for Tacitus' use of *ius adipiscendorum honorum* to mean *latus clavus*, *Ann.* 14.50.1. See Millar, *Emperor*, 293.
210 *Ibid.*, 290.
211 *Ibid.*, 290f.

extent that the emperor was formally responsible for the grant of the *latus clavus*. But perhaps the statement places too much emphasis on the emperor at the expense of the mediators. Unless we believe that the *latus clavus* was granted in the main to brave provincials who physically approached the emperor unaccompanied and unintroduced, then we must assign the primary role in the selection of new men to patrons such as Pliny who brought Voconius Romanus to the attention of Trajan (whether successfully or not in this case is unimportant).[212] After all, it would be a mistake to see the gradual expansion of Roman rights as a phenomenon confined to the Principate. As Claudius himself noted, the process of patrons introducing new men from increasingly distant regions and lower status groups into the Roman state and senate had deep roots in the Republic.[213] On the other hand, it is true that the pace of the process quickened in the Principate: by putting the final decision in the hands of the emperor, the obstacles of developing popular support in the assemblies and overcoming opposition from other senators were removed. The emperor did not have a vested interest in limiting the roll of those eligible for senatorial office in the way that Republican senators did.

Our description of the various types of patronage bonds helps to add concrete content to the frequently expressed idea that provincials received citizenship and higher honors when they became Romanized.[214] Romanization entailed participation by the local élites in imperial culture, which in turn provided opportunities for initiating personal friendships with influential senators and equestrians. Once the entry of Africans into the imperial aristocracy got under way, what was the relative importance of the cultural institutions as opposed to ascriptive relationships in providing access to honors and offices? Modern Mediterranean studies emphasize the importance of education and the army in opening alternative avenues of access. In recent years on Malta, for example, better education of villagers has broken down the dominating role of the priest as the only broker in the village capable of dealing with the central government.[215] Twentieth-century Jordan supplies another illustration: the patronage networks used to be strictly hierarchical, monopolized at each stage by one man and allowing no alternatives; army careers began after 1923 to offer opportunities for opting out of the old hierarchy.[216] It is tempting to see army and education playing a similar role in

---

212 *Ep.* 10.4 for example.
213 *ILS* 212 (M. Smallwood, *Documents illustrating the Principates of Gaius, Claudius and Nero,* 369 = *CIL* XIII. 1688).
214 For a general overview concerning Romanization, P.A. Brunt, 'The Romanization of the local ruling classes in the Roman Empire' in *Assimilation et résistance à la culture gréco-romaine dans le monde ancien,* ed. D.M. Pippidi, 161-73.
215 Boissevain, 'When the saints go marching out', in *Patrons and Clients,* ed. Gellner and Waterbury, 87f.
216 A. Farrag, 'The wastah among Jordanian villagers', in *Patrons and Clients,* ed. Gellner and Waterbury, 229.

the Roman empire, and to some extent they did. Millar has heavily emphasized education and literary culture in the initiation of personal contacts. With regard to the

complex network of relationships which bound the emperor to the educated bourgeoisie of the cities,... cultural factors were of all-embracing, though not exclusive, importance. It was the rhetoricians, the poets, grammarians and philosophers of the provincial cities who, after his senatorial 'friends', had the easiest access to the emperor... it was from these educated provincials that, apart from a brief moment of glory for the imperial freedmen, the emperor's assistants and secretaries were drawn; and it was they who were most successful in channelling benefits to their protégés and native cities. The eventual detachment of the emperor from the social context of the city meant on the one hand closer attachment to the army, but on the other his capture by the educated provincials, mainly Greek, who now staffed his court.[217]

It may be argued that this emphasis derives partially from a reliance on the Greek literary sources, and that the African epigraphic evidence supplies a useful counterweight. Our findings indicate that by far the majority of inscriptions to non-official patrons in imperial circles were dedicated to men with ascriptive ties (kinsmen and fellow townsmen). Though I would not want to argue that this is fully representative of the network and patterns of distribution of favors, there is possibly one test (not foolproof) to help decide between the emphases: the distribution of procuratorships. It is a reasonably good test insofar as procuratorial service was in no sense hereditary and so constantly involved fresh distributions to new families. Now Millar's claim is that the mainly Greek litterateurs were 'most successful in channelling benefits to their protégés and native cities'. This is certainly what we would expect if education were the most important feature in the network,[218] but in fact even in the Severan period, as far as we can tell, provincials from the Latin-speaking part of the empire still were far more successful in securing procuratorships. According to Pflaum's figures for 193 to 260, 54 came from the West (including 24 from Africa) in comparison with only 23 from the Greek East.[219] While the descriptions of the Greek sophists' successes by Philostratus may attract more attention, it seems that the personal relationships described on the banal African stones may be more representative of the personal networks which extended from the emperor to the provinces, drawing new families into the imperial aristocracy.

Perhaps this is not surprising, in view of the fact that our comparison between the Roman aristocracy and modern Mediterranean peoples has one major flaw: the Jordanian army and Maltese education permitted their

217 *Emperor*, 9.
218 See Barnes, *Tertullian*, 187ff. for the dominance of Greek literary education.
219 *Procurateurs*, 260f.

participants to break out of the hierarchy economically with sources of income other than their inherited family plot.[220] Since land continued to be the major source of wealth for the Roman aristocracy, required in large quantity for promotion into higher *ordines*, ascriptive ties seem to have remained of paramount, though by no means exclusive, importance. A man normally had to keep in more than just casual contact with his kin (with whom he was involved in the maintenance and inheritance of family estates) and his *patria* (where he continued to hold the estates which supported him).

Finally, as more Africans entered the imperial aristocracy, what were the implications of the historical trend for provincial administration? In an important article about the early Principate Brunt argued forcefully against the presumption that the Principate was a period of vastly improved provincial administration. After carefully reviewing the evidence of maladministration under the emperors up to Trajan, he concluded that 'in truth the most conscientious Emperors could hardly maintain generally high standards of administration. Augustus reformed the state: he could not reform society. Public morality remained what it had been under the Republic.'[221] Arguing from a handful of examples to general historical trends is extremely problematic, but the problem becomes much worse in the second century after the evidence of Tacitus and Pliny, who are the sole sources for three-quarters of Brunt's examples, runs out. We are left essentially to our *a priori* generalizations (such as Augustus 'could not reform society').

There seems to me at least one *a priori* reason for suspecting that provincial administration in Africa was less rapacious in the second century. In a recent article S. Khalaf pointed out a difference between government in Lebanon and that in other parts of the Ottoman Empire. In most areas a *multazim* from outside was sent in to govern a district. 'He developed little interest in the welfare of his subjects and tried instead to enrich himself at their expense.' In Lebanon, by contrast, governing was left to the *muqata'ji* (local feudal chieftain) who lived in and administered his own village; his 'power and economic well-being depended on the continuous support and loyalty of his *atba'*. Accordingly, he was less likely to be oppressive and rapacious towards them.'[222] Here Khalaf presents a theme which in a general form runs throughout patronage studies: patronage relationships give the weak a means

---

220 Farrag notes the importance of the economic factor in Jordan: after the 1920s 'sons who previously had little chance of escaping their father's economic domination now began to enter the army. This decreased the father's economic control as sons earned their independent salaries' (229f.). The land allotted to veterans in the Principate perhaps makes the case of the Roman peasant more closely analogous to that of the Jordanians.
221 'Charges of provincial maladministration under the early Principate', *Historia* 10 (1961), 221.
222 'Changing forms of political patronage in Lebanon', in *Patrons and Clients*, ed. Gellner and Waterbury, 189.

of influencing the powerful. In 'predatory states' where officials are sent in from the outside, they are not linked to their subjects by any sort of bonds which permit the latter to influence or limit the arbitrariness of the former. The influx of provincials into the imperial aristocracy not only meant that they began at times to govern their home provinces. Perhaps more importantly, provincials entered patronal networks of the imperial aristocracy so that even officials from other regions of the empire were no longer governing complete strangers, but kin and friends of their senatorial and equestrian colleagues. Fronto's *commendationes* to governors in Africa on behalf of his friends illustrate the way in which provincials could influence Roman officials. As more provincials entered the imperial aristocracy, more influence could be brought to bear by more people.

Two qualifications need to be added to this suggestion. The first is that most of the links between the imperial aristocracy and provincials were with the municipal élite. They were the ones most likely to benefit from greater opportunities for influencing officials: the *saltus Burunitanus* case illustrates with great clarity how patronage or collusion between Roman officials and wealthy provincials could lead to increased oppression of the weak. The second qualification derives from Gilsenan's warning in a recent essay that emphasis on 'vertical' patronage networks which cut across classes should not be allowed to blind us to the basic structure of exploitation. With reference to a study of a Sardinian village he wrote: 'the most important element... is the cementing of ties between the favour givers who have a common interest (and structural position) in excluding favour seekers and keeping them dependent... In other words, we are dealing with the crystallization and consolidation by the dominant group of shared class position at either end of the stratification scale. There is a reinforcement of the horizontal dimension rather than a cross-cutting'.[223] A careful weighing of the effects of vertical patronal ties against class interests for the Roman empire would require another study of some length. But the example of the Thorigny Marble indicates that Gilsenan's warning must be taken seriously. There we saw a case of a senatorial and an equestrian governor closing ranks to protect the senator from a threatened prosecution by leading provincials. The tone of the former equestrian governor's letter leaves little doubt that he perceived the common interests of the ruling class as overshadowing any benign vertical ties with the subjects.[224] Both of these qualifications indicate that it would be a mistake to think of Roman provincial administration as altogether fair and equitable. Nevertheless, it seems likely that the arbitrariness was partially limited by the increased ability of provincials to bring social pressures to bear on their officials.

223 'Against patron-client relations', in *Patrons and Clients*, ed. Gellner and Waterbury, 182.
224 *CIL* XIII. 3162; see above, p.132.

Finally, I want to give very brief consideration to a second possible trend during the Principate in the light of findings in the comparative material of the effects of bureaucratization on patronage. There seems to be general agreement that increasing bureaucratization in various parts of the Mediterranean has not eliminated patrons and clients (as it did not in the later Empire), but it has altered the form of the relationships and the types of patrons needed.[225] Today government in many areas is expanding and making itself felt to a much greater segment of the population in a greater variety of ways. With expansion has come a more formally developed hierarchy with more decision-making by committees rather than single powerful individuals. This process, together with modernization, has entailed specialization. These changes in government have introduced great changes in the kinds of patrons needed. Gone (for the most part) are the days of the single powerful brokers (e.g., priests) who mediated in all contacts between villagers and the outside world. Villagers need to approach government more often now for a greater number of favors (e.g., water and electricity supplies). They require a variety of specialist brokers who know the technicalities of how to negotiate with various branches of a specialized and complex bureaucracy. This comparative evidence highlights how little Roman patronage changed and how limited was the degree of bureaucratization in the Principate. The only important specialization of organization came with the separation of financial from other gubernatorial duties. This did not introduce enough complexity to require specialization of patrons; the traditional multi-purpose patron remained entirely adequate, as demonstrated by Fronto's patronage of the *conductor IIII publicorum Africae*.[226] Not only the form, but also the content of the exchange relationships remained essentially unchanged from the Republic. Cicero's and Fronto's *commendationes* to provincial governors look very much alike; both request favorable judicial decisions, help with their client's *negotia*, etc. Provincials increasingly sought higher statuses and more offices, but this represented a quantitative, not a qualitative change and certainly did not require any change in the type of patron needed.

The comparative material, with its emphasis on increasing governmental provision of goods and services to the entire population, also highlights the

---

225 *Patrons and Clients, passim,* esp. Boissevain, 'When the saints go marching out'. Though the bureaucracy increased in the later Roman Empire and increased governmental interference perhaps made patronage more valuable, the administration did not specialize in such a way as to cause extensive specialization of patrons. As in the Principate, proximity to the emperor remained the most important factor. As Jones noted with respect to appointments, 'in general *suffragium* was a very haphazard business. What a candidate for office required was the voice of someone in the inner circle of the court who could press his claims, and it did not matter much what office the *suffragator* held, or indeed if he held any office at all, so long as he had access to the emperor' (*Later Roman Empire,* 392).
226 See above, p.174.

relatively limited degree to which the imperial government of Rome was involved with the mass of provincials. This means that the kind of patronage we have considered in this chapter — that between the municipal and Roman aristocracies — represents only the thin, upper crust of patronage relationships. By all criteria which a recent collection of studies has listed as conducive to patronage between landowners and the laboring classes, conditions were ripe throughout the empire for patronage to permeate the society from top to bottom. We can catch only the briefest glimpses of patronage relationships with the lower classes — for example, a dedication to M. Asinius Rufinus Valerius Verus Sabinianus from his *cultores domus ob merita*.[227] That is unfortunate, because it was these relationships which provided the crucial economic and social infrastructure for the élite patronage which we have studied here.

APPENDIX 5

The epigraphic evidence from North Africa

At the outset of this study the prospects seemed good that an examination of the large bulk of inscriptions from North Africa would reveal networks of families, friends, patrons and clients. Unfortunately, the value of the epigraphic evidence has turned out to be less than hoped for because of the low survival rate of inscribed stones: the 30,000 extant inscriptions from the region probably represent less than ten percent of the number originally set up.[228] Nevertheless, the fraction which has survived provides important support for some arguments and corroboration for others in this chapter. On the following pages is a summary of the main body of evidence on which the study is based — a table of all private patronage inscriptions from North Africa which I have been able to find (excluding dedications from *liberti* to ex-masters). 'Patronage inscriptions' here include (1) all private dedications with the word *patronus*, (2) private dedications with the word *amicus* reflecting *amicitia* between social unequals, and (3) inscriptions which indicate an exchange relationship by language such as *ob beneficium* or *ob meritum*. Inscriptions dedicated to *patroni* by *curiae* and *collegia* have already been collected by G. Clemente and there is no reason to repeat his list here.[229]

The table comprises 53 inscriptions. At first sight such a small number out of the 30,000 inscriptions from North Africa may seem to argue for the insignificance of

227 *AE* (1954), 58.
228 Duncan-Jones cautiously suggests that the maximum survival rate was probably 5.1% in *The Economy of the Roman Empire*, 360f. He is not quite consistent in his calculations: on the one hand, he excludes two of a Thamugadi priest's four dedications on the grounds that two dedications is the expected average; on the other hand, he says that 5.1% 'is probably a maximum, since the original number of commemorations may have been higher than two per man'. There are other possible sources of error in the calculation: e.g., significant error could be introduced if for some political or social reason the provincial priests were concentrated in some city unusually well or poorly represented in the epigraphic record (e.g., Carthage). Even a higher survival rate would still play havoc with any attempt to reconstruct networks.
229 Guido Clemente, 'Il patronato nei collegia dell' impero romano', *SCO* 21 (1972), 142-229; T. Kotula, *Les curies municipales en Afrique romaine*.

Table III: North African patronage inscriptions

Patronus	Cliens	Dedication	Reference
1 Q. Aelius Q.f. Rufinus Polianus, trib. mil.	T. Atilius P.f. Iuvenalis, praef. coh.	amico et municipi fraternae adfectionis dilecto	CIL VIII.4292 (Batna)
2 M. Aemilius Macer Dinarchus, son of legatus pr. pr.		patrono	AE (1946), 64 (Thamugadi)
3 Q. Anicius Faustus, cos.	M. Sedius Rufus, adv., fl. pp., IIvir	patrono	AE (1911), 99 (Lambaesis)
4 M. Annaeus Maximus Aquila Fulvianus, c.p.	Fulviani maiores	patrono	CIL VIII. 12065 (Muzuc)
5 Armenia Paulina, c.f., coniunx Anni Flaviani, proc. tract. Kart.	C. Vibius Marinus, centurio leg. III Aug.	amicus et municeps mariti eius	Pflaum, Carr. no. 202, 2 (Thamugadi)
6 Annius Armenius Donatus, c.p., son of above	C. Vibius Marinus, pp. leg. III Aug.	amicus et municeps eius patris	AE (1901), 195 (Thamugadi)
7 Annius Postumus, proc. a byblio.	Horatius Marcianus	amico indulgentissimo ob beneficia quae in se contulit	CIL VIII. 20684 (Saldae)
8 C. Annius Titianus, fl. pp., IIvir, eq. R.	Bennius Rufus Pacatianus, aed. des. and Gallius Renatus Tessellius	amico rarissimi exempli	AE (1955), 151 (Hippo Regius)
9 Arrius Antoninus, praetor	C. Iulius Libo, trierchus (sic) classis novae Lybice	patrono	ILS 1119 = CIL VIII.7030 (Cirta)
10 C. Arrius Longinus, c.p., son of C. Arrius Honoratus	L. Magnius Saturninus Sedianus Iunior	patrono amantissimo	AE (1915), 23 (Thuburbo Maius)
11 M. Atilius Metilius Bradua Caucidius Tertullus Claudius Atticus Vibullius Pollio Gavidius Latiarius Atrius Bassus, procos.	D. Iunius Crescens, Q. Calpurnius Capito, L. Plautius Octavianus, D. Iunius Galba	patrono	IRT 517 (Lepcis Magna)

Table III, cont.

Patronus	Cliens	Dedication	Reference
12 M. Aurelius Cominius Cassianus, leg. pr. pr.	L. Valerius Optatianus, adv., eq. R.	patrono... ob insignem eius erga se dignationem	*AE* (1917-18), 73 (Lambaesis)
13 M. Aurelius Cominius Cassianus	C. Iulius Rogatianus, dec. al. Fl.	ex corniculario provectus ab eo	*AE* (1917-18), 74-5 (Lambaesis)
14 M. Aurelius Cominius Cassianus	T. Fl. Silvanus, eq. R., advoc., Q. Pinarius Urbanus IIvir, L. Gargilius Felix fl. pp.	qui iu[dicia] eius for[i iustitiamque] tot[ies admirati sunt]	*CIL* VIII.2734 (Lambaesis)
15 Aurelius Zeno Ianuarius, c.v.	Iulius Antoninus, a militiis	ob merita	*CIL* VIII.10982 (Caesarea)
16 C. Caerellius Pollittanus, c.v.	Bonicii Victorinus Iulianus et Germanus Venussianus ex Africa	ob innumeribilia eius in se beneficia	*CIL* VI.1366 (Rome)
17 L. Calpurnius Fidus Aemilianus, trib. pl.	P. Sicinius Pescennius Hilarianus	candidat. eius amico incompar.	*CIL* VIII.25382 (Utica)
18 Aelia Flavina, coniunx Classici proc. Aug.	Caninia Salsa	ob merita	*AE* (1902), 13 (Chercel)
19 M. Coculnius Sex. f. Quintillianus, c.v., quaest. des.	Florus, princeps et undecim primus gentis Saboidum	amico merenti de suo...	*ILAlg.* II.i. 626 (Cirta)
20 M. Cornelius Octavianus, proc. Mauret. Caes. and family	... Saturninus dec. alae et... candd. eorum	candd. eorum patronis dignissimis	*AE* (1954), 136 (Chercel)
21 P. Curius P.f. Servilius Draco, scrib. q., eq. pub.	Servilius Primus	patrono	*ILTun.* 15 (Gigthis)
22 C. Fabricius Felix Salvianus, praet.	Maurelius Marcus (?)	incomparabili viro	*ILTun.* 83 (Thaenae)
23 M. Flavius T.f. Postumus, praetor	M. Paccius Rufinus, Q. Aemilius, P. Nonius Silvanus, A. Publicius Pontianus, C. Iulius Gargilianus	patrono optimo	*ILAlg.* II.i.630 (Cirta)
24 T. Flavius Serenus, praeses of both Mauretanias	Iulii Sabinus, a militiis, et Pontianus ex decurione adiutor et strator eius	patrono incompar.	*CIL* VIII.9002 (Rusuccurru)

Table III, cont.

Patronus	Cliens	Dedication	Reference
25 Ti. Flavius Umbrius Antistius Saturninus Fortunatianus, c.v.	Aemilius...	patrono	CIL VIII.61 (Hadrumetum)
26 Iulius Q.f. Clemens, IIvir qq., fl. Aug.	L. Sempronius Venustus	amico ob merita	CIL VIII.21452 (Gunugu, Mauret. Caes.)
27 Vergilia Florentina, coniunx Iuli Fortunatiani, leg. pr. pr.	Aemilius Florus, domicurator	patronis	AE (1917-18), 52 (Lambaesis)
28 C. Iulis Lepidus Tertullus, leg. pr. pr.	M. Aemilius M.f. Felix, aedil. q.p. praef. i.d.	patrono optimo	AE (1934), 26 (Diana Veteranorum)
29 Ti. Iulius Pollienus Auspex, leg. pr. pr.	C. Publilius Septtiminius (sic), centurio	candidatus eius	AE (1917-18), 50 (Lambaesis)
30 Ti. Iulius Pollienus Auspex	Sinicii Rufus et Fortunatus, advocati	patrono	CIL VIII.2743 (Lambaesis)
31 T. Iulius Tertullus Antiochus	L. Valerius Optatianus, eq. R., advoc.	cliens eius... ob insignem in se dignationem	CIL VIII.2393 (Thamugadi)
32 T. Licinius Hierocles, proc. Mauretan. Caes.	M. Aelius Saturninus, veteranus ex. dec. al.	patrono dignissimo	CIL VIII.20996 (Caesarea)
33 T. Licinius Hierocles	Servianus	patrono dignissimo	CIL VIII.20995 (Caesarea)
34 L. Maecilius P.f. Nepos, fl. pp., eq. pub. exornatus, omnib. honoribus functus in IIII col.	P. Paconius Cerealis	amico optimo et merenti	ILAlg. II.i.690 (Cirta)
35 C. Memmius C.f. Fidus Iulius Albius cos.	C. Annius Iulius Secundus	amico rarissimo ob eximiam erga se benivolentiam	CIL VIII.12442 (Vina)
36 Memmius C.f. Messius Pacatus, fl. pp., honoribus in patria functus	fullones eius domus	optimo patrono	ILAfr. 22 (Gigthis)

Table III, cont.

	Patronus	Cliens	Dedication	Reference
37	C. Mevius Silius Crescens Fortunatianus, c.p., son of C. Iulius Fortunatianus, e.v.	Sex. Volussius Maximus	patrono (filius patroni)	CIL VIII.610 = 11773 (Mididi)
38	L. Naevius Flavius Iulianus Tertullus Aquilinus, c.p.	C. Maecius Titianus Iunior, eq. R.	patrono incomparabil.	ILAlg. I.7 (Hippo Regius)
39	Q. Octavius Rufus Erucianus, e.v.	L. Sallustius Saturninus, omnib. honorib. functus	iusto viro ob notissimam omnibus in se bonitatem qua in perpetuum est reservatus	CIL VIII.1646 (Sicca Veneria)
40	Q. Octavius Q.f. Erucianus Stella Stratonianus, c.i. (son of above)	C. Cerficius Victor	patrono ob eximiam Eruciani patris in se benignitatem qua sunt in perpetuum reservati	CIL VIII.15885 (Sicca Veneria)
41	M. Plotius Faustus, praef. alae, fl. pp.	Plotius Thallus, alumnus	patrono benignissimo	CIL VIII.2394 (Thamugadi)
42	Quintianus, e.R., fl. pp.	C. Papirius Fortunatus	amico simplicissimo	CIL VIII.2408 (Thamugadi)
43	C. Pomponius Magnus, leg. pr. pr.	P. Geminius Gallonianus, domicurator	patrono incompar... promotus ab eo	AE (1917-18), 76 (Lambaesis)
44	... Pomponius C.f.L... murianus, proc. tract. Kart.	L. Valgius..., fisci advocatus	ob eximiam condisc... ratus adfectionem	CIL VIII.11341 (Sufetula)
45	C. Pontianus Ulpius Verus ... nianus Victor, c.p., son of C. Pontius Victor Verianus, v.e., fl. pp.	Q. Hammonius Donatianus, q., praef. i.d.	patrono	CIL VIII.2400 (Thamugadi)
46	C. Postumius Saturninus Flavianus, proc. reg. Hadrimetinae	L. Sempronius Maximus, fl. pp.	patrono	CIL VIII.11174 (Segermes)

Table III, cont.

Patronus	Cliens	Dedication	Reference
47 C. Postumius Saturninus Flavianus	Victor, lib. Augg.	cliens	CIL VIII.11175 (Segermes)
48 C. Sulpicia C.f. Dymiana, c.f., coniunx Quintii Victorini c.v.	Calpurnius Gabinius	patronae	AE (1964), 179 (Utica)
49 Q. Rupilius Q.f. Honoratus, in equestres turmas adl., fl. pp.	L. Popilius Saturninus	patrono incomparab.	CIL VIII.627 (Mactar)
50 Q. Sallustius Macrinianus, proc. of both Mauretanias, Q. Sallustius Macrianianus, c.v., son, commilito, and Q. Sallustius Macrinianus, nepos	Anullius Geta	ob insignem eorum erga se humanitatem	CIL VIII.9371 (Caesarea)
51 L. Titinius Clodianus, proc. and praeses of Numidia	C. Vibius Maximus, eq.R., fisci adv.	candidatus eius patrono rarissimo	AE (1917-18), 85 (Lambaesis)
52 M. Valerius Maximianus, leg. pr. pr.	Aquili Restutus, fl. pp., IIvir qq., praef. i.d. et Marcianus, IIvir	patrono	CIL VIII.4600 (Diana Veteranorum)
53 Virria Flavia Severina Petronia, M. Virri Fl. Iugurthae eq. R., fl. pp., filia	Pompeii Fuscus et Felix	fidem paternae amicitiae ista memoriae per- petuitate testantes	AE (1909), 156 (Thamugadi)

patronage. Further thought, however, suggests that such a conclusion would be unwarranted. The proportion of the total number is unimportant since the great majority of the 30,000 are brief funerary dedications. The absolute number is also not significant: the number of surviving *patronus* inscriptions from the Republic (excluding those from *liberti*) can be counted on one hand and no one doubts the importance of patronage in that era.[230] If the survival rate estimated by Duncan-Jones is close to the mark, these 50 stones represent some 1,000 originally erected in the provinces of North Africa — a number from which we could construct a comprehensive and persuasive picture of the importance of patronage. Finally, these 'patronage inscriptions' represent only the tip of the iceberg. Behind the hundreds of other simple dedications there may stand patron-client relationships, but the stones do not provide sufficient information for us to be certain.[231]

The dedicators of these stones rarely indicated precisely why they put them up (though there may be clear hints) and so some might be inclined to think of the stones as banal formalities. It is impossible to disprove this view conclusively, but two considerations militate against it. First, the stones were too expensive to be frivolous. Duncan-Jones gives 400HS as the price of a relatively inexpensive statue base with an inscription of fourteen lines.[232] This represents something on the order of several weeks' income for a decurion.[233] Secondly, these dedications need to be placed in the context of the reciprocity ethic of Roman patronage and *amicitia*. As stressed in the first chapter, exchange of concrete *beneficia* was an indispensable ingredient of these relationships. There may not have been a precisely equal *quid pro quo*, but we would expect that there would usually be a substantial *beneficium* from the patron to merit an expensive dedication in return. The wording of inscriptions suggests three occasions on which a dedication might be appropriate: (1) the death of a patron, calling for a memorial stone;[234] (2) after a *beneficium* from a patron as a sign of gratitude;[235] (3) the promotion of a patron-official when congratulations were in order.[236]

I have included in the table of inscriptions only those in which patronage relationships are explicit in the language. In other inscriptions the attestation of kinship ties between imperial and local aristocrats, together with the award of imperial *beneficia*, points implicitly to patronal exchange involved in kinship relations of different types. A review of this evidence shows that the pattern of success enjoyed by the Septimii was not unusual. Owing to a series of seven inscriptions found at the baths in Lambaesis, a stemma covering three generations can be constructed for the family of P. Aelius Q.f. Lem. Menecratianus Zita, settled in Lambaesis.[237] Zita, a centurion, had a daughter and three sons, one of whom was responsible for the series of inscriptions.

---

230 De Grassi, *ILLRP* 341, 382, 386, 432, 433. I can find no others in *CIL* I.
231 E.g., it was tempting to include *AE* (1917-18), 71 and *AE* (1939), 38 in the table.
232 Duncan-Jones, *Economy*, 78.
233 Arbitrarily taking a decurion worth 100,000 HS who achieves a 10% return on his property investment.
234 E.g., *CIL* VIII.10982: 'Memoriae Aurelii Zenonis Ianuari...' On the importance of showing gratitude to dead friends, Pliny, *Ep.* 6.10.
235 E.g. *CIL* VIII.20684: '... amico indulgentissimo ob beneficia quae in se contulit...'
236 Inscriptions put up for an official of the province and listing the official's next appointment seem likely instances of this (e.g., *AE* (1922), 19).
237 N.-E. Weydert, 'Inscriptions des Thermes de Lambese', *BACTH* (1912), 345-55.

The daughter, Aelia Menecratilla, was probably the link which permitted the family upward mobility. She married P. Maevius Saturninus Honoratianus, a *procurator Augusti* and a *clarissimus vir*, probably also from Lambaesis.[238] Their son, P. Maevius Saturninus Honoratianus, proceeded to a senatorial career, receiving the *latus clavus* and holding a tribunate in *legio XI Claudia*. Aelia's three brothers probably enjoyed the benefits of having a member of the imperial aristocracy as a brother-in-law. D. Aelius Menecratianus passed through the equestrian *militiae* and then between 197 and 202 went on to hold a legionary tribunate. Of Aelius Procles Menecratianus we know neither his praenomen nor anything else. The third brother, P. Aelius Menecrates Florianus, paid for the erection of the series of inscriptions in 197 and is described as *exornatus equo publico*. The following stemma can be constructed.[239]

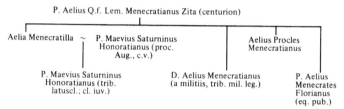

P. Aelius Q.f. Lem. Menecratianus Zita (centurion)

Aelia Menecratilla ~	P. Maevius Saturninus Honoratianus (proc. Aug., c.v.)		Aelius Procles Menecratianus
P. Maevius Saturninus Honoratianus (trib. latuscl.; cl. iuv.)		D. Aelius Menecratianus (a militiis, trib. mil. leg.)	P. Aelius Menecrates Florianus (eq. pub.)

Given the brevity of the inscriptions, it is impossible to prove conclusively that Aelia's husband was responsible for her two brothers' receiving offices and honors from the emperor. But Honoratianus' patronage seems very likely: he and his senatorial son are the most prominent figures in Florianus' series of dedications and the chronology of the marriage and offices is consistent with this suggestion.[240] N. Weydert, who published the inscriptions, made another interesting suggestion: 'il convient de rappeler le nom de Aelius Florianus, *vir perfectissimus*, qui fut préfet de vigiles entre 226 et 244. Ce personnage pourrait être un fils de P. Aelius Menecrates Florianus.'[241] The suggestion seems plausible from a chronological standpoint and the name of Aelius Florianus is not common. If Weydert is right, we have here a situation parallel to that of the Septimii with patronage links between collateral lines. However likely this conjecture, the certain part of the stemma illustrates a kinship pattern found elsewhere in which families of the imperial aristocracy are linked by marriage to families from their *patria*.

The next illustration of the pattern comes from a leading family of Cuicul and Cirta. Probably in the early second century C. Iulius Crescens was the first man from Cuicul to hold the post of *flamen Augustalis provinciae Africae*.[242] His daughter, Iulia Ingenua, married Q. Iulius Crescentianus, of whom we know nothing more than his name. Their son, C. Iulius Crescens Didius Crescentianus, was *flamen perpetuus* of both Cuicul and

238 The only Maevii Saturnini that I am able to find in the indices of *CIL* come from Africa: one from Lambaesis (VIII.3184, 4073); one from Theveste (VIII.16589); and one from Uchi Maius (VIII.26349).

239 Weydert, 'Thermes de Lambese', 353. Weydert notes that Zita is an African name indicating African roots of the family.

240 In 197 when the inscriptions were erected, Menecratilla and Honoratianus must have been married about twenty years (to allow time for a son to grow up and reach a tribunate) — plenty of time in which to fit D. Aelius Menecratianus' *militiae*.

241 Weydert, 'Thermes de Lambese', 353.

242 For all references, see *PIR²* I. 284.

Cirta and became tribune of a cohort. He and his wife Naevia had three children: one of their daughters, Didia Cornelia, married into a senatorial family (*clarissima femina*) and their son, C. Didius Maximus, was *exornatus equo publico*. I have reproduced the stemma from *PIR²*.

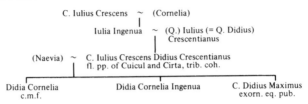

C. Iulius Crescens ~ (Cornelia)

Iulia Ingenua ~ (Q.) Iulius (= Q. Didius)
                   Crescentianus

(Naevia) ~ C. Iulius Crescens Didius Crescentianus
             fl. pp. of Cuicul and Cirta, trib. coh.

Didia Cornelia   Didia Cornelia Ingenua   C. Didius Maximus
   c.m.f.   exorn. eq. pub.

In some respects the pattern here is similar to that of Menecratianus and his family: a daughter marrying into a family (unnamed in this case) of the imperial aristocracy. But here the situation is complicated by the fact that there may have been another source of patronage for the family. Jarrett has suggested that the positions of influence of Q. Lollius Urbicus and Fronto explain 'the fact that three men from Cuicul obtained equestrian commissions under Pius. The connection between Cuicul and the four colonies of the Cirtan federation was extremely close, many men serving as decurions and magistrates in both places.'[243] One of these three men is our C. Iulius Crescens Didius Crescentianus. He certainly held magistracies in both cities and it may have been the Cirtan connection which yielded the *equus publicus* and tribunate. But the chronology does not allow Jarrett's precise interpretation. *CIL* VIII. 8318 and 8319 were erected in 169 when Urbicus and probably Fronto were dead:[244] these inscriptions provide full details of Crescentianus' magistracies and his *equus publicus*, but give no hint that he had held the tribunate at this point. A more likely source of patronage is the senatorial family of Didia Cornelia's husband (who could have been from Cirta for all we know). The chronology of this conjecture is more plausible. Crescentianus' tribunate came after his daughter's marriage (and her death, which would not necessarily have broken off the relationship between the two families).[245] Didia Cornelia in her will stipulated that an honorary inscription be erected to her brother, Maximus; perhaps the same concern for his *dignitas* motivated the successful petition to the emperor through her husband's family for the *equus publicus*.[246] There is no chronological reason why her father's public horse could not have come through the same channels, although it is quite possible that a leading provincial family like the Crescentiani would have had other connections. In any case, the Jarrett conjecture gives warning against the facile association of the award of honors with the few big men whom we know about from the same area. We are dealing here with a large, complex web of kinship, friendship and patronage relations: only a fraction of it is visible to us and so there were many more links available to provincials trying to influence decisions at Rome than we can know about.

243 'African Contribution', 220.
244 *PIR²* L.8327 and Champlin, 'The chronology of Fronto', 137ff. (Acceptance of Champlin's arguments about the date of Fronto's death need not entail acceptance of his arguments about the date and addressee of *Ad Amic.* 1.9.)
245 The tribunate is not mentioned in *AE* (1913), 21.
246 *AE* (1916), 13.

The reverse of the above pattern can also be found, that is, a provincial male marrying a senatorial sister or daughter and so benefiting. Q. Asturnius Lappianus from Rusicade was a municipal magistrate at Cirta (*III vir IIII coloniarum* and *praefectus IIII coloniarum*) and received the public horse. The latter honor may be explained by the fact that he had the good fortune to marry Claudia Gallitta, sister of Tiberius Claudius Claudianus, a consular who served as imperial legate of the two Pannonias.[247] Given the possibilities for profit, it is not surprising to find local people dedicating honorary inscriptions to their important affines and so advertising their own importance by association while publicly keeping up the exchange relationship with their relatives. *CIL* VIII. 8934 is probably another example of this phenomenon. P. Blaesius Felix, a centurion and probably from Saldae,[248] dedicated an inscription to his *adfinis* Sextus Cornelius Dexter, a high-ranking procurator of the Antonine period, also from Saldae. He set up a stone in honor of Dexter *ob merita*, perhaps out of gratitude for his centurionate. (It is easier to believe that a woman of an important equestrian family married a well-off local who received his commission by patronage rather than a soldier who had worked his way up through the ranks.)[249]

One other variation on this kinship theme appears in the African evidence: a provincial sister and/or her children advertising the maintenance of contact with a senatorial or procuratorial brother. Egnatuleia Sabina, L. Egnatuleius Sabinus and Calidius Proculus dedicated a stone to their procuratorial brother, tutor and maternal uncle, respectively.[250] Later another family of the municipal aristocracy, this time of Lepcis Magna, set up an inscription in honor of one Fulvius, *procurator XX hereditatium*.[251] The family included Fulvius' sister, husband and their two sons. The relationship between the people named in a damaged stone from Madauros (later third century) is less clear: 'T. Iulio Sabino Victoriano, eq. R., fl. pp., centenario viro gloriosae innocentiae, probatae fidei, Q. Calpurnius Honoratus fl. pp., [T. Fl]avi[us] Victorianus, [T. F]laviu[s...]ianus fl. pp... Iuliu[s Ve]nustus... Cornel. Salvius Cha[e]re[as p]arentes laudibil[i...a]vo et [avunculo...].'[252] Given that no other evidence is available concerning the relationships among these men, it is not clear why *avunculo* should be a compelling restoration (though it seems to be repeated without question).[253] But that is unimportant for our purposes: it still illustrates the continuing connections between the *parentes* at home and a *centenarius vir probatae fidei*. Unfortunately, there is no hint of what form any *officia*, the expressions of familial *fides*, might have taken.

To complete the description of kinship relationships found in the African evidence, we should include fictive kinship. Two dedications to M. Plotius Faustus illustrate a situation for Africa which is familiar from Pliny's passages about fictive and adopted

---

247 *ILAlg.* II.i.29 (= *CIL* VIII.7978 = *ILS* 1147).
248 For the other Blaesii from Saldae see *CIL* VIII.8944, 20688.
249 See Pliny, *Ep.* 6.25 for the centurionate commission by patronage.
250 *CIL* VIII.10500 (= *ILS* 1409, of second-century date).
251 *AE* (1931), 2.
252 *AE* (1920), 17.
253 Pflaum and Jarrett both print *avunculo* in their collections (*Carrières*, no. 245a and 'Album', no. 87).

sons.[254] Faustus, a municipal aristocrat and local priest from Thamugadi, passed through the *tres militiae* about the beginning of the second century. It seems that he and his wife Cornelia Valentina Tucciana did not have children and instead adopted one or perhaps two sons, Plotius Thallus, an *alumnus*, and M. Pompeius Quintianus, an *eques Romanus* who described them as *parentes*.[255] Leschi makes an interesting and plausible guess about the relationships.

> Ne voyons-nous pas le flamine et la flaminique donner leur nom à un personnage Plotius Thallus qui se dit leur *alumnus* et qui, avec sa fille Plotia Faustiana, les appelle ses *patroni*. *Alumnus* désigne l'enfant étranger recueilli en bas âge et élevé dans la famille. Thallus était sans doute d'origine humble, sinon servile. Il n'en était pas de même de Quintianus. Sa promotion au rang de chevalier romain, alors que son père n'était qu'un *veteranus*, laisse croire qu'il a été richement doté par les généraux Thamugadiens à qui il a tenu à témoigner sa reconnaissance.[256]

The suggestion that Faustus gave Quintianus the requisite wealth for equestrian census is attractive and reminiscent of Pliny's relationship with Romatius Firmus.[257] Unfortunately, no later inscriptions inform us whether Quintianus was able to draw on Faustus' connections to obtain some sort of commission or honor from Rome.

In some respects these inscriptions only reveal the obvious: kinship ties between imperial and municipal aristocrats were one consequence of individual provincials winning entry into imperial offices at Rome. But, as Apuleius' uneven relationship with his stepson illustrates, kinship ties need not be warm, enduring and useful for provincials aspiring to imperial offices and honors. It is for this that these inscriptions, only a fraction of those erected, provide evidence.

254 See above, p.143.
255 No. 41 in the table of patronage inscriptions for Thallus; *AE* (1946), 65-6; *CIL* VIII.17904 (=*ILS* 2751), 17905, 2408, cf. 2372 and pp. 951, 1693 for Quintianus.
256 *BACTH* (1946), 31.
257 *Ep.* 1.19.

Conclusion:
Patronage in perspective

In this study we have sought to discover in what aspects of Roman life patronage played a part and how it functioned during the early Empire. The evidence suggests that exchange between patrons and clients was of considerable importance in political, legal, social and economic affairs. The aristocratic social milieu of the Republic continued into the Principate, and with it the basic notion that a man's social status was reflected in the size of his following — a large clientèle symbolizing his power to give inferiors what they needed. If a man's *clientela* was indicative of his current status, his potential for mobility depended on the effectiveness of his patrons, whose wealth and political connections could be indispensable. Perhaps partly because of the unchanging social structure and values, financial institutions developed little, and so Romans appear to have continued to rely largely on patrons, clients and friends for loans or gifts in time of need, and assistance in financial activities.

Within the sphere of politics and administration, patron-client relations supply part of the answer to the question of how such a large empire was governed by so small an administration. The emperor had at his disposal formal organizations to meet his primary needs of the maintenance of law and order and the collection of taxes: here patron-client relations allowed manipulation of administrative activities, but did not in themselves fulfill governmental functions. With regard to the recruitment of administrators, on the other hand, Rome during the Principate had markedly little formal machinery by comparison with other great, enduring pre-industrial empires (e.g. the Chinese and Ottoman).[1] Rather than developing palace schools or competitive examinations (as in Turkey and China, respectively), emperors relied on a network of private connections to bring leading candidates to their attention. While the emperor had a limited bureaucracy through which he could reach his subjects, there were few formal, impersonal mechanisms through which the subjects could initiate contacts with the central government.

1 For the Chinese system of recruitment see Appendix 3A; for the Ottoman Empire, A.H. Lybyer, *The Government of the Ottoman Empire in the Time of Suleiman the Magnificent*, 71ff.

Hence, many of these contacts, which in a more developed bureaucracy would take the form of written applications, could be made only through patron-client networks in the Roman empire. As a result, these networks are essential to an understanding of how provincials related to Rome.

It was suggested in the introduction that a monograph on a single social institution or custom risks distortion by its concentration, and the reader has no doubt been aware of the limitations of this study. First, patronage has been treated as a static custom for the period of the Principate; the only development discussed in detail was the increasing integration of provincials into aristocratic networks. The stress on continuity has been intentional, in part as a counterweight to previous arguments for change which have been based on changes in the kind of extant evidence examined. The corpus of Cicero's writings, with one hundred letters of recommendation, constitutes the bulk of our evidence for the late Republic, whereas for the early Empire we are much more dependent on inscriptions. The fact that the former mention patronal exchange frequently while the latter do not should not be allowed to mislead us into believing that patronage changed or declined. Like kinds of evidence should be compared, and when this is done, as de Ste Croix noted, little change can be detected between Cicero's and Fronto's *commendationes*.[2] On the other hand, there was a standard form for letters of recommendation, so these letters cannot be assumed simply to reflect the realities of patronal exchange. We would expect patronage to have evolved in response to political, economic and social developments. When the Principate was established and the popular assemblies became unimportant, the configuration of political patronage was altered as connections with the emperor, direct or indirect, became vital for political success, and the need for popularity in the assemblies declined. Three centuries later another major reform in the organization of government was reflected in patronal relations. The institution of a new system of taxation and growing pressure for collection increased the value of the great patrons able to supply protection to those who worked the land.[3] Thus rural patronage, which no doubt existed throughout Roman history, took on a new importance. It was perceived as a threat to the government, and for the first time emperors attempted to suppress patronage of this kind insofar as it interfered with the collection of revenues. Other kinds of patronal exchange continued unhindered, though some emperors attempted to clarify the legal ramifications of venal *suffragium* used to secure official appointments.[4] Within the period of the Principate, it is difficult to discover any specific events or reforms which demonstrably affected patron-client relations in the way

2 'Suffragium', 43.
3 See above, p.112.
4 Walter Goffart, 'Did Julian combat venal suffragium? A note on C.Th. 2.29.1', *Cl.Ph.* 65 (1970), 145ff.; T.D. Barnes, 'A law of Julian', *Cl.Ph.* 69 (1974), 288ff.

that the *iugatio-capitatio* tax system did. More subtle trends, such as the supply and demand for labor and land, the intensity of competition for high office, and the desire to avoid municipal obligations, probably influenced how and for what purposes patron-client bonds were formed, but these trends are often impossible to measure, much less to relate convincingly to the evolution of patronal relations. In general, where sources have been available, we have been able to document similar exchanges from the reign of Augustus to the Severan period.

The second major limitation has been that of scope: we have focused on a single type of reciprocal exchange out of the range of Roman social relations. Other personal relations, such as family and friendships with men of similar social station, were also important, but because of the great inequalities of wealth, power and status in the Roman world, personal bonds between unequals were of special significance. As R. Kaufman pointed out with reference to Latin America, in societies 'which, by all other evidence that can be mustered, should have torn themselves to pieces long ago, societies characterized by atomization, by parochialism and mistrust, by profound status inequalities', a study of patron-client networks promises 'some insight into the question of why [these] societies hang together at all'.[5] At the same time, Kaufman warned against the indiscriminate use of the concept of patronage to explain all social behavior. An echo of this warning can be found in a recent review by Brunt, criticizing 'the modern dogma of the all-importance of "Nah-und-Treuverhältnisse" in general, or of clientage in particular'.[6] With regard to the Principate, Brunt expressed reservations about the importance of the patronal ideology to the position of the emperor: 'the emperors could not rely on any ancient equivalent of the traditional sentiment that mediaeval and modern kingship inspired; both the army and the higher classes, among whom they had to select counsellors and agents, required satisfaction of material interests and compliance with accepted political, social and moral principles; the title *"pater patriae"*...only represented genuine devotion where an emperor fulfilled these obligations'.[7] Brunt's remarks seem to me to be sound, and so the emphasis of this study has been placed on *beneficia* rather than *fides*. The emperor satisfied the material interests of different subjects in different ways. The army's interests were satisfied largely in an impersonal way through benefactions and salaries paid to all soldiers. We have seen that the upper classes' interests, by contrast, were met by personal gifts and grants in relationships that were conceived to involve reciprocal (though unequal) exchange. Therefore, the web of patron-client relationships emanating from the emperor is one vital element (and only one)

5 'The patron-client concept', 286f.
6 Review of Strasburger, *Zum antiken Gesellschaftsideals*, *Gnomon* 51 (1979), 447.
7 *Ibid.*, 448.

in our understanding of the emperor's position. More generally, patronage was not all-important in Roman imperial society, but it (especially its non-political aspects) has surely suffered more from lack of attention in social histories of the Principate than from an exaggerated estimate of its significance. It is hoped that this study has provided something of a corrective which will improve our perspectives on the continuities in the many social, economic and political institutions affected by patronage.

Bibliography

Abbott, F. and A. C. Johnson. *Municipal Administration in the Roman Empire* (New York, 1926).

Alföldy, G. 'Consuls and consulars under the Antonines; prosopography and history', *Anc Soc* 7 (1976), 263-99.

Konsulat und Senatorenstand unter den Antoninen (Bonn, 1977).

Römische Sozialgeschichte (Wiesbaden, 1975).

Armstrong, J.A. *The European Administrative Elite* (Princeton, 1973).

Aylmer, G.E. *The King's Servants: the Civil Servants of Charles I* (London, 1961).

Badian, E. *Foreign Clientelae* (Oxford, 1958).

Balsdon, J.P.V.D. *Roman Women* (London, 1962).

Barnes, T.D. 'The family and career of Septimius Severus', *Historia* 16 (1967), 87-107.

'A law of Julian', *CPh* 69 (1974), 288-91.

Tertullian (Oxford, 1971).

Benabou, M. 'Proconsul et légat en Afrique. Le témoignage de Tacite', *Ant. Afr.* 6 (1972), 129-36.

Benveniste, E. *Indo-European Language and Society*, transl. E. Palmer (London, 1973).

Béranger, J. *Recherches sur l'aspect idéologique du Principat* (Basel, 1953).

Berchem, D. Van. *Les distributions de blé et d'argent à la plèbe romaine sous l'Empire* (Geneva, 1939).

Birley, A.R. 'The coups d'état of the year 193', *BJ* 169 (1969), 247-80.

'The Governors of Roman Britain', *Epigraphische Studien* 4 (1967), 63-102.

Septimius Severus: The African Emperor (London, 1971).

'Some notes on HA Severus 1-4', *Bonner Historia-Augusta-Colloquium 1968/69* (1970), 59-78.

'Some teachers of M. Aurelius', *Bonner Historia-Augusta-Colloquium 1966/67* (1968), 39-42.

Birley, E. 'The Governors of Numidia, A.D. 193-268', *JRS* 40 (1950), 60-8.

'Promotions and transfers in the Roman army II: The centurionate', *Carnuntum Jahrbuch* 7 (1963-4), 21-33.

Roman Britain and the Roman Army (Kendal, 1953).

'Senators in the emperor's service', *PBA* (1953), 197-214.

Blau, P.M. *The Dynamics of Bureaucracy*, 2nd ed. (London, 1967).

Blok, A. 'Variations in patronage', *Sociologische Gids* 16 (1969), 365-78.

Boissevain, J. *Friends of Friends* (Oxford, 1974).

Boissevain. J. and J.C. Mitchell (ed.). *Network Analysis: Studies in Human Interaction* (The Hague, 1973).

Boissevain, J. 'Patronage in Sicily', *Man* n.s.1 (1966), 18-33.

Boulvert, G. *Esclaves et affranchis impériaux sous le Haut-Empire romain: rôle politique et administratif* (Naples, 1970).

Bowersock, G.W. *Greek Sophists in the Roman Empire* (Oxford, 1969).

Broughton, T.R.S. *The Romanization of Africa Proconsularis* (London, 1929).

Brown, R. *Social Psychology* (London, 1965).

Brunt, P.A. 'The administrators of Roman Egypt', *JRS* 65 (1975), 124-47.

'"Amicitia" in the late Roman Republic', *PCRhS* n.s.11 (1965), 1-20 (reprinted in *The Crisis of the Roman Republic*, ed. R. Seager (Cambridge, 1969), 199-218).

'Charges of provincial maladministration under the Early Principate' *Historia* 10 (1961), 189-223.

'The Equites in the late Republic', in *The Crisis of the Roman Republic*, ed. R. Seager (Cambridge, 1969), 83-103.

Italian Manpower, 225 B.C.-A.D. 14 (Oxford, 1971).

'Procuratorial jurisdiction', *Latomus* 25 (1966), 461-89.

'The romanization of the local ruling classes in the Roman Empire', in *Assimilation et résistance à la culture gréco-romaine dans le monde ancien*, ed. D.M. Pippidi (Paris, 1976), 161-73.

Review of H. Strasburger, *Zum antiken Gesellschaftideal*, in *Gnomon* 51 (1979), 443-8.

Burton, G. 'Powers and functions of Proconsuls in the Roman Empire, 70-260 A.D.' (unpublished Oxford D. Phil. diss., 1973).

'Proconsuls, assizes and the administration of justice under the Empire', *JRS* 65 (1975) 92-106.

'Slaves, freedmen and monarchy' (review of Boulvert, *Esclaves et affranchis impériaux sous le Haut-Empire romain: rôle politique et administratif* and *Domestique et fonctionnaire sous le Haut-Empire romain: la condition de l'affranchi et de l'esclave du prince*), *JRS* 67 (1977), 162-6.

Campbell, B. 'Who were the "viri militares"?', *JRS* 65 (1975), 11-31.

Campbell, J.K. *Honour, Family and Patronage* (Oxford, 1964).

Carney, T.F. *Bureaucracy in Traditional Society* (Lawrence, Kans., 1971).

Champlin, E.J. 'The chronology of Fronto', *JRS* 64 (1974), 136-59.

Fronto and Antonine Rome (Cambridge, Mass., 1980).

Chastagnol, A. 'Le laticlave de Vespasien', *Historia* 25 (1976), 253-6.

'"Latus Clavus" et "Adlectio"', *RD* 53 (1975), 375-94.

'Les modes d'accès au Sénat romain au début de l'Empire: remarques à propos de la Table Claudienne de Lyon', *BSAF* (1971), 282-310.

'La naissance de l'ordo senatorius', *MEFR* (1973), 2, 583-607.

'Les sénateurs d'origine provinciale sous le règne d'Auguste', in *Mélanges de philosophie, de littérature et d'histoire ancienne offerts à Pierre Boyancé* (Rome, 1974), 163-71.

Chang Chung-li. *The Chinese Gentry: Studies on their Role in Nineteenth Century*

Chinese Society (Seattle, 1955).

Clemente, G. 'Il patronato nei Collegia dell'Impero Romano', *SCO* 21 (1972), 142-229.

Cohen, E.W. *The Growth of the British Civil Service 1780-1939* (London, 1941).

Crook, J.A. *Consilium Principis* (Cambridge, 1955).

Law and Life of Rome (London, 1967).

Dobson, B. 'The centurionate and social mobility during the Principate', in *Recherches sur les structures sociales dans l'antiquité classique*, ed. C. Nicolet (Paris, 1970), 99-116.

'The Praefectus Fabrum in the Early Principate', in *Britain and Rome*, ed. M.G. Jarrett and B. Dobson (Kendal, 1965), 61-84.

'The significance of the centurion and "primipilaris" in the Roman army and administration', *Aufstieg und Niedergang der römischen Welt* II.1, ed. H. Temporini (Berlin, 1974), 392-434.

Domaszewski, A. von. *Die Rangordnung des römischen Heeres*, rev. ed. B. Dobson (Köln, 1967).

Duff, A.M. *Freedmen in the Roman Empire* (Oxford, 1928).

Duncan-Jones, R. *The Economy of the Roman Empire: Quantitative Studies* (Cambridge, 1974).

'Equestrian rank in the cities of the African provinces under the Principate: An epigraphic survey', *PBSR* 35 (1967), 147-88.

'Patronage and city privileges — the case of Guifi', *Epigraphische Studien* 9 (1972), 12-16.

Eck, W. 'Beförderungskriterien innerhalb der senatorischen Laufbahn, dargestellt an der Zeit von 69 bis 138 n. Chr.' *Aufstieg und Niedergang der römischen Welt* II.1, ed. H.Temporini (Berlin, 1974), 158-228.

'Zu den prokonsularen Legationen in der Kaiserzeit', *Epigraphische Studien* 9 (1972), 24ff.

Eisenstadt, S.N. *The Political Systems of Empires* (New York, 1963).

Evans, J.K. 'The role of *suffragium* in imperial political decision-making: a Flavian example', *Historia* 27 (1978), 102-28.

Finley, M.I. *The Ancient Economy* (London, 1973).

Aspects of Antiquity (London, 1967).

'Empire in the Greco-Roman world', *G&R* 25 (1978), 1-15.

Fishwick, D. and B.D. Shaw. 'The formation of Africa Proconsularis', *Hermes* 105 (1977), 369-80.

'Ptolemy of Mauretania and the conspiracy of Gaetulicus', *Historia* 25 (1976), 491-4.

Floud, R. *An Introduction to Quantitative Methods for Historians* (Cambridge, 1973).

Frederiksen, M.W. 'Caesar, Cicero and the problem of debt', *JRS* 56 (1966), 128-41.

Friedlaender, L. *Roman Life and Manners under the Early Empire*, 7th ed. transl. by J.H. Freese (London).

Fritz, K. von. 'Tacitus, Agricola, Domitian, and the problem of the Principate', *CPh* 52 (1957), 73-97.

Fustel de Coulanges, N.M. *Les origines du système féodal* (Paris, 1890).

Gagé, J. *Les classes sociales dans l'Empire romain* (Paris, 1964).

Garnsey, P. 'Rome's African Empire under the Principate', in *Imperialism in the Ancient World*, ed. C.R. Whittaker and P. Garnsey (Cambridge, 1978).

Social Status and Legal Privilege in the Roman Empire (Oxford, 1970).

'*Taxatio* and *Pollicitatio* in Roman Africa', *JRS* 61 (1971), 116-29.

Garzetti, A. *From Tiberius to the Antonines*, transl. by J.R. Foster (London, 1974).

Gascou, J. *La politique municipale de l'empire romain en Afrique proconsulaire de Trajan à Septime-Sévere*, Coll. Éc. Fr. de Rome (Rome, 1972).

Gaudemet, J. *Indulgentia Principis* (Publication no. 3, 1962, of the Istituto di storia del diritto, University of Trieste).

'Testamenta ingrata et pietas Augusti', *Studi Arangio-Ruiz* (Naples, 1953) vol. 3, 115ff.

Gellner, E. and J. Waterbury (ed.). *Patrons and Clients in Mediterranean Societies* (London, 1977).

Gelzer, M. *The Roman Nobility*, transl. by R. Seager (Oxford, 1969).

Gérard, J. *Juvénal et la réalité contemporaine* (Paris, 1976).

Goffart, W. 'Did Julian combat venal suffragium? A note on C.Th. 2.29.1', *CPh* 65 (1970), 145-51.

Griffin, M. *Seneca: A Philosopher in Politics* (Oxford, 1976).

Hammond, M. 'Composition of the Senate, A.D. 68-235', *JRS* 47 (1957), 74-81.

'Septimius Severus, Roman bureaucrat', *HSPh* 51 (1940), 137-73.

Hands, A.R. *Charities and Social Aid in Greece and Rome* (London, 1968).

Harmand, L. *Un aspect social et politique du monde romain: le patronat sur les collectivités des origines au Bas-Empire* (Paris, 1957).

Haywood, R.M. 'The African policy of Septimius Severus', *TAPhA* 71 (1940), 175-85.

Heath, A. *Rational Choice and Social Exchange: A Critique of Exchange Theory* (Cambridge, 1976).

Hellegouarc'h, J. *Le vocabulaire latin des relations et des partis politiques sous la république* (Paris, 1963).

Honoré, A.M. *Tribonian* (London, 1978).

Hopkins, M.K. 'The age of Roman girls at marriage', *Population Studies* 18 (1964-5), 309-27.

'Elite mobility in the Roman Empire', *P&P* 32 (Dec. 1965), 12-26.

'Eunuchs in politics in the Later Roman Empire', *PCPhS* n.s.9 (1963), 62-80.

Review of F. Millar, *The Emperor in the Roman World*, in *JRS* 68 (1978), 178-86.

'Social mobility in the Later Roman Empire: the evidence of Ausonius', *CQ* n.s. 11 (1961), 239-49.

Hsu, F.L.K. 'Social mobility in China', *Amer. Soc. Rev.* 14 (1949), 764-71.

Jarrett, M.G. 'The African contribution to the Imperial Civil Service', *Historia* 12 (1963), 209-26.

'An album of the equestrians from North Africa in the emperor's service', *Epigraphische Studien* 9 (1972), 146-232.

'The career of L. Titinius Clodianus', *Latomus* 21 (1962), 855-9.

Jones, A.H.M. *The Later Roman Empire, 284-602* (Oxford, 1964).

Studies in Roman Government and Law (Oxford, 1968).

Jones, C.P. 'A new commentary on the Letters of Pliny', *Phoenix* 22 (1968), 111-42.

Plutarch and Rome (Oxford, 1971).

The Roman World of Dio Chrysostom (London, 1978).

Kaufman, R.R. 'The patron-client concept and macro-politics: prospects and problems', *CSSH* 16 (1974), 284-308.

Kelly, J.M. *Roman Litigation* (Oxford, 1966).

Kelsall, R.K. *Higher Civil Servants in Britain from 1870 to the Present Day* (London, 1955).

Kloft, H. *Liberalitas Principis* (Böhlau, 1970).

Kotula, T. *Les curies municipales en Afrique romaine* (Warsaw, 1968).

Kracke, E.A. Jr. *Civil Service in Early Sung China, 960-1067* (Cambridge, Mass., 1953).

'Family vs. merit in the Chinese Civil Service examinations during the Empire', *Harvard Journal of Asiatic Studies* 10 (1947), 103-23.

Laet, S.J. De. *Portorium* (Brugge, 1949).

LaFleur, R.A. 'Amicitia and the unity of Juvenal's First Book', *ICS* 4 (1979), 158-77.

Landé, C.H. 'Networks and groups in Southeast Asia: Some observations on the group theory of politics', *Am. Pol. Sci. Rev.* 67 (March 1973), 103-27.

Le Gall, J. 'La "nouvelle plèbe", et la sportule quotidienne', in *Mélanges d'archéologie et d'histoire offerts à A. Piganiol*, ed. R. Chevallier (Paris, 1966), 1, 449-53.

Leglay, M. 'La vie intellectuelle d'une cité africaine des confins de l'Aurés', in *Hommages à L. Herrman*, Coll. Lat.′44 (1960), 485-91.

Levick, B. 'Imperial control of the elections under the early Principate: commendatio, suffragatio, and "nominatio" ', *Historia* 16 (1967), 207-30.

Libanius: *Discours sur les patronages*, ed., transl. with commentary by L. Harmand (Paris, 1955).

Lipset, S.M. and A. Solari (ed.). *Elites in Latin America* (New York, 1967).

Lybyer, A.H. *The Government of the Ottoman Empire of the Time of Suleiman the Magnificent* (Cambridge, Mass., 1913).

McAlindon, D. 'Entry to the Senate in the Early Empire', *JRS* 47 (1957), 191-5.

MacMullen, R. 'Market days in the Roman Empire', *Phoenix* 24 (1970), 333-41.

Roman Government's Response to Crisis (New Haven, Conn., 1976).

Roman Social Relations, 50 B.C. to A.D. 284 (New Haven, Conn., 1974).

Marache, R. 'La revendication sociale chez Martial et Juvénal', *RCCM* 3 (1961), 30-67.

Matthews, J. *Western Aristocracies and the Imperial Court A.D. 364-425* (Oxford, 1975).

Mauss, M. *The Gift*, transl. by I. Cumnison (London, 1966).

Menzel, J. (ed.). *The Chinese Civil Service* (Boston, 1963).

Michel, J. *Gratuité en droit romain* (Brussels, 1962).

Millar, F. *The Emperor in the Roman World* (London, 1977).

'Emperors at work', *JRS* 57 (1967), 9-19.

'Epictetus and the Imperial Court', *JRS* 55 (1965), 141-8.

Review of Pflaum, *Les carrières procuratoriennes équestres*, in *JRS* 53 (1963), 194-200.

A Study of Cassius Dio (Oxford, 1964).

Mitchell, S. 'Requisitioned transport in the Roman Empire: a new inscription from

Pisidia', *JRS* 66 (1976), 106-31.

Mitchell, T.N. *Cicero: the Ascending Years* (New Haven, Conn., 1979).

Mommsen, T. *Römische Staatesrecht*, 3rd ed. (Leipzig, 1887).

'Vitorius Marcellus', *Gesammelte Schriften* VII (Berlin, 1965), 221-3.

Morris, J. 'Leges Annales under the Principate', *LF* 87 (1964), 316-37 and 88 (1965), 22-31.

Moussy, C. *Gratia et sa famille* (Paris, 1966).

Neuhauser, W. *Patronus und Orator* (Innsbruck, 1958).

Nicols, J. *Vespasian and the Partes Flavianae*, Historia Einzelschriften 28 (Wiesbaden, 1978).

Nutton, V. 'The beneficial ideology', in *Imperialism in the Ancient World*, ed. C.R. Whittaker and P. Garnsey (Cambridge, 1978), 209-21.

'L. Gellius Maximus, physician and procurator', *CQ* n.s. 21 (1971), 262-72.

'Two notes on immunities: Digest 27.1.6.10 and 11', *JRS* 61 (1971), 52-63.

Oost, S.I. 'The career of M. Antonius Pallas', *AJPh* 79 (1958), 113-39.

Patlagean, E. *Pauvreté économique et pauvreté sociale à Byzance 4e-7e siècles* (Paris, 1977).

Pavis d'Escurac, H. 'Pour une étude sociale de l'apologie d'Apulée', *Ant. Afr.* 8 (1974), 89-101.

La préfecture de l'annone, service administratif impérial d'Auguste à Constantin (Rome, 1976).

Pedersen, F.S. 'On professional qualifications for public posts in late antiquity', *C & M* 31 (1970), 161-213.

Pelletier, A. 'Les sénateurs d'Afrique proconsulaire d'Auguste à Gallien', *Latomus* 23 (1964), 511-31.

Peristiany, J.G. (ed.). *Honour and Shame* (London, 1965).

Petit, P. *Pax Romana*, transl. J. Willis (London, 1976) (orig. publ. as *La paix romaine* [Paris, 1967]).

Pflaum, H.-G. *Abrégé des procurateurs équestres* (Paris, 1972).

'À propos de la date de la création de la province de Numidie', *Libyca* 5 (1957), 61-75.

Les carrières procuratoriennes équestres sous le Haut-Empire romain (Paris, 1960-61).

'Les correspondants de l'orateur M. Cornelius Fronto de Cirta', in *Hommages à J. Bayet*, Coll. Lat. 70 (Brussels, 1964), 544-66.

'Les juges des cinq décuries originaires d'Afrique romaine', *Ant. Afr.* 2 (1968), 153-95.

'Une lettre de promotion de l'empereur Marc Aurèle pour un procurateur ducénaire de Gaule Narbonaise', *BJ* 171 (1971), 349-66.

Le Marbre de Thorigny (Paris, 1948).

Les procurateurs équestres sous le Haut-Empire romain (Paris, 1950).

Picard, G.C. 'Deux sénateurs romains inconnus', *Karthago* 4 (1953), 119-35.

La civilisation de l'Afrique romaine (Paris, 1959).

Pitt-Rivers, J. *The Fate of Shechem, or the Politics of Sex* (Cambridge, 1977).

The People of the Sierra, 2nd ed. (Chicago, 1971).

Pöschl, V. *Grundwerte römischer Staatsgesinnung in den Geschichtswerken des Sallust*

(Berlin, 1940).

Premerstein, A. Von. *Vom Werden und Wesen des augusteischen Prinzipats* (Munich, 1937).

Reischauer, E. and J. Fairbank. *East Asia: The Great Tradition* (London, 1960).

Rogers, R.S. 'The Emperor's displeasure — amicitiam renuntiare', *TAPhA* 90 (1959), 224-37.

'The Roman emperors as heirs and legatees', *TAPhA* 78 (1947), 140-58.

Rosenberg, H. *Bureaucracy, Aristocracy, and Autocracy: The Prussian Experience, 1660-1815* (Cambridge, Mass., 1958).

Rostovtzeff, M.I. *Social and Economic History of the Roman Empire*, rev. ed. P. Fraser (Oxford, 1957).

Studien zur Geschichte des römischen Kolonates (Berlin 1910).

Ryberg, I.S. *Rites of the State Religion in Roman Art* (Memoirs of the American Academy in Rome, 1955).

Sahlins, M.D. 'On the sociology of primitive exchange', in *The Relevance of Models for Social Anthropology*, ed. Michael Banton (London, 1965).

Saller, R.P. 'Anecdotes as evidence for Roman imperial history', *G&R* 2nd ser. 27 (1980), 69-83.

Ste Croix, G.E.M. de. 'Suffragium: from vote to patronage', *British Journal of Sociology* 5 (1954), 33-48.

Seager, R. 'Amicitia in Tacitus and Juvenal', *AJAH* 2 (1977), 40-50.

Seston, W. and M. Euzennat. 'Un dossier de la chancellerie romaine: la Tabula Banasitana', *CRAI* (1971), 468-90.

Sewell, W.H. Jr. 'Marc Bloch and the logic of comparative history', *History and Theory* 6 (1967), 208-18.

Shackleton Bailey, D.R. *Cicero: Epistulae ad Familiares* (Cambridge, 1977).

Cicero's Letters to Atticus (Cambridge, 1966).

Shatzman, I. *Senatorial Wealth and Roman Politics* (Brussels, 1975).

Shaw, B.D. 'Pastoralists, peasants, and politics in Roman North Africa' (unpublished Cambridge Ph. D. diss., 1978).

Sherwin-White, A.N. *Letters of Pliny* (Oxford, 1966).

'*Procurator Augusti*', *PBSR* 15 (1939), 11-26.

Speidel, M. 'The singulares of Africa and the establishment of Numidia as a province', *Historia* 22 (1973), 125-7.

Starr, C. 'Epictetus and the tyrant', *CPh* 44 (1949), 20-9.

Stein, A. *Der römische Ritterstand* (Munich, 1927).

Stirling, P. 'Impartiality and personal morality', in *Contributions to Mediterranean Sociology*, ed. J.-G. Peristiany (Paris, 1968), 49-64.

Stockton, D. *Cicero: A Political Biography* (London, 1971).

Syme, R. *Ammianus and the Historia Augusta* (Oxford, 1968).

Emperors and Biography (Oxford, 1971).

History in Ovid (Oxford, 1978).

'The Jurist Neratius Priscus', *Hermes* 85 (1957), 480-93.

'People in Pliny', *JRS* 58 (1968), 135-51.

'Pliny the Procurator', *HSPh* 73 (1969), 201-36.

'Pliny's less successful friends', *Historia* 9 (1960), 362-79.

The Roman Revolution (Oxford, 1939).

'Some friends of the Caesars', *AJPh* 77 (1956), 264-73.

Tacitus (Oxford, 1958).

Thomasson, B.E. *Die Statthalter der römischen Provinzen Nordafrikas von Augustus bis Diocletianus* (Lund, 1960).

Torelli, M. 'Per una storia della classe dirigente di Leptis Magna', *RAL* 28 (1973), 377-410.

Veyne, P. *Le pain et le cirque* (Paris, 1976).

Volkmann, H. 'Griechische Rhetorik oder römische Politik?', *Hermes* 82 (1954), 465-76.

Warmington, B.H. 'The municipal patrons of Roman North Africa', *PBSR* n.s. 9 (1954), 39-55.

The North African Provinces from Diocletian to the Vandal Conquest (Cambridge, 1954).

Watson, G.R. *The Roman Soldier* (London, 1969).

Weaver, P.R.C. *Familia Caesaris* (Cambridge, 1972).

'Social mobility in the early Roman Empire: the evidence of the imperial freedmen and slaves', *P&P* 37 (1967), 3-20.

Weber, M. *Economy and Society*, ed. and transl. G. Roth and C. Wittich (New York, 1968).

Theory of Social and Economic Organization (Glencoe, Ill., 1947).

Weydert, N.-É. 'Inscriptions des Thermes de Lambèse', *BCTH* (1912), 345-55.

White, P. '*Amicitia* and the profession of poetry in early imperial Rome', *JRS* 68 (1978), 74-92.

'The friends of Martial, Statius, and Pliny, and the dispersal of patronage', *HSPh* 79 (1975), 265-300.

Williams, W. 'The *libellus* procedure and the Severan papyri', *JRS* 64 (1974), 86-103.

Wilson, P. (ed.) *Rationality* (Oxford, 1970).

Wiseman, T.P. 'The definition of "eques romanus" in the late Republic and early Empire', *Historia* 19 (1970), 67-83.

New Men in the Roman Senate, 139 B.C.-A.D. 14 (London, 1971).

Wistrand, E. *Opera Selecta* (Stockholm, 1972).

Wittfogel, K. 'Public office in the Liao dynasty and the Chinese examination system', *Harvard Journal of Asiatic Studies* 10 (1947), 13-40.

Wolf, E. 'Kinship, friendship and patron-client relations', in *The Social Anthropology of Complex Societies*, ed. M. Banton (London, 1966).

Yavetz, Z. *Princeps and Plebs* (Oxford, 1969).

Zuckermann, L. 'Essai sur les fonctions des procurateurs de la province de Bithynie - Pont sous le Haut-Empire', *PBPh* 46 (1968), 42-58.

Index

Made in the USA
Middletown, DE
26 September 2023

39451163R00139